California's
SOUTH SIERRA
SECOND EDITION

Best SHORT HIKES in

California's
SOUTH SIERRA

SECOND EDITION

KAREN AND TERRY WHITEHILL
REVISED BY PAUL RICHINS JR.

THE MOUNTAINEERS BOOKS

Published by
The Mountaineers Books
1001 SW Klickitat Way, Suite 201
Seattle, WA 98134

First edition: first printing 1991, second printing 1992, third printing 1994,
fourth printing 1997, fifth printing 1999
Second edition: 2003

Published simultaneously in Great Britain by Cordee, 3a DeMontfort Street,
Leicester, England, LE1 7HD

Manufactured in Canada

Project Editor: Laura Slavik
Copy Editor: Eric Lucas
Cover and Book Design: The Mountaineers Books
Layout: Mayumi Thompson
Mapmaker: Jim Miller/Fennana Design
Photographers: Paul Richins Jr., and Karen & Terry Whitehill

Cover photograph: © Paul Richins Jr.
Frontispiece: *Hungry Packer Lake with Picture Peak* (Hike 43). Photo by Paul Richins Jr.

Library of Congress Cataloging-in-Publication Data
Whitehill, Karen, 1957–
  Best short hikes in California's south Sierra : a guide to day hikes
near campgrounds / by Karen and Terry Whitehill ; revised by Paul
Richins Jr.—2nd ed.
    p. cm.
  Rev. ed. of: Best short hikes in California's southern Sierra. c1991.
  Includes bibliographical references (p.   ) and index.
  ISBN 0-89886-282-5 (pbk.)
  1. Hiking—Sierra Nevada (Calif. and Nev.)—Guidebooks. 2. Sierra
Nevada (Calif. and Nev.)—Guidebooks. I. Whitehill, Terry, 1954–II.
Richins, Paul, 1949–III. Whitehill, Karen, 1957–Best short hikes in
California's south Sierra. IV. Title.
  GV199.42.S55 W49 2003
  917.94'4—dc21
                                    2002012282

CONTENTS

EASTSIDE TRAILHEADS

Mount Whitney Area ■ 113

Bishop Area ■ 150

Mammoth Lakes Area ■ 195

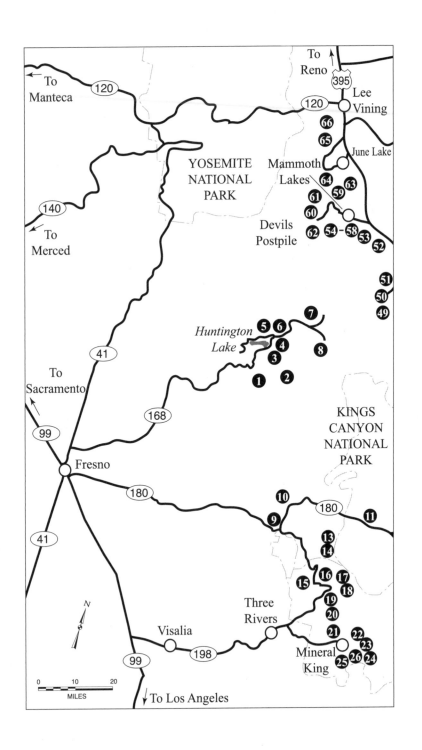

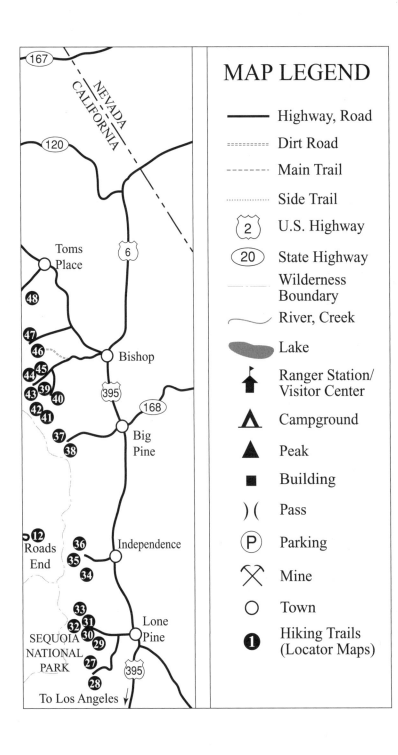

MAP LEGEND

——————	Highway, Road
==========	Dirt Road
- - - - - -	Main Trail
··············	Side Trail
(2)	U.S. Highway
(20)	State Highway
·············	Wilderness Boundary
⌒⌒	River, Creek
▬▬	Lake
⚑	Ranger Station/ Visitor Center
▲	Campground
▲	Peak
■	Building
)(	Pass
(P)	Parking
✕	Mine
○	Town
❶	Hiking Trails (Locator Maps)

PREFACE TO THE SECOND EDITION

The Sierra Nevada wilderness possesses riches beyond one's wildest dreams—lush meadows, picturesque alpine lakes and streams, wild and scenic rivers, turbulent cataracts, saw-toothed ridges, sheer granite walls, and majestic mountain summits. The drives to the various trailheads will take you past the largest trees in the world, provide dramatic views of some of the deepest canyons in the United States, and reveal glimpses of the highest peak in the Lower 48.

This guidebook has been written to help hikers of all ages and abilities experience these wonders. With easy automobile access, excellent trails, and comfortable campgrounds, no one is too young or too old to enjoy the splendor, charm, and rugged beauty of the Sierra Nevada's high alpine environment. The guide includes easy hikes from 2 to 6 miles for families with children and those who do not plan to spend an entire day hiking up a challenging trail. Also sprinkled throughout are excellent hikes for the adventurous who seek to explore a little farther into the wilderness. For those considering camping, the guide offers information about the campgrounds located near each trailhead.

The first edition of Karen and Terry Whitehill's *Best Short Hikes in California's Southern Sierra* was published in 1991. Second, third, fourth, and fifth printings quickly followed, demonstrating the popularity and value of this guidebook among hikers and backpackers. The second edition has been updated with extensive new material. Discussions of hypothermia, mountain sickness, giardia, water purification, and how to keep safe in a lightning storm have been added (see Backcountry Travel in the Sierra). Each hike's "in a nutshell" information block has been expanded, providing additional summary data for quick reference. The description of each campground and hike has been carefully updated. Several hikes have been deleted and new ones added to improve the overall selection.

Many of the original outings have been expanded to include two destinations—a shorter one and a longer one. With the addition of a second objective, you now have a palette of more than 100 treks to select from when planning your adventure. Part of your party may choose an easier half-day walk while others in your group may want a more challenging excursion; both are possible from the same trailhead.

The new outings that have been added include, to name a few, Bald Mountain Lookout, Pear Lake, and Franklin Lakes in Sequoia National Park; New Army Pass, Mountaineers Route, Whitney Portal National Recreation Trail, Golden Trout Lake, and Kearsarge Lakes in the Mount Whitney area; Finger Lake, Honeymoon Lake, Hungry Packer Lake, and Midnight Lake in the Bishop area; and Ediza Lake and Upper Sardine Lake in the Mammoth Lakes area. Each is a special destination in a spectacular setting.

For well-conditioned hikers interested in climbing Mount Whitney, Hike 32 contains new information that will increase your chances of success. A moonlight ascent of Whitney is also described.

Six new appendixes have been added; they provide essential information for planning an excursion to the mountains, including important phone numbers, websites, and mailing addresses. Valuable instructions for making campground reservations, securing wilderness permits, contacting the Forest Service or the National Park Service, finding the correct maps, locating shuttle services, and determining what equipment to take are specified. What you may find most helpful are the summary tables of each hike's mileage, elevation gain, level of difficulty, and nearest town (Appendix 3). The summary tables and the list of authors' favorites and family-friendly hikes (Appendix 4) are handy tools to help you select a hike that is just right for your group. I hope you will have many opportunities to explore the boundless riches of the Sierra Nevada. In so doing, your spirit will be renewed and perhaps inspired to new heights.

Your comments are appreciated. Send them to prichins@jps.net, or *http://pweb.jps.net/~prichins/backcountry_resource_center.htm*.

Happy hiking,
Paul Richins Jr.

A REMINDER TO HIKERS AND CAMPERS: TREAD LIGHTLY

The Sierra Nevada has become a favorite of sightseers, campers, and backcountry hikers. With this popularity comes the added responsibility for those visiting the area to protect the fragile alpine ecology. We must all do our part to keep the area unspoiled by following the few simple rules of wilderness conduct established by the National Park Service and the U.S. Forest Service. The mountains' fragile alpine ecology is neither limitless nor eternal. This delicate wilderness balance is wounded each time a wildflower is trampled beneath a hiker's boot, whenever a stand of trees is reduced to ashes by a carelessly discarded match, and any time a trout dies in a polluted stream. Tread lightly while you explore the wilderness: stay on designated trails, do not cut switchbacks, and walk carefully near streams, lakes, and meadows. Touch the treasure joyfully, take photographs for enduring memories, and leave it as you found it: a legacy for those who will follow. The matchless beauty and unique wonders of the Sierra Nevada are treasures worth preserving for the generations that will follow.

A NOTE ABOUT SAFETY

Safety is an important concern in outdoor activities. No guidebook can alert you to every hazard or anticipate the limitations of each reader. Therefore, the descriptions of roads, trails, routes, and natural features in this guidebook are not guarantees that a particular place or excursion will be safe for your party. While the author and publisher have done their best to provide accurate information, conditions change from day to day and from year to year. It is presumed that the users of this guide possess the requisite hiking, climbing, backpacking, and cross-country navigational skills for safe travel in the mountains. When you follow the routes described herein, you assume responsibility for your own safety. Under normal conditions, such excursions require the usual attention to traffic, road and trail conditions, weather, terrain, objective danger, and the capabilities of your party. Under adverse conditions, a relatively easy hike may become a serious challenge, and potentially unsafe. Keeping informed on current conditions and exercising common sense are the keys to a safe, enjoyable outing.

—*The Mountaineers Books*

BACKCOUNTRY TRAVEL IN THE SIERRA

ABOUT THE SIERRA NEVADA

California's Sierra Nevada is a unique and unforgettable land of high adventure and enjoyment, a hiker's playground spanning nearly the length of the state. From south of Lassen Volcanic National Park to Mount Whitney and another 80 miles south to Tehachapi Pass, this spectacular chain of mountains offers an endless variety of outdoor opportunities. Picturesque alpine lakes, peaceful streams, lush meadows, colorful wildflowers, cascading waterfalls, deep canyons, immense glacial cirques, lofty mountain passes, and splendid summits inspire the wilderness traveler to action.

Thousands of eager prospectors hastened to California during the gold and silver rushes of the nineteenth century. They came to claim their fortunes, but the mountains and streams bestowed their favors haphazardly. Some who made the long journey found their dreams of wealth and glory; others were less fortunate.

Today, millions pilgrimage to the Sierra Nevada. These current-day prospectors are searching for something just as precious as silver and gold: they seek the timeless beauty and the unspoiled serenity of the mountains. And they do not go away disappointed. Each returns home renewed and strengthened, steeped in the backcountry's incredible riches.

The Sierra Nevada was formed over many millions of years through a series of uplifts that pushed the great Sierra Block upward and tilted it toward the west. From a geologic perspective, the range is essentially a gigantic granite block 350 miles long and 40 to 80 miles wide that has been tilted on its side. While the Sierra Block was being pushed upward, the land to the east began to drop thousands of feet, creating the impressive east face of the range that is readily seen from U.S. Highway 395. This explains why the east side of this range is so rugged, whereas the slopes on the west gradually rise to the crest over many miles.

The range runs generally north and south along the eastern boundary of the state, forming California's geographic backbone. The Sierra Nevada gradually increases in elevation from north to south in a surprisingly orderly manner. The highest peaks in the north, near the small town of Quincy, barely reach 8000 feet. Moving south, higher

The sheer east face of Mount Whitney (Hike 33). Paul Richins Jr.

and higher peaks are encountered: 10,000-foot peaks appear for the first time near Lake Tahoe, 11,000-foot peaks near Sonora Pass (Highway 108), 12,000-footers emerge east of Bridgeport in the Sawtooth Range, and 13,000-foot summits arise in Yosemite National Park's high country.

The first 14,000-footer is not encountered until the Palisades region, 250 miles south of the beginning of the range. Five of the Sierra Nevada's eleven 14,000-foot peaks are located in the Palisades region (west of the town of Big Pine). These magnificent peaks are soon followed by the remaining six 14,000-foot peaks of the Mount Whitney region (west of the towns of Lone Pine and Independence). The Sierra Nevada culminates atop Mount Whitney; six miles to the south is Mount Langley, the last 14,000-foot peak in the Sierra Nevada. From this point, the peaks rapidly decrease in elevation, and the Sierra Nevada ends near the Mojave Desert.

The beauty and size of the mountain range are unparalleled. The Sierra Nevada's splendor is exemplified by Lake Tahoe and three magnificent national parks: Yosemite National Park, Sequoia National Park, and Kings Canyon National Park. The range is enormous—to provide a sense of geographic perspective, the Sierra Nevada easily exceeds the size of the entire European Alps: the French, Swiss, Austrian, and Italian Alps combined.

One of the most amazing things about the southern half of the Sierra Nevada is that not a single road crosses from one side to the other for about 160 miles. From Yosemite National Park and Tioga Pass Road (Highway 120) in the north to Walker Pass (Highway 178) in the south, no road bisects this vast wilderness: one must explore the area on foot or horseback. This vast roadless region south of Yosemite National Park is the focus of this guidebook.

HOW TO USE THIS GUIDEBOOK

The guide covers trailheads originating on both the west side and east side of the Sierra Nevada south of Yosemite National Park. Whereas this guidebook covers the southern portion of the Sierra Nevada, a companion trail guide, *Best Short Hikes in California's North Sierra* (The Mountaineers Books, 2003), covers the northern portion of the range and is quite useful.

Best Short Hikes in California's South Sierra is dedicated to helping modern-day prospectors stake their claim to the treasures of the Sierra Nevada. This guidebook is for anyone who has the desire to explore these beautiful mountains, streams, meadows, and lakes.

The focus is on day hikes, although many of the outings will appeal to backpackers as well. Hikes range from short trips of less than 5 miles to all-day treks of 15 miles or more. Some hikes lead to alpine lakes, others climb to lofty passes, and still others end on mountaintops.

A few of the book's sixty-six hikes may be too difficult for all but the most energetic outdoor enthusiast. Other hikes may seem too tame for visitors who seek a more physical challenge. Fortunately, with so many trips to choose from, there is a wide assortment of treks to fit everyone's personal preferences. The table in Appendix 3 summarizes each hike including mileage, elevation gain, and level of difficulty.

Because many visitors come to camp as well as hike, a secondary focus is on public campgrounds. A list of campgrounds accompanies each grouping of hikes. Beginning with the Huntington Lake area, the sixty-six hikes and their corresponding campgrounds are arranged in geographic clusters. From Huntington Lake, the hike groupings move in a counterclockwise direction, south along the west side of the Sierra Nevada and then north up its eastern flank along Highway 395.

The sixty-six hikes are arranged in two sections: Westside Trail-heads and Eastside Trailheads. Hikes 1–26 originate on the west side of the Sierra Nevada. These trails are accessed from the towns of Fresno and Visalia on Highway 99; hikers then head east toward the Sierra Nevada on Highways 168, 180, and 198.

Hikes 27–66 begin on the east side of the range. Whitney Portal Road (Lone Pine), Onion Valley Road (Independence), Big Pine Creek Road (Big Pine), Highway 168 (Bishop), Rock Creek Road (Toms Place), Convict Lake Road (near the Mammoth Lake Airport), Highway 203 (Mammoth Lakes), and Highway 158 (June Lake) provide east/west access from Highway 395 to these trailheads.

Information Blocks

Each hike begins with a block of information or "in a nutshell" overview of the hike. Some hikes may have two (or more) primary destinations. If there are two or more, the hikes will be summarized in the information block as shown in the example below and fully described in the text.

Distance	▪	4.2 miles round trip (Alpenglow Lake) / 8 miles round trip (Round Robin Lake)
Difficulty	▪	Easy / Moderate
Starting elevation	▪	7240 feet / 7240 feet
High point	▪	8780 feet / 9600 feet
Elevation gain	▪	540 feet / 1360 feet
Trail grade	▪	205 feet per mile / 340 feet per mile
Maps	▪	USGS Lodgepole 7.5' or Mount Whitney High Country Trail Map (Tom Harrison Maps)
Access road/town	▪	Highway 395 to Onion Valley Road / Independence

The "Information Block" for each hike starts with the distance, given in miles. All distances are specified as either one-way, loop, or round-trip mileage. Each hike is also rated for difficulty: *easy*, *moderate*, or *strenuous*. Hikes 6 miles or less in length gaining less than 1000 feet were assessed as *easy*. Hikes ranging from 6 to 12 miles gaining less than 2000 feet were considered *moderate*, and those over 12 miles and gaining more than 2000 feet were considered *strenuous*. Hikes that are within the mileage criterion but gain considerably more elevation than these guidelines were placed in the next higher rating. For example, a short hike of 5 miles that gains 1500 feet would be rated *moderate* rather than *easy*.

The elevation of the starting point and high point for each hike is listed in feet. The elevation gain will include the major ups and downs of the trail. Consequently, the total elevation gain may be greater than the difference between the starting point and high point.

The grade or steepness of the trail is an average over the one-way distance of the trip. In the example, the one-way distance to Alpenglow Lake is 2.1 miles with an elevation gain of 540 feet. The trail grade is 540 feet divided by 2.1 miles, equaling 205 feet per mile. Since this is an average, sections of the trail will be flatter or steeper than indicated by the trail grade. However, this provides a comparison among the trails for planning purposes.

To gauge the relative grade or slope of a trail, the following general guidelines are offered:

0–200 feet per mile: flat or nearly flat walking
201–500 feet per mile: gentle hiking
501–800 feet per mile: moderately steep
801–1200 feet per mile: steep

The maps provided in the guide are for general reference. They include the various trails in the area and geographic features such as prominent lakes, streams, meadows, ridges, and peaks. These small maps can be used if you plan to stay on the described trails, but if you deviate from the book's routes or want to explore through some cross-country ramblings, more detailed maps are needed.

The "Information Block" for each hike lists the appropriate U.S. Geological Survey (USGS) map (7.5-minute series). Unfortunately, the USGS no longer produces the 15-minute series where an inch equals about a mile. The scale of these maps is ideal for hikers and backpackers. The new USGS 7.5-minute maps, where 2.6 inches equal a mile, provide more detail than is necessary. Fortunately, there are several excellent sources available to replace the USGS 15-minute series maps, such as the Tom Harrison Maps. The "Information Block" includes the Tom Harrison Map recommended for the outing. These maps are on a scale of one inch to the mile or one inch to two miles. Because of the scale and the layout, one map covers a large geographic area and numerous trails described in this guidebook. Wilderness Press, Wildflower Productions (*TOPO! Interactive Maps on CD-ROM*), and the Forest Service/National Park Service are other sources of maps. Various maps can be purchased at Inyo, Sierra, and Sequoia National Forest Service District Offices, Sequoia and Kings Canyon National Parks Visitor Centers, Sequoia Natural History Association (see Appendix 2), and backpacking stores.

The information block also includes the major access road(s) to the trailhead and the closest town, place, or visitor center where a limited number of supplies may be purchased.

When to Go

Because winter weather conditions and the depth of the snowpack vary considerably from year to year, it is not possible to predict with accuracy when each trail will be open for exploration. The best advice is to check with the Forest Service or National Park Service on trail conditions (see Appendix 1 for list of phone numbers and websites). That said, the primary hiking season is June through October, with the most popular months being July and August.

Generally speaking, all but the highest trails will be open in June. Many trails and campgrounds are quite popular on the weekends. The best way to avoid the crowds is to go during the week in peak season, or in early summer or fall. Additionally, many of the trails, even the high-altitude ones, can be hot even in October. To avoid the heat, plan an early morning start.

There is no bad time to plan a hike during these months. Each month has unique characteristics that make a trip during that particular time a rewarding experience. However, two favorite seasons are early summer (June/early July) and early fall (September/October). In early summer the creeks and waterfalls are overflowing with rushing water from snowmelt, the meadows are plush with flowers, and the wildlife is plentiful. September and October are also wonderful times for exploring the Sierra Nevada. The crowds are dwindling; the leaves of the quaking aspen trees are turning all shades of red, yellow, and gold; the mosquitoes and bugs are gone; the threat of afternoon thunderstorms has passed; and bear activity is on the decline. In the frosty fall mornings, skiffs of ice form on the lakes and streams but quickly melt in the morning sun. And in the evenings, the crisp autumn air signals the rapid approach of winter.

Trip Descriptions

The sixty-six hike descriptions are designed with several purposes in mind. First, the text for each hike will help you decide if it's a trek for you. Read through the text to learn about each hike, and consult Appendixes 3 and 4. Appendix 3 contains an especially helpful summary of all the hikes—including the mileage, elevation gain, and difficulty of each trip—packed into a single table. Appendix 4 lists the authors' favorite hikes and family-friendly hikes. Then, decide which trip is right for you.

Second, the goal of each hike description is to guide you to the trailhead, lead you smoothly through the journey's twists and turns and junctions, and deposit you happily (and without unwanted detours) at your goal. Along the way, commentary on the surrounding scenery will inform and enhance your experience.

Wilderness Permits

While the National Park Service and the Forest Service believe that the details of their respective permit systems will be in place for many years to come, they are also open to suggestions for improving the system and may make adjustments to it from time to time. Check with the Forest Service and National Park Service for current procedures, as the permit requirements and the quota season vary considerably. That said, the wilderness permit requirements, at this writing, are briefly summarized below.

A wilderness permit is not required for day hikes. The lone exception is the Mount Whitney Trail (Hike 32) beyond Lone Pine Lake. All overnight trips require a wilderness permit any time of the year. The Forest Service's wilderness permit quota system is in place between the last Friday in June and September 15 for some trails and from May 1 to November 1 on other trails. For hikes originating in the Sequoia and Kings Canyon National Parks, the wilderness permit quota system is in place from May 21 through September 21. For hikes requiring a wilderness permit, advance reservations are recommended during the quota season.

Due to the popularity of the Mount Whitney Trail (Hike 32), the quota system is in place from May 1 through November 1. Additionally, the Forest Service has implemented a lottery system to issue wilderness permits. Permit applications for the lottery must be postmarked by February 28 for the upcoming hiking season.

Wilderness permits, maps, books, trail and campground conditions, and other information can be obtained from the various Forest Service and National Park Service offices listed in Appendixes 1 and 2. Check with the appropriate Forest Service or National Park Service Ranger Station for current trail conditions and trail permit requirements.

Campground Listings

Camping in the Sierra Nevada is an inexpensive and enjoyable alternative to motels or inns. Best of all for hikers, campgrounds usually offer the best access to the trailheads. Each section describes a few campgrounds that provide convenient access to the trails. Driving directions for campgrounds are combined with information about fees, reservations, the number of campsites, and types of facilities. To obtain more specific camping information, please refer to the appropriate section and the campground listing for the area you plan to visit. See also Appendix 1 for campground reservation information.

Many campgrounds are extremely busy on Fridays and weekends. It is recommended that you secure advance reservations for campgrounds where reservations are accepted or arrive at the campground on Friday for your weekend stay.

Many other excellent campgrounds have not been included due to space limitations. A more complete list of campgrounds can be secured from the appropriate National Park Visitor Center or Forest Service office (see Appendix 1). You may also consider purchasing a California campground guide. One source that is extremely helpful is Tom Stienstra's *California Camping, the Complete Guide to California's Recreation Areas* (see Appendix 6).

BEING PREPARED

By knowing in advance what to expect and then being prepared, the potential dangers of mountain travel can be avoided and the problems mastered before they become serious. Hypothermia, mountain sickness, lightning, adverse weather, routefinding difficulties, bears, and other mischievous critters may be encountered on your hike. The following provides advice on what to take and how to cope with each eventuality.

Always hike with one or more companions. However, if you must enter the mountains alone, always notify someone of your intended route, destination, departure and return time, and the license number of your automobile. Leave a note on your tent when you leave the campground, or share a morning chat with the campground host. Twisted ankles, mountain sickness, unexpected changes in the weather, hypothermia—any of these can leave a solitary hiker stranded and in trouble. If someone else knows about your plans, you will have backup when you get into a jam.

What to Take

Always carry the Ten Essentials, no matter how brief the distance or how tame the destination. Refer to Appendix 5 (Equipment Checklist for Day Hikes) for a complete list of items to include in your pack. Make sure you take a map and compass, extra clothing, matches (in a waterproof container) and/or a lighter, a knife, a flashlight, some form of firestarter (for igniting wet wood), a first-aid kit, sunglasses, and extra food. And don't forget one more essential item—strong sunscreen. Use a sunblock that provides the greatest amount of protection (SPF 40 or greater). Sunblock in conjunction with a wide-brimmed hat(s) and fabric that hangs around the neck and face is most effective in preventing sunburn to the face and neck.

Water

The question of whether the water from mountain streams and alpine lakes in the Sierra Nevada is safe to drink has been a major concern over the years. Ask the average outdoorsperson about *Giardia lamblia* or giardiasis, and they have certainly heard about it. Almost always, however, they are misinformed about the organism's prevalence in wilderness water and the seriousness of the disease. The U.S. Forest Service and National Park Service have issued warnings advising campers and hikers to filter, treat with iodine, or boil all surface water before drinking. This advice does not appear to be based on scientific research, but a desire to err on the side of caution.

In 1987, 1996, and 1997, Dr. Robert L. Rockwell conducted extensive scholarly, peer-reviewed research on *giardia* in the Sierra Nevada and concluded that you can indeed contract giardiasis on visits to the Sierra Nevada, but it won't be from the water. Proper personal hygiene is far more important in avoiding giardiasis than treating the water.

The medical literature does not support the widely held perception that giardiasis is a significant risk to hikers and campers in the Sierra Nevada or the United States. To further support this conclusion, the National Park Service and the U.S. Forest Service have filtered hundreds of gallons of water from wilderness streams and have found few organisms (far less than enough to be infective).

When one acknowledges that Sierra Nevada water has fewer *giardia* cysts than the municipal water supply of San Francisco and Los Angeles, it becomes apparent that *giardia* is not a serious threat to those who drink from a Sierra Nevada stream or lake. Below are some typical *giardia* cyst concentrations (cysts per liter) measured throughout California.

~1000 = Typical swimming pool contamination
~100 = Giardiasis is plausible
~10 = Minimum needed to contract giardiasis
~1 = Some wilderness water outside California
0.12 = San Francisco water
0.108 = Worst Sierra Nevada water measured
0.030 = Los Angeles water
0.013 = Trail Camp on the Mount Whitney Trail
0.003 = Whitney Portal

Sierra Nevada water has far too few *giardia* cysts to cause an infestation. Even if you go somewhere where the concentration is high, you probably won't get giardiasis. If you do get giardiasis, you probably won't have any symptoms. If you have symptoms, they will probably go away by themselves in a week or so. If they don't or you develop serious persistent symptoms, you should seek medical treatment. Finally, those contracting giardiasis may develop immunity to it, thus lowering the likelihood they will get it again.

Good sanitation is probably the best preventative measure against contracting *giardia*. Health experts estimate that one out of five people carry *giardia*. Asymptomatic carriers can spread the disease unknowingly. Cooks and food handlers can easily spread *giardia* when good hygiene is not practiced. This is consistent with the finding that a majority of giardiasis cases are caused by fecal-oral or foodborne transmission. In the backcountry it is wise to use antibacterial waterless soap after each nature call and before preparing a meal/eating.

However, if you still have concerns and want to take extra precautionary measures, boil, filter, or use iodine tablets to treat the water.

Iodine is more effective than filtering the water, is less expensive, a lot less work, and much lighter in your pack than an expensive and cumbersome water filter.

Hypothermia
Mountain weather can change rapidly. Many of the hikes attain elevations of 10,000 feet, where snow, sleet, and hail can be encountered during a summer storm.

A primary concern during the summer is afternoon thunderstorms. Without the proper clothing, such wet and windy conditions can quickly lead to hypothermia. Hypothermia can be a serious medical problem in the mountains. If a hiker becomes wet, the wind can quickly strip the body of its core heat. A low wind speed of 10 to 20 miles per hour can have a dramatic and potentially fatal effect on a wet hiker. Furthermore, hypothermia often occurs at ambient air temperatures above freezing. The best prevention is to not get wet in the first place by bringing windproof and water-repellent outer clothing like ponchos, parkas, or other water-protective garments.

The symptoms of hypothermia are decreased mental acuity, reduced physical ability, slowness, tiredness, confusion, and, after shivering has ceased, coma and death. A hiker is at risk for hypothermia when wet and tired. Wet falling snow, sleet, hail, or rain from a summer thunderstorm can quickly soak a hiker. For further reading on the field management of hypothermia, see *Backcountry Medical Guide* by Peter Steele, M.D. (Appendix 6).

Mountain Sickness
In addition to hypothermia, another concern for those hiking above 8000 feet is mountain/altitude sickness. The rapid rise in elevation is the primary cause, with 10 to 40 percent of hikers experiencing symptoms. The deck is stacked against a hiker who drives from near sea level to a high-elevation trailhead and immediately sets out. Many robust hikers may quickly develop a splitting headache, nausea, dizziness, and no energy or desire to continue.

Mountain sickness is not a specific disorder but a group of symptoms caused by a rapid rise in elevation that vary widely in severity and consequences. What begins as a mild problem may progress into something much worse. Acute mountain sickness (AMS), generalized edema, disordered sleep, high-altitude pulmonary edema (HAPE), and high altitude cerebral edema (HACE) represent the spectrum of altitude-related problems from the less serious (mild AMS) to the often-fatal (HAPE or HACE). Although individual susceptibility to mountain sickness varies, hikers who have had one or more episodes, young children, and women in the premenstrual phase are at highest risk.

Symptoms of mild AMS are similar to those of a hangover or the flu: lack of energy, loss of appetite, mild headache, nausea, dizziness, shortness of breath, general feeling of lassitude, and disturbed sleep. These symptoms generally resolve over twenty-four to forty-eight hours at a given altitude and resolve more quickly if one descends. A 125-mg dose of Acetazolamide (a mild diuretic that acidifies the blood) taken twice a day may help those who suffer repeatedly from unpleasant symptoms despite a slow ascent. This prescription medication should be taken only until maximum altitude is attained or for 2 days, whichever is less. It will lessen your chances of getting AMS. Side effects include tingling of the face and fingers and frequent urination. Victims experiencing moderate mountain sickness involving severe headache, nausea, and vomiting must descend immediately.

General edema is a harmless disorder occurring within the first week at high altitude. Edema is an abnormal collection of fluid in the extracellular, extravascular compartment, typically in dependent parts of the extremities. Edema probably is caused by the increased permeability of small blood vessels and reduced kidney function resulting from reduced oxygen concentrations in the blood. This fluid retention can cause a noticeable weight gain of four or more pounds. The excess fluid retention can cause swelling of the face, eyelids, ankles, feet, fingers, and hands. Urine output may be scanty despite adequate fluid intake. In the absence of AMS, edema can be treated effectively with a diuretic.

A much more serious form of mountain sickness is HAPE. Symptoms are inordinate shortness of breath and a dry, nonproductive cough or a cough producing a small amount of pink-tinged sputum (caused by blood from the lungs). HAPE results in the lungs' air sacs filling with fluid that has oozed through the walls of the pulmonary capillaries. As more air sacs fill with fluid, the oxygen transfer to the pulmonary capillaries is blocked, resulting in cyanosis (a bluish cast to the lips and nail beds caused by decreased oxygen saturation of hemoglobin). Without immediate treatment, HAPE may eventually lead to severe hypoxia, coma, and death. Treatment is immediate descent. If descent is not possible, supplemental oxygen administered at a rate of 4–6 liters per minute may be helpful along with nifedipine (20 mg, slow release, given every six hours).

High-Altitude Cerebral Edema is another serious form of mountain sickness. It is characterized by severe headache, nausea, vomiting, mental confusion, poor judgment, ataxia (clumsy or uncoordinated gait), and eventually coma and death. In the case of HACE, fluid is retained in the brain cavity, causing swelling inside the skull. Both HAPE and HACE are rare in the Sierra Nevada, occurring in only about 0.5 percent and 0.1 percent, respectively, of hikers venturing above 8500 feet. Both HAPE and HACE are true emergencies necessitating immediate descent and immediate medical attention. Lowering a climber 1000–3000 feet often can make a significant difference.

There are several things you can do to prevent or reduce the severity of mountain sickness. The most important is to take your time. It is helpful to camp at the end of the road or as high as possible for one or two nights before beginning your hike from a trailhead above 8000–9000 feet. This will help your body adjust to the higher altitude.

Drink plenty of water or your favorite sport drink. Research suggests that there is a direct correlation between fluid intake and susceptibility to altitude sickness. Ample fluid intake is essential to preventing dehydration and altitude sickness.

The following measures will help alleviate the discomfort associated with mountain sickness and may promote recovery.

■ Avoid heavy exertion; maintain light activity (such as walking) to increase circulation. The natural tendency is to lie down and rest, but this reduces circulation.
■ Drink plenty of water—more than you think is necessary. A sport drink also is beneficial.
■ Eat light meals, avoiding too much fat. Warm soups are excellent.
■ Take aspirin, acetaminophen, or ibuprofen for symptom relief.

Monitor closely for HAPE or HACE. If early signs are apparent, the victim must be taken 2000–3000 feet lower. If an immediate improvement is not observed, remove the victim from the mountain.

Lightning

Although not one of the main concerns of hikers, lightning has caused a number of serious (and mostly avoidable) accidents in the Sierra Nevada and should be taken seriously when thunderheads form (primarily in July and August). Many outings place hikers in vulnerable spots that are the most frequent targets of lightning: high and exposed passes and ridges.

The stone hut on the summit of Mount Whitney was built in 1908 for scientific study by the Smithsonian Institution. A hiker seeking refuge in this hut was killed by a lightening strike. Paul Richins Jr.

If caught in a lightning storm, avoid areas that might be hit by lightning. Seek a location with nearby projections or masses that are significantly higher and closer than one's head to any clouds. In a forest, the best place is among the shorter trees. Along a ridge, the best location is in the middle because the ends are more exposed and susceptible to strikes. The following are some useful tips for hikers caught in a lightning storm:

- If a lightning storm is approaching, descend quickly to a safe location away from the summit and off exposed ridges.
- If caught unexpectedly by a lightning storm in an exposed position, seek a location with nearby projections or masses that are significantly higher than your head.
- Avoid moist areas, including crevices and gullies.
- Sit, crouch, or stand on an insulating object such as a pack, sleeping bag, or sleeping pad.
- Occupy as small an area as possible. Keep your feet close together and hands off the ground.
- Stay out of small depressions; choose instead a narrow, slight rise to avoid ground currents. A small detached rock on a scree slope is excellent.

■ Stay away from overhangs and out of small caves.

■ When on a ledge, crouch at the outer edge, at least 4 feet from the rock wall.

Routefinding

The majority of the trails described in this guide are well defined and easy to follow. However, some trails cut across bare slabs of granite or receive such little use that they're partially overrun by vegetation. If you are familiar with some simple "signposts," you will be able to follow the intended route more easily.

Ducks, also called rock cairns, are an invaluable aid to routefinding. Usually consisting of a few flat stones piled one atop another, ducks often mark the passage of a trail across barren expanses of granite. If the trail disappears when it hits a continuous slab of granite, look for irregularly spaced piles of rocks to mark the way. Another method of trail marking involves outlining a route with a border of stones or logs. Again, this routefinding aid is useful when a trail crosses barren granite or when the path is somewhat overgrown.

Tree blazes are another method for marking the trails. These shallow cuts are made in the trunks of trees, usually at eye level or above.

As mentioned earlier, a good map is a must for every hiker. Refer to your map whenever you have a question. Always be alert to your surroundings. Don't venture far from the trail unless you're an experienced scrambler, equipped with a map and compass.

Aches and Pains

Many will experience aches, pains, and sore muscles during and after their hike. Ibuprofen and naproxen are the wonder drugs for hikers and backpackers. Taken with food once or twice during the day, these over-the-counter miracle drugs help ease the aches, pains, and soreness associated with strenuous hiking. A tablet at midday acts as a powerful second wind for the tired and sore hiker. Another tablet taken before bed helps reduce stiffness and improves the quality of sleep. Five to ten minutes of stretching exercises at the end of the hike as part of the cooling-down process, and then again before bedtime, also may help to reduce stiffness.

FLORA AND FAUNA

One of the wondrous things about the south Sierra Nevada is the presence of majestic groves of giant sequoias. These magnificent forest specimens, with their massive red-hued trunks, are ageless wonders that have survived droughts, disease, and forest fires. The giant sequoia speaks of timelessness, strength, and the incredible diversity of nature.

Clustered around the sequoias is an amazing variety of fir, pine, and cedar trees. The sugar pine boasts the longest pinecone in the world. The sequoia claims the largest trunk. The incense cedar wears its bark like a shaggy coat. The Jeffrey pine has a tantalizing odor.

Immerse yourself in the trees, bushes, and wildflowers. The more you know about this vegetation, the more you will appreciate what you see. Trailside flora has been noted, but specialized guidebooks will enhance your identification efforts. Refer to Appendix 6 for further reading on the subject.

Even if you're not ready to begin toting several extra books with you on the trail, you can make use of the free handouts provided in most Forest Service or National Park Service offices. The informative fact sheets on trees and wildflowers make a good addition to any hiker's pack.

You may also want to ask the park ranger about poison oak. Poison oak is prevalent on the west side of the Sierra Nevada at elevations below 7000 feet, predominantly on sunny slopes. At higher elevations it is rare.

In addition to the flora, you will see many life forms that aren't rooted to the ground during your time in the Sierra, ranging in size from tiny chipmunks to graceful deer. Again, Forest Service fliers can help you differentiate between a tree squirrel and a golden-mantled ground squirrel or identify a Clark's nutcracker or a Steller's jay. If you're visiting with young children, Forest Service offices stock an assortment of wonderful coloring books about the Sierra's plants and animals as well.

It's easy to stay in harmony with the vegetation. Don't pick the flowers, don't trample the meadows, stay on existing trails and don't cut the switchback, and don't let a sugar pinecone hit you on the head. But what about keeping the peace with the animals?

The sugar pine produces the longest pinecone in the world. Karen & Terry Whitehill

The delicate blossoms of Labrador tea add their own unique beauty to Sierra hiking. Karen & Terry Whitehill

Here's some advice to ensure good relations between you and your native hosts.

Bears and Other Mischievous Critters

Adult black bears roaming the Sierra Nevada and other parts of California weigh up to 350 pounds and come in many shades of brown, black, and cinnamon. Generally, they are not as dangerous or aggressive as the grizzly bear, but they can inflict serious damage on parked cars (in search of hidden victuals) and can devour a week's supply of food in a matter of minutes.

Most people's first concern is about bears. Will you see one while you're hiking? Probably not. Most bear encounters occur in campgrounds or at backpackers' campsites, not on the trail. Still, it is wise to keep an eye on the assorted footprints on the trail when you're out hiking. If you spot bear tracks, stay alert and pick up your conversation level by several decibels.

When staying at campgrounds, be responsible with your food. Don't blame the bears for choosing a goodie-laden cooler over a dried-up thimbleberry bush. Never leave groceries on your picnic table, and don't take food into your tent at night. Dispose of all garbage promptly; your discards may just be a bear's buffet. If your campsite has a bear box, use it.

When bears repeatedly raid campsites and garbage cans, these intelligent animals quickly learn that human food is much easier to obtain and tastier than their natural diet. Once they taste our food they begin to crave it and in the process become less fearful. A fearless bear may become destructive and dangerous. To help avoid this problem, proper food storage is required by federal regulations and feeding wildlife is prohibited.

Bears are an ever-present problem at certain trailhead parking lots. Check with the Forest Service or National Park Service to determine if bears have been a concern at the trailhead parking lot you plan to use. Do not leave food, toiletries, sunscreen, soap, garbage, empty ice chests, or anything with a smell in a parked car. Bears have learned to recognize the shape of ice chests and have broken into cars for empty ones. Any empty ice chest left in a parked car should be concealed.

Although not a serious concern, you may want to ask the park ranger about mountain lions in the area. There have been several mountain lion attacks in the more populated foothills of California, although not in the higher elevations covered by this guidebook.

Certain trailhead parking areas, especially those at Mineral King (Hikes 21–26), are plagued by marmots. Marmots have been known to damage cars by climbing into the engine compartments and eating hoses and wires. If you park your car for any length of time where there is a history of marmot problems, consider placing chicken wire or mesh completely around it to keep the marmots out. Ask the Forest Service or National Park Service for information on trailhead conditions and advice about marmot damage to parked cars.

Mosquitoes, Ticks, and Snakes

Mosquitoes, biting midges, and gnats can be a problem early in the hiking season near meadows and along creeks, or anywhere standing water exists. Be sure to pack mosquito repellent (or sunscreen with an added mosquito repellent) for hikes in June and July. By August and September the problem resolves itself. Ticks are a bit more worrisome—but most of the hikes in this guide are above the tick level, so encounters should be infrequent. Ticks are rare above 7000 feet. Still, you will want to keep an eye out for the little beasties whenever you're in the mountains.

Do a "tick check" at the end of every hiking day. Comb or brush your hair thoroughly, and visually examine every inch of skin. Check your clothes and bedding, too. Ticks often survey their surroundings for a while before digging in. If you do find a tick that has already embedded itself in your skin, remove it promptly and completely.

Tweezers may work if the tick isn't in too deep. If you can't get the tick out easily, if the area around the bite is inflamed or sore, or if redness or swelling appears later on, consult a doctor immediately.

Another concern is the threat of rattlesnakes. Like ticks, rattlesnakes are seldom seen at higher elevations. If you're hiking below 7000 feet, you can lessen your chances of an unhappy encounter with a rattlesnake by staying out of brush and rocks, keeping on the trail, and always watching where you step and where you put your hands.

Pack Animals

If you do much hiking you will surely meet some of the sturdy beasts that carry food, equipment, and saddle-sore tourists into the

High above Ruby Lake, a string of pack mules head to Mono Pass (Hike 50). Paul Richins Jr.

backcountry. Pack animals are a common fixture on some of the trails covered in this guidebook.

If you follow some simple rules for peaceful coexistence with the humble pack animals, you shouldn't have any problems sharing your way with them. Pack animals always have the right-of-way. If you are approached or overtaken by a string of mules or horses, it's your responsibility to give way. Leave the trail on the uphill side, and avoid loud noises or sudden gestures. Inexperienced riders usually have their hands full, and a startled horse or mule is dangerous to everyone in the vicinity.

Opposite: *A small pond near Long Lake with Mount Goode in the background (Hike 41). Paul Richins Jr.*

WESTSIDE
TRAILHEADS

The hikes on the west side of the Sierra Nevada (Hikes 1–26) are located east of the San Joaquin Valley towns of Fresno and Visalia with their trailheads in or near Sequoia and Kings Canyon National Parks. Hikes 1–8 are situated north of the park in the Sierra National Forest near Huntington Lake. Hikes 10, 13, and 14 are located just west of the park in Sequoia National Forest. The remainder of the trails (Hikes 9, 11, 12, 15–26) are in the Sequoia and Kings Canyon National Parks.

In the late 1800s, cattle grazing, logging, and mining threatened the lands that are today encompassed by Sequoia and Kings Canyon National Parks. On September 25, 1890, Sequoia National Park was established as the nation's second national park (shortly after the designation of Yellowstone as a national park). One week later the Grant Grove was added and the area of the park was tripled in size to ensure further protection of this magnificent natural resource from the ever-encroaching lumberjacks of the day. On March 4, 1940, Kings Canyon National Park was created. To protect Mineral King from future development, Congress transferred the management of the Mineral King area from the Forest Service to Sequoia National Park on November 10, 1978.

Sequoia and Kings Canyon National Parks contain the deepest canyons in North America, the highest peak in the contiguous forty-eight states, and the largest living thing on earth. The Kings Canyon reaches a depth of 8200 feet near the confluence of the middle and south forks of the Kings River. The depth of this canyon is without peer in North America. It is deeper than Hells Canyon in Idaho and the Grand Canyon in Arizona. At Roads End, the start of Hike 12, one can stand in the flat, glacial valley and peer up at the canyon walls rising nearly a mile overhead.

Mount Whitney, 14,491 feet, is the highest peak in the Lower 48. It is located on the eastern boundary of Sequoia National Park on the Sierra Nevada crest west of Lone Pine. The peak is highly coveted by hikers and peakbaggers. Each year about 30,000 hikers and climbers attempt its summit. Hike 32 describes the 22-mile round trip to the summit and back.

The giant sequoia is not the tallest tree, nor the oldest tree, but it is one of the largest of all living things. Its near-conical trunk is more like a club than a walking stick. Giant sequoias grow naturally only in one area of the world, the western slope of the Sierra Nevada between 5000 feet and 7000 feet. There are only seventy-five groves in this narrow climatic zone. These giant sequoia trees are commonly called Bigtrees or Sierra Redwoods, but are distinctly different from the coastal redwoods of California. The giant sequoia has a columnlike trunk, huge stout branches, and cinnamon-colored bark. The taller and more slender coastal redwood is more coniferlike in shape.

John Muir explored the Sequoia and Kings Canyon areas before they were designated national parks, and named the Giant Forest, where four of the world's five largest trees stand. His writings and descriptions of the canyons, giant sequoia groves, and lofty summits were partially responsible for the area being designated a national park.

After extensive exploration Muir, in November 1891, penned an article for the *Century Illustrated Monthly Magazine* titled "The Cañon of the South Fork of Kings River: A Rival of the Yosemite," in which he wrote:

> *In the vast Sierra wilderness far to the southward of the famous Yosemite Valley, there is a yet grander valley of the same kind. It is situated on the south fork of King's River, above the most extensive groves and forests of the giant sequoia, and beneath the shadows of the highest mountains in the range, where the cañons are deepest and the snow-laden peaks are crowded most closely together. It is called the Big King's River Cañon, or King's River Yosemite. It is about ten miles long, half a mile wide, and the stupendous rocks of purplish gray granite that form the walls are from 2500 to 5000 feet in height, while the depth of the valley below the general surface of the mountain mass from which it has been carved is considerably more than a mile. Thus it appears that this new Yosemite is longer and deeper, and lies embedded in grander mountains, than the well-known Yosemite of the Merced. Their general characters, however are wonderfully alike, and they bear the same relationship to the fountains of the ancient glaciers above them.*

To the east of the park's deep canyons and majestic groves of giant sequoia are magnificent mountains, lush meadows, glaciated cirques, and beautiful alpine lakes. This area is excellent for exploring, hiking, fishing, mountain climbing, ski mountaineering, and simply enjoying the scenery.

HUNTINGTON LAKE AREA

Because of its easy access, ample modern facilities, and abundance of outdoor opportunities, the area around Shaver and Huntington Lakes is popular with recreation-seekers. It offers many opportunities for hiking, camping, horseback riding, fishing, boating, water-skiing, sailing, hunting, and four-wheeling. There are many developed and undeveloped campgrounds in the area, as well as cabins, resorts, and lodges. Supplies are abundant at Shaver Lake and Huntington Lake but are limited as you venture deeper into the mountains along Kaiser Pass Road.

This guide focuses on the hiking and backpacking opportunities along Highway 168 and Kaiser Pass Road between Shaver Lake and Florence Lake. However, a trip into the backcountry could easily be coupled with any one of the many other enjoyable activities that are so popular in the area.

Hikes in this area offer a wide variety of outings for all interests and age groups. A short 1.6-mile round trip to a beautiful waterfall, a short ascent to an abandoned fire-prevention lookout station, a 7-mile loop

Huntington Lake from near the trailhead for Kaiser Peak (Hike 5).
Paul Richins Jr.

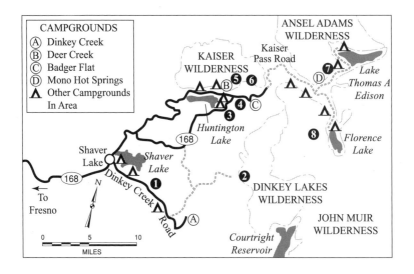

CAMPGROUNDS

(A) Dinkey Creek
(B) Deer Creek
(C) Badger Flat
(D) Mono Hot Springs
▲ Other Campgrounds
   In Area

trip to four beautiful lakes, or a challenging 10.6-mile round trip excursion to the top of a wonderful peak with panoramic views of the Sierra Nevada can be found in the Huntington Lake area (Hikes 1–8).

From Fresno, access to this multi-use area is northeast on Highway 168. Highway 168 is a two-lane paved road that ends at Huntington Lake. The road is kept open year-round for winter snow activities. Hikes 1–5 are located near Shaver Lake and Huntington Lake. To reach the more remote adventures (Hikes 6–8), drive to Huntington Lake and turn onto Kaiser Pass Road. This narrow, winding road soon becomes a dirt road and continues to Florence Lake. Access to the trailheads is along Kaiser Pass Road.

Trails in the Shaver/Huntington Lakes area head into four different wildernesses—the Dinkey Lakes Wilderness, the Kaiser Wilderness, the Ansel Adams Wilderness, and the John Muir Wilderness. The Dinkey Lakes Wilderness is adjacent to the John Muir Wilderness, separated only by the Ershim-Dusy Off-Highway Vehicle Route (a popular haunt for four-wheel-drive vehicle users). The wilderness is named for the delightful Dinkey Lakes, which, according to popular lore, honors a lonely trapper's faithful dog, Dinkey (see Hike 2).

The 22,700-acre Kaiser Wilderness is named for rugged Kaiser Ridge (Hike 5—Kaiser Peak), which acts as a geologic dividing line for the area. Located just north of Huntington Lake, the Kaiser Wilderness includes dense forests, beautiful meadows, and countless subalpine lakes and streams.

The trek to Doris Lake and Tule Lake (Hike 7) crosses into the Ansel Adams Wilderness, a vast area of more than 200,000 acres that encompasses the former Minarets Wilderness. The Ansel Adams Wilderness contains the headwaters of the Middle Fork and the North Fork of the San Joaquin River.

The fourth wilderness area approached via Kaiser Pass Road is the John Muir Wilderness, totaling 584,000 acres. Crater Lake (Hike 8) is on the western edge of the wilderness area. Mount Whitney (14,491 feet), the highest summit in the Lower 48, is located on its eastern edge.

Seasonal Forest Service offices are open from Memorial Day to Labor Day at the Highway 168–Kaiser Pass Road junction and on Kaiser Pass Road east of the Kaiser Pass summit. For a listing of the appropriate Sierra National Forest offices, refer to Appendix 1.

CAMPGROUNDS

Dinkey Creek Campground *(Hikes 1 and 2)*. Dinkey Creek Campground contains 128 sites for tents and RVs, spaced along beautiful Dinkey Creek. With flush toilets, piped water, firepits, picnic tables, and a nearby grocery store, the campground is less than rustic. The campground's rising popularity has contributed to the establishment of a reservation system for campsites. See Appendix 1 to make reservations.

To reach Dinkey Creek Campground, proceed along Highway 168 to the south end of the small community of Shaver Lake and turn east onto Dinkey Creek Road. Follow this paved road for about 14 miles to the campground.

Dinkey Creek Campground is open May to October. Reservations accepted. Moderate fee required.

Deer Creek Campground *(Hikes 3–5)*. This popular campground on Huntington Lake has 28 shaded sites for tents and RVs with piped water, picnic tables, and firepits. Convenient lake access and flush toilets contribute to its popularity.

To find Deer Creek Campground, drive Highway 168 to Huntington Lake and turn left onto Huntington Lake Road at the junction with Kaiser Pass Road. Continue 0.9 mile along the lakeshore to the campground.

Not only is this campground close to trailheads in the Huntington Lake area, it is also on the way to an interesting geologic formation known as Mushroom Rock—a massive wind-carved pinnacle of stone. Mushroom Rock commands a lofty view of Shaver Lake and the San Joaquin Valley.

Reach Mushroom Rock by driving Huntington Lake Road for 6.2 miles beyond the lake's lodge and post office. Go right on the unpaved Road 8S32 (signed for Mushroom Rock Vista) and continue 4.4 miles to the parking area.

Deer Creek Campground is open June to October. Reservations accepted. Moderate fee.

Badger Flat Campground *(Hike 6)*. Rustic Badger Flat Campground is a super spot. It offers access to the trailhead for Twin Lakes and is roomy and pleasant. Fish-rich Rancheria Creek is nearby. Add a wildflower meadow filled with a colorful constellation of shooting stars and this campground is hard to beat.

To find Badger Flat Campground, drive Highway 168 to the shore of Huntington Lake and turn right onto the Kaiser Pass Road (toward Mono Hot Springs and Florence Lake). Continue 5 miles and turn right into the campground. There are approximately 15 campsites for tents or RVs. You will have to provide your own drinking water.

Shaded sites offer picnic tables, firepits, and non-flush toilets. Be careful with your foodstuff (and at all campgrounds in the area), as bears are occasional visitors.

Badger Flat Campground is open June to October. No reservations. Moderate fee.

Mono Hot Springs Campground *(Hikes 7 and 8)*. Although it's a long drive to Mono Hot Springs Campground, this pleasant spot on the South Fork of the San Joaquin River attracts many campers, swimmers, and anglers. Come early in the day if you're hoping for a weekend site.

Mono Hot Springs Campground's 31 tent platforms include piped water, picnic tables, firepits, and non-flush toilets. The campground is a short walk from Mono Hot Springs Resort (with a spa and grocery store), and it's just a brief stroll to the trailhead for Hike 7.

To reach the campground, proceed on Highway 168 to the shore of Huntington Lake and turn right onto Kaiser Pass Road (signed for Mono Hot Springs and Florence Lake). Continue 5.7 miles on this good two-lane road, and then continue for 11.2 miles on a roughly paved one-lane road (not recommended for RVs).

At the junction to Mono Hot Springs and Florence Lake, turn left to Mono Hot Springs. Drive 1.7 miles to another hot springs sign and go left. It's 0.2 mile to the campground (18.8 miles total from Highway 168).

Mono Hot Springs Campground is open June to September. Reservations accepted. Moderate fee.

1. BALD MOUNTAIN LOOKOUT

Distance	■	3.5 miles round trip
Difficulty	■	Moderate
Starting point	■	6533 feet
High point	■	7826 feet
Elevation gain	■	1293 feet
Trail grade	■	720 feet per mile
Maps	■	USGS Dinkey Creek (1:24000) or Sierra National Forest Map (US Forest Service)
Access road/town	■	Highway 168 to Dinkey Creek Road/ Shaver Lake

This is one of the easier summit hikes described in this guidebook as well as one of the more rewarding summit outings. The hike is short (it can be completed in half a day or less), is not overly challenging, and has fantastic views—and the summit includes an old Forest Service fire lookout. The hike will take you through various stands of pine and fir, wildflowers, ferns, brush, and a vast array of glaciated granite formations.

From the small community of Shaver Lake turn east off Highway 168 onto the Dinkey Creek Road. Travel about 8 miles to the road summit and park on the north side of Dinkey Creek Road. The start of the trail is marked.

The trail begins in a thick grove of mature pine and fir trees with numerous varieties of wildflowers and ferns dotting the forest floor. The trail climbs steadily up the west ridge of Bald Mountain. As one ascends the ridge the trees become scattered and the glaciated granite, the namesake of Bald Mountain, is the principal element. After about 0.5 mile of hiking, the trail merges into the Bald Mountain Off-Highway Vehicle route. Follow the road for 1.3 miles to the top.

Do not let the fact that the trail joins an off-road vehicle route discourage you from this hike, as few vehicles should be encountered and one does not have to go as high as the 4x4 road to enjoy the superb views of Dinkey Creek. However, if you choose to continue to the unique upper rock formations, superb views of Shaver Lake, Blue Canyon, Pine Flat Lake, upper Dinkey Creek, the Three Sisters, Nelson Mountain, Eagle Peak, much of Sequoia National Park, the Central Valley, and the Coast Range make the climb to the top a worthy goal. An added bonus is the chance to explore the site of the old fire lookout.

*Bald Mountain and the old Bald Mountain Lookout, as viewed from Dinkey
Creek Road. Paul Richins Jr.*

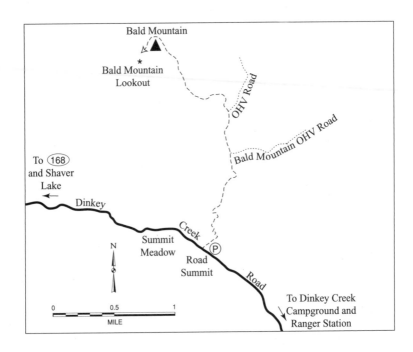

9. MYSTERY LAKE AND DINKEY LAKES

Distance ■	3.8 miles round trip (Mystery Lake) / 7 miles (First Dinkey Lake loop)
Difficulty ■	Easy / Moderate
Starting point ■	8590 feet / 8590 feet
High point ■	8960 feet / 9380 feet
Elevation gain ■	370 feet / 790 feet
Trail grade ■	185 feet per mile / 226 feet per mile
Maps ■	USGS Dogtooth Peak (1:24000) or Dinkey Lakes Wilderness (US Forest Service Map)
Access road/town ■	Highway 168 to Dinkey Creek Road/ Shaver Lake

This delightful hike is especially enjoyable in July and August when the delicate wildflowers and lush meadows are at their finest. Once Mystery Lake is reached, a new lake is passed every half mile or so.

To reach the trailhead, turn off Highway 168 at the south end of the small community of Shaver Lake and drive along the Dinkey Creek Road for about 10 miles. Turn left onto a paved road to the Dinkey

Lakes trailhead. This turnoff is about 3 miles west of the Dinkey Creek Ranger Station and 4 miles west of the Dinkey Creek Campground. Continue 6 miles to another junction and turn right. Stay on the main road for 4.7 miles (shunning branches to the left and right). At a three-way junction, make a hard right to the Dinkey Lakes trailhead. Continue the final 2.2 miles to the parking area.

Begin the hike with a short descent to the columbine-decked banks of Dinkey Creek. Cross the waterway and climb gently away from the creek. You will quickly regain the creek at 0.3 mile. Enjoy level walking through lodgepole pines and blossom-covered Labrador tea.

Recross Dinkey Creek and reach the sign for the Dinkey Lakes Wilderness at 0.5 mile. Continue gently uphill alongside the creek. Watch for the blooms of mountain pennyroyal, meadow penstemon, sticky cinquefoil, and golden brodiaea as you walk to a junction at 1.3 miles. Turn right toward Mystery Lake and recross Dinkey Creek.

It's a steady climb to the shore of Mystery Lake at the 1.6-mile point. Hike along the meadowy lakeshore, stealing views out across the water. There are many excellent spots to stop and enjoy the lake. If you have little time or want to shorten the hike, Mystery Lake or Swede Lake are good places to turn around. If you plan to continue on the loop to First Dinkey Lake, leave Mystery Lake at 2 miles and cross the creek descending from Swede Lake.

The trail climbs steeply for about 0.3 mile, ascending a series of switchbacks and finally arriving at Swede Lake. What a lovely spot to catch your breath! Of the four lakes in this loop, Swede Lake is the

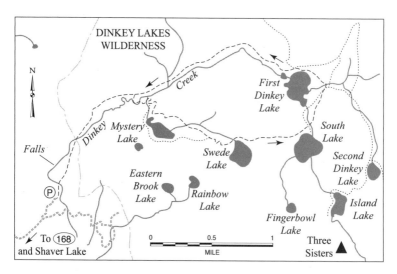

The Dinkey Lake loop includes four picturesque lakes. Paul Richins Jr.

most picturesque, has many campsites for the overnight backpacker, and has the best area for swimming with a nice sandy beach extending out into the lake. With a shoreline of Labrador tea, lodgepole pine, and mountain hemlock, Swede Lake paints a serene picture.

After you've rested, continue on by crossing an outlet creek choked with shooting star and tiger lily. Hike along the shore and resume climbing at 2.7 miles. A brief uphill climb melts into a short descent to South Lake at the 3.2-mile point. This large lake includes a score of camp spots, good fishing, and an impressive granite backdrop.

Cross over South Lake's outlet creek and follow the trail to First Dinkey Lake. You will quickly arrive on First Dinkey Lake's meadowy shores. If you time your hike for the height of the wildflower season, you will be treated to Lemmon's paintbrush, bistort, primrose monkeyflower, meadow penstemon, and shooting star—to name just a few of the area's treasures.

With the meadow in the foreground, the view toward 10,612-foot Three Sisters Peak is a scene to remember. Take in First Dinkey Lake's calm beauty and then press on to another junction at 4.1 miles. Keep left along the shore and begin a gradual descent beside Dinkey Creek.

Close the loop at 5.7 miles. A final 1.3 miles leads to the trailhead parking lot. The memory of this loop's matchless scenery will linger throughout your drive home.

3. INDIAN POOLS

Distance	■	1.4 miles round trip
Difficulty	■	Easy
Starting point	■	7050 feet
High point	■	7120 feet
Elevation gain	■	70 feet
Trail grade	■	100 feet per mile
Map	■	USGS Huntington Lake 7.5'
Access road/town	■	Highway 168 / Huntington Lake

The hike to Indian Pools along cascade-filled Big Creek is an ideal outing for families with young hikers. It is short and level and has scores of opportunities for picnicking and wading. Small children will be able to do most of the walk themselves. However, the trail is a bit rough in spots, so short-legged walkers may need a boost now and then. The hike is best enjoyed May–July when the creek's pools are brimming with snowmelt from the mountains high above. In late summer, the flow in Big Creek slows to a trickle, making the pools less inviting.

To reach the trailhead, drive Highway 168 toward Huntington Lake. About 1.5 miles south of the Kaiser Pass Road junction turn east into the Sierra Summit Ski Area area. Proceed 0.5 mile to the east end of the parking lot. Park at the far end of the lot, and look for a small sign for Indian Pools.

Set out on foot, following trail signs along a private road past several mobile homes. You will spy an official trailhead sign at 0.1

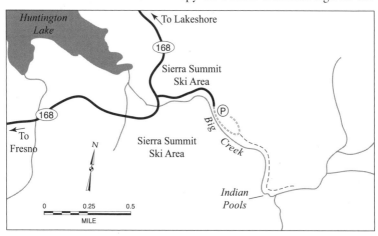

An inquisitive ground squirrel searches for a handout. Karen & Terry Whitehill

mile and gain a level trail through a forest of lodgepole pines and white firs. Early in the season, the way will be brightened by blossoms of larkspur, golden brodiaea, and bistort.

Reach the first of many pools along Big Creek at 0.4 mile. More pools lie ahead, so continue upstream. Scattered rocky sections will slow you just enough to allow you to delight in the abundance of azaleas in bloom along the creek.

The end of the official trail comes at 0.7 mile with the largest pool—clear and cold, overhung with incense cedars and Jeffrey pines and lined with sweet-smelling azaleas and mountain heather. This is a comfortable spot to enjoy your lunch and take a dip in the pool. If you desire a bit more privacy, continue upstream in search of smaller and quieter pools.

4. RANCHERIA FALLS

Distance ■	1.6 miles round trip
Difficulty ■	Easy
Starting point ■	7600 feet
High point ■	7800 feet
Elevation gain ■	200 feet
Trail grade ■	250 feet per mile
Maps ■	USGS Huntington Lake 7.5' and USGS Kaiser Peak 7.5'
Access road/town ■	Highway 168/Huntington Lake

Like the trek to Indian Pools (Hike 3), the walk to Rancheria Falls is an ideal family outing. It is short and easy, with a climb that youngsters can handle without difficulty. The waterfall is at its finest in the spring and early summer, as it may be up to 50 feet wide overflowing with snowmelt from the mountains high above. By the end of July and August the waterfall is reduced to a trickle.

To reach the trailhead, drive along Highway 168 toward Huntington Lake. Turn off at the sign for Rancheria Falls, about 0.5 mile south of the junction with Kaiser Pass Road. Leave the pavement and follow the dirt road 1.2 miles to the trailhead parking.

Begin your hike with a gentle climb. Your way will be decorated with broadleaf lupine, pearly everlasting, and gayophytum in July. The

Even in the summer, Rancheria Falls is a beautiful sight. In the spring, when the stream overflows with snowmelt, the falls impress even more. Paul Richins Jr.

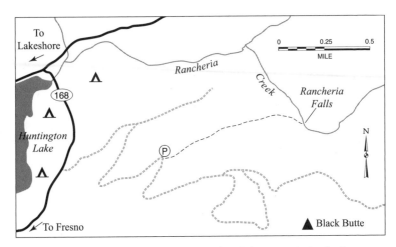

incline eases at 0.2 mile and white and red firs cast their shadows on the trail. A gentle climb intensifies slightly at 0.6 mile. Soon the sound of the falls will be apparent.

Catch your first look at the 150-foot-high Rancheria Falls at 0.7 mile and descend briefly to reach the water. This lively waterfall is a welcome sight, especially on a hot summer afternoon. The froth-flecked water fans out across a wide granite wall as though it were a glistening wedding veil, tossing icy spray like handfuls of white rice in the faces of its visitors.

A score of large boulders piled at the base of the waterfall provide sun-warmed perches for relaxation.

5. KAISER PEAK

Distance ■	10.6 miles round trip
Difficulty ■	Strenuous
Starting point ■	7150 feet
High point ■	10,320 feet
Elevation gain ■	3170 feet
Trail grade ■	598 feet per mile
Maps ■	USGS Kaiser Peak 7.5' or Kaiser Wilderness (US Forest Service)
Access road/town ■	Highway 168 / Huntington Lake

This hike to the summit of Kaiser Peak stands out from all the other outings in the Huntington Lake area. Although the hike is strenuous, the views of the Sierra Nevada from the summit are spectacular. Start early, bring plenty of water and a windbreaker, and you will agree it is worth the effort.

To reach the Kaiser Peak trailhead, drive Highway 168 to Huntington Lake. Turn left onto Huntington Lake Road at the junction with Kaiser Pass Road. Continue to Upper Deer Creek Lane (just before Kinnikinnick Campground) and turn right. Follow signs to D&F Stables. It is about 0.6 mile to the hikers' parking area located along the road just before the stables.

Walk through the pack station to its upper side to the start of the

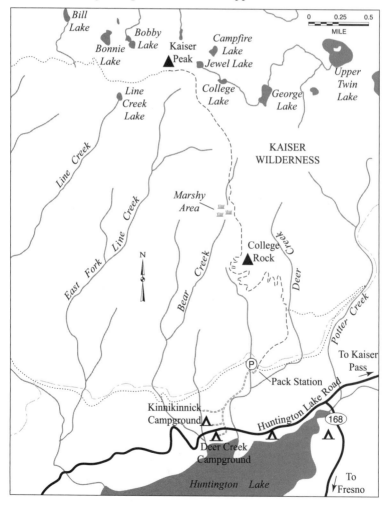

Rehydrating on the summit of Kaiser Peak. Karen & Terry Whitehill

Kaiser Loop Trail. The uphill climb begins immediately. Soon you will pass a sign marking the boundary of the Kaiser Wilderness area.

Ascend steadily on the trail shaded by white and red firs. The climb is continuous but the tiny white blossoms of gayophytum will cheer your upward progress. Walk beside a small creek at 0.6 mile and pass an unmarked trail to the right (it goes to Potter Pass).

You will see the tracks of many horses and an occasional deer as you climb a series of switchbacks through open areas of pinemat manzanita and chinquapin. Enjoy a wide panorama of Huntington Lake after 1.5 miles. The shade grows more scarce as you traverse a boulder-strewn hillside.

A rocky outcropping provides an excellent view of Huntington Lake at 1.9 miles. Watch for another viewpoint alongside a lone Jeffrey pine at 2.2 miles. Pause for a breather and gaze down at the tiny white sails of countless sailboats slicing through the surface of the lake like a score of shark fins.

Ascend a winding trail through a red fir forest as you push onward to the massive rock outcropping known as College Rock at 3 miles. It's a bit of a scramble to the top of the rock, but you will have views of distant eastern peaks in addition to Huntington Lake from this lofty perch.

Resume climbing to reach a flower-flooded marshy area at 3.5 miles. The trail levels off at last as you wade through a knee-deep jumble of shooting star, Indian paintbrush, Sierra wallflower, and single-stem groundsel.

Negotiate a steep pitch as the trail follows a streambed up to a lofty saddle at 4.3 miles. From this point you will get your first look at Kaiser Peak. Savor the break in the ascent and the far-ranging vistas to the west. Steal a peek at distant Mount Ritter to the north just before you descend to cross a small gully and look for Lake Thomas

A. Edison to the right at the bottom of the dip. At this point the trail steepens for 0.3 mile before a brief level stretch at the 4.8-mile point convinces you that you might make it after all.

The final assault on Kaiser Peak's elusive summit leads to a small sign for Kaiser Peak at 5.3 miles. Follow a rocky trail to reach the high point of your climb. Rest your legs and savor a 360-degree panorama unmatched anywhere in this area of the Sierra.

On a clear day, the view to the north will reach to the Minarets and Mount Ritter. You will see Mammoth Pool Reservoir to the northwest, Huntington Lake to the south, Mount Goddard to the southeast, and Mount Humphreys to the east. A host of smaller peaks completes the vista.

6. TWIN LAKES AND GEORGE LAKE

Distance	▪	7.2 miles round trip (Twin Lakes)/ 9.4 miles round trip (George Lake)
Difficulty	▪	Moderate / Moderate
Starting point	▪	8280 feet / 8280 feet
High point	▪	8980 feet / 9120 feet
Elevation gain	▪	1100 feet / 1600 feet
Trail grade	▪	306 feet per mile / 340 feet per mile
Maps	▪	USGS Kaiser Peak 7.5' and USGS Mount Givens 7.5', or Kaiser Wilderness (US Forest Service)
Access road/town	▪	Highway 168 to Kaiser Pass Road / Huntington Lake

The hike to Twin Lakes and George Lake offers both tantalizing lakeside destinations and an extra dose of scenery. The trail is challenging as it runs up and over 8980-foot Potter Pass, but not so difficult that it becomes discouraging. The surroundings offer ample reward for your efforts. An alternate trail that is shorter and requires less elevation gain is described at the end of this trail description.

To reach the Twin Lakes trailhead, drive along Highway 168 to Huntington Lake and turn right onto the Kaiser Pass Road (signed for Mono Hot Springs and Florence Lake). Continue 4.8 miles to riding and hiking trail 24E03. There is trailhead parking on the south side of the road. Cross the road to the Twin Lakes–Potter Pass Trail located on the north side.

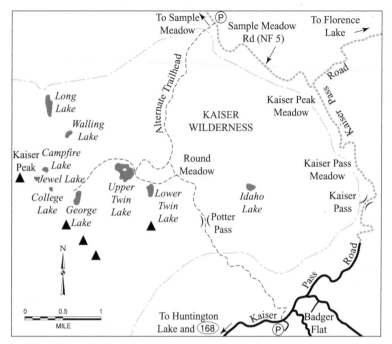

Begin climbing immediately, ascending a lodgepole-covered hill-side in a series of switchbacks. You will be glad for the shade of scattered Jeffrey pines, Sierra junipers, and red firs as you begin the climb over the first 0.4 mile.

Enjoy easier hiking for a short time and then resume climbing to a stream crossing at 1 mile. A flower-filled meadow is alive with shooting star, bistort, Sierra wallflower, and Macloskey's violet.

Climb gently to a saddle and then savor more level walking through a red fir forest. You will catch a wonderful view toward Huntington Lake at 1.6 miles as you cross an open hillside decorated with broadleaf lupine, mule ears, and bright purple larkspur.

The ascent continues to the crest of Potter Pass at 2.1 miles. If you are hiking on a clear day, you will want to linger, as the vista from the pass is magnificent, extending north to the Minarets and 13,157-foot Mount Ritter. The view is even more spectacular from a small knoll near the pass (on the left as you approach the saddle).

Enter the Kaiser Wilderness as you begin descending on a rocky trail through an avalanche of wildflowers. Your downhill tumble will ease at 2.5 miles, as you continue through a flower-covered basin. Reach a junction at 2.8 miles and turn left toward Twin Lakes, climbing moderately with fine views north toward the Minarets.

You will reach the shore of granite-backed Lower Twin Lake at 3.3 miles, but don't break out your picnic yet—Upper Twin Lake is the real treasure of this outing. Continue along the level trail to find this rocky gem at the 3.6-mile point.

Kaiser Peak dominates the scene above the lake and a large rock island lures hearty swimmers to its shores. Check out the lake's remarkable outlet stream. It dives underground as it exits the lake and then reappears a little farther downstream.

Tiger lilies in the grass along the trail. Karen & Terry Whitehill

If you want to make a longer day of it and have the energy, head to George Lake. This will add 2.2 miles to the round trip.

An alternate trail can be used to reach Upper Twin Lake and George Lake that is considerably shorter with less elevation gain than the hike described above. This route requires the effort of a 5-mile round trip with 800-foot elevation gain to reach Upper Twin Lake and a 7.2-mile round trip and 1300-foot climb to attain George Lake. This route does not go over Potter Pass so it is a bit more direct with less elevation gain.

To reach this alternate trailhead, drive to Kaiser Pass and continue on the Kaiser Pass Road in a northwesterly direction for about 3 miles. Turn left onto the dirt road to Sample Meadow Campground (Road NF 5). In 2.1 miles, park in the trailhead parking area on the northeast side of the road. The trail begins on the opposite side of the road.

7. DORIS LAKE AND TULE LAKE

Distance	■	1.8 miles round trip (Doris Lake) / 4 miles round trip (Tule Lake)
Difficulty	■	Easy / Easy
Starting point	■	6550 feet / 6550 feet
High point	■	6920 feet / 6920 feet
Elevation gain	■	370 feet / 370 feet
Trail grade	■	185 feet per mile / 185 feet per mile
Map	■	USGS Mount Givens 7.5'
Access road/town	■	Highway 168 to Kaiser Pass Road / Huntington Lake

This is a pleasant walk and is ideal for families with young children. The walk can be shortened further by hiking only to Doris Lake.

To reach the trailhead, refer to the driving directions at the beginning of this section for Mono Hot Springs Campground. Once at the Mono Hot Springs Resort, continue through the resort to the spur road for the trailhead. This road junction is just before the second entrance to the campground.

The spur road is extremely rough, so it may be best to leave your vehicle in the resort's day-use parking area or along the roadside near the spur road. The calculation of the hike's mileage begins from this point.

Set out walking on the dusty secondary road, and enjoy the blossoms of meadow penstemon, meadow goldenrod, cinquefoil, yampah, and wild rose. You will spot the official Tule Lake–Doris Lake trailhead in 0.4 mile.

Abandon the roadway and climb to a junction and a sign for the Ansel Adams Wilderness. Go left for Doris and Tule Lakes, and continue ascending through a landscape of manzanita, sage, and rock. Arrive at a second junction at 0.7 mile, and veer right for Doris Lake. If you're doing the entire hike and would prefer to end your trek with a refreshing swim, you can reverse the route and visit Tule Lake first before dipping into lovely Doris Lake.

Climb steeply from the junction following a creek up more gently to a flat basin filled with Jeffrey pines and Sierra junipers. Arrive at Doris Lake in only 0.9 mile.

Backed by a canvas of distant mountains, this sparkling gem is

A rocky shoreline cradles little Doris Lake. Karen & Terry Whitehill

definitely a swimmer's paradise. Its unique shoreline boasts steep rock embankments with sheer drops into the water that are sure to tempt the adventurous on a warm summer day. Use caution as you enjoy the lake and never dive without making certain of the depth of the water.

If you can tear yourself away from the beauty of Doris Lake, backtrack to the junction for Tule Lake to continue your trek. Turn right, taking the trail to Tule Lake, and climb a rocky route lined with sage and manzanita. The terrain levels off at the 1.4-mile point and you will descend to pass a pothole lake at 1.6 miles.

Enjoy easy walking to a junction at 1.8 miles and angle left for Hell Meadow. Follow the undulating trail to a rose-scented meadow. You will continue on beside a vast tule marsh before arriving at the aptly named Tule Lake at 2.2 miles.

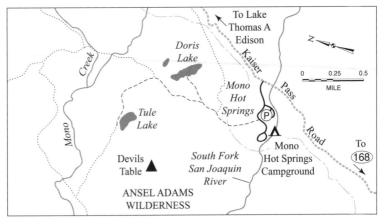

Although not particularly scenic, this petite lake (with a tule-lined shore) does have good fishing opportunities. Scramblers can add a detour to the top of the nearby Devils Table, a lava formation dusted with volcanic ash. Devils Table provides an excellent view of the surrounding area.

8. CRATER LAKE

Distance ■	8 miles round trip
Difficulty ■	Moderate
Starting point ■	7350 feet
High point ■	9380 feet
Elevation gain ■	2030 feet
Trail grade ■	508 feet per mile
Maps ■	USGS Dogtooth Peak 7.5', USGS Mount Givens 7.5', and USGS Florence Lake 7.5'
Access road/town ■	Highway 168 to Kaiser Pass Road / Huntington Lake

Although a bit of a drive to the trailhead, the setting for Crater Lake is superb. The lake is nestled into an impressive granite basin. Fishing and camping opportunities abound, and Crater Lake provides a fine backdrop for a picnic and relaxation.

To reach the Crater Lake trailhead, drive Highway 168 to the shore of Huntington Lake and turn right onto Kaiser Pass Road (toward Florence Lake). Continue 5.7 miles on the two-lane road and then continue 11.2 miles on a narrow one-lane road (not recommended for RVs). Arrive at the junction signed for Mono Hot Springs and

Florence Lake. Stay right for Florence Lake and drive 6.1 miles to a large day-use parking area.

The Crater Lake trailhead is at the far end of the day-use parking lot. Start ascending a rocky trail lined with Sierra junipers and manzanita. You will enter the John Muir Wilderness right away. Savor the shade of white firs, Jeffrey pines, and Sierra junipers. Unfortunately, the trees are much too scarce on this sun-exposed hillside.

It's a steady climb for 1.5 miles but then the grade mellows. The uphill climb covers some rocky terrain and lousy footing. Watch for rock cairns to guide you in spots where the trail grows faint. Continue upward, winding through a lodgepole pine forest, and regain open granite terrain at the 1.8-mile point. Again, you will need to watch for rock cairns to help you find the way. Look for stonecrop, mountain pride penstemon, and meadow penstemon, and lift your eyes for stunning views of distant mountains as you ascend the trail.

The grade intensifies at 2.2 miles. Ascend through trees to reach Dutch Lake and the crest of this section of your climb at 2.6 miles. Large but shallow, Dutch Lake is ringed by trees and a host of tule weeds. If the bugs are buzzing, you probably won't want to linger.

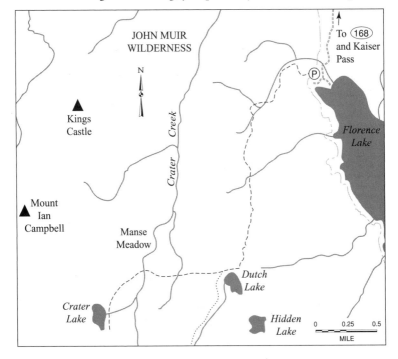

Go right with the trail along the lakeshore and arrive at a trail junction at 2.8 miles. Keep right for Crater Lake. You will enjoy level walking through trees and cross a stream lined with wildflowers at 3.4 miles. From this point, the climb to Crater Lake resumes.

Ascend gently at first, delighting in a ground cover of Brewer's lupine, and then begin working harder as the grade intensifies across a rocky hillside. You will have a fine view of surrounding peaks from the ridgeline just before Crater Lake. Arrive at the lakeshore at 4 miles.

The lake is set into a granite amphitheater dominated by a single peak. The scene is almost churchlike; the lone rock spire is reminiscent of a stout cathedral tower. Peel off your shoes, lean back, and enjoy the lake and its scenery.

Crater Lake. Karen & Terry Whitehill

SEQUOIA AND KINGS CANYON NATIONAL PARKS

Hikes described in this section (Hikes 9–26) originate in Sequoia National Forest and Sequoia and Kings Canyon National Parks. Hikes 10, 13, and 14 are in Sequoia National Forest, Hikes 9, 11, and 12 start in Kings Canyon National Park, Hikes 15–20 in Sequoia National Park, and Hikes 21–26 in the Mineral King area of Sequoia National Park.

There are three main roads that provide access into the area. Visitors traveling from the north via Highway 99 will turn east on Highway 180 at Fresno. If approaching from the south, turn off Highway 99 near Visalia and head to the mountains on Highway 198. Highway 198 enters Sequoia National Park from the south at Ash Mountain and works its way east and then north to Highway 180 and Kings Canyon National Park, thus forming a loop through the park.

The third approach is the Mineral King Road. It departs Highway 198 east of the small community of Three Rivers just before the Ash Mountain entrance into Sequoia National Park. This paved, twisting, narrow 25-mile-long paved road is the only access to remote Mineral King Valley. In the 1870s, the Mineral King Road was built by miners and few improvements,

Watchtower as viewed at sunrise on the Pear Lake Trail (Hike 18). Paul Richins Jr.

other than paving, have occurred over the years. This tediously slow drive may help preserve this priceless corner of the wilderness from being trampled by admirers.

Forest Service offices and National Park Visitor Centers contain a wealth of information. (Appendix 1 contains a list of the visitor centers). Grant Grove Visitor Center is located near the northern entrance (Highway 180) to Sequoia and Kings Canyon National Parks. The Ash Mountain Visitor Center is reached immediately after passing the south entrance (Highway 198/Ash Mountain). Much farther up the road the Lodgepole Visitor Center and Campground is a hub of activity. Maps, brochures, campground listings, and hiking advice are all readily available. Visitor center personnel will also let you know about ranger-led hikes and fireside talks. Look for schedules of activities in the parks' newspaper, *The Sequoia Bark* (see Appendix 2).

It is difficult to speak about Sequoia National Park without referring to Kings Canyon National Park in the same breath. The two share such close association, both geographically and administratively, that most visitors think of the 864,000-acre package as a single, yet widely diverse, park.

Sequoia and Kings Canyon National Parks are certainly popular, attracting more than two million visitors each year. This sounds like a lot of visitors, and it is, but the area seems almost deserted by comparison to crowded Yosemite National Park. Although the parks are busy in the summer months, opportunities for solitude abound in their vast wildernesses.

Both Sequoia National Park and Kings Canyon National Park possess some of the finest giant sequoias to be found anywhere. Hikes 9, 10, 15, 19, 20, and 21 provide tours through impressive groves. The Giant Forest grove in Kings Canyon National Park (Hike 9) includes four of the five largest giant sequoias in the world, and the forest possesses a serene beauty that visitors will long remember. A network of well-maintained, self-guiding trails leads to scores of impressive forest giants as well as to the remnants of logging operations that once threatened their existence. Families will find many opportunities for both recreation and education.

The namesake of Kings Canyon National Park is the canyon of the Kings River, whose south and middle forks cut an awesome swath through the wilderness. Kings Canyon is more than 8000 feet deep at the confluence of the south and middle forks of the Kings River. The Junction View overlook (see the information on Sentinel Campground)

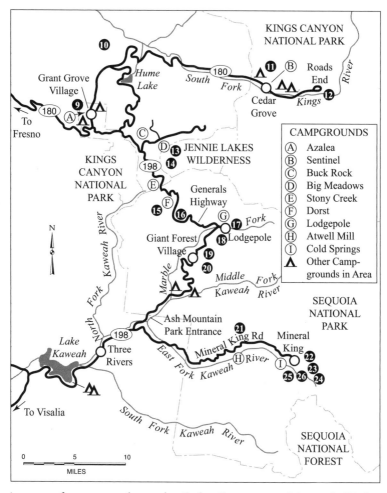

is a must for any traveler to the Cedar Grove area of the park. Highway 180 descends into this mighty canyon and contains many vista points along the road to Cedar Grove/Roads End.

The Mineral King area located in a remote southern corner of Sequoia National Park has its own unique history. A mining rush in the 1870s brought bevies of prospectors to the valley in search of silver ore. Many mines were established in the early 1870s but long winters, devastating avalanches, and disappointing yields contributed to the bust of the mining boom less than ten years later.

Fortunately for Mineral King, the United States government gained interest in the area, even as the miners lost it. Mineral King was made part of the Sierra Forest Preserve in 1893. All wasn't smooth sailing as the area nearly fell victim to development of a large commercial ski area by the Disney Corporation in the 1960s and 1970s. Opponents stalled the process with lawsuits and Congress declared the area a part of Sequoia National Park in 1978.

Arm yourself with bug repellent: mosquitoes are a problem April–July. Because the heat can be intense in summer, plan your hikes for early in the day. You will also have to guard your food closely in the campgrounds. Ground squirrels will carry away anything that's edible, and bears can cause havoc if food is not stored properly in bear-proof food boxes. In the Mineral King Valley munching marmots are an annoyance and have been known to eat the hoses and wires of parked cars. Refer to the discussion of bears and other mischievous critters in the Flora and Fauna section.

CAMPGROUNDS

Azalea Campground, Kings Canyon National Park *(Hikes 9 and 10).* This large campground near the Big Stump Entrance Station to Kings Canyon National Park is convenient for hikers and sightseers. With 113 sites for tents and RVs, Azalea Campground can absorb a lot of visitors. Even so, it's best to come early to claim a spot.

To reach Azalea Campground, drive east on Highway 180 from Fresno and enter Kings Canyon National Park at the Big Stump Entrance Station. Continue 1.6 miles and turn left toward Cedar Grove. In another 1.4 miles the Grant Grove Visitor Center is reached. From the visitor center, proceed 0.3 mile to the turnoff for Azalea Campground and the Grant Tree. Turn left and then turn in to the campground. An easy footpath from Azalea Campground leads to the General Grant Tree and the start of Hike 9, North Grove Loop.

Sites offer firepits, picnic tables, piped water, flush toilets, and bear-proof food storage boxes. Beware of marauding ground squirrels. The campground is near restaurants, a market, gift shops, showers, horseback riding, and RV disposal at the visitor center.

Azalea Campground is open all year. No reservations. Moderate fee.

Sentinel Campground, Kings Canyon National Park *(Hikes 11 and 12).* Tucked in the deep recesses of Kings Canyon National Park, Sentinel Campground is surrounded by deep granite walls. The outstanding scenery, coupled with the nearby trails, make Sentinel Campground an ideal spot to pound in your tent stakes and stay awhile.

To reach Sentinel Campground, drive Highway 180 from Fresno and enter Kings Canyon National Park at the Big Stump Entrance Station. Continue 1.6 miles, turn left toward Cedar Grove and drive 1.4 miles to the Grant Grove Visitor Center. From the visitor center, proceed 29.2 miles on often-winding but beautiful Highway 180 to Cedar Grove Village. Be sure to pause along the way to enjoy Junction View, a wonderful vista point above the confluence of the south and middle forks of the Kings River. The viewpoint is 10.8 miles from the Grant Grove Visitor Center.

Sentinel Campground has 82 sites for tents and RVs, scattered along a shaded shore of the south fork of the Kings River. The campground offers firepits, picnic tables, piped water, flush toilets, and bear-proof food storage boxes. A market, restaurant, gift shop, showers, laundry, RV disposal, and horseback riding are located 0.25 mile away in Cedar Grove. Other equally nice campgrounds in the Cedar Grove area include Canyon View (37 sites), Moraine (120 sites), and Sheep Creek (111 sites).

Sentinel Campground is open April to October. No reservations. Moderate fee.

Buck Rock Campground, Sequoia National Forest *(Hikes 13 and 14)*. Besides an easy access to the trailhead for Jennie and Weaver Lakes, rustic Buck Rock Campground has another plus to its credit: it's on the way to Buck Rock Lookout. This is an attraction visitors to the area won't want to miss.

To reach Buck Rock Campground, proceed east on Highway 180 from Fresno and enter Kings Canyon National Park at the Big Stump Entrance Station. Continue for 1.6 miles and turn right to Sequoia National Park and Giant Grove. Proceed 7 miles and turn left on Big Meadows Road. Drive the paved road toward Big Meadows for 2.9 miles and turn left to Buck Rock Campground. The campground will be reached in 0.4 mile.

This primitive campground has a handful of shaded sites scattered along the road. There is no drinking water but picnic tables, firepits, and non-flush toilets are available. If you're visiting during the height of mosquito season (June through early August) be sure to bring repellent—the bugs can be nasty.

While at Buck Rock Campground, visit the impressive Buck Rock Lookout. It's only a couple of miles from the campground. Continue on the unpaved road. Turn right at a major fork in the road and continue to the designated parking area. Walk the level, gated road to the base of Buck Rock. The lookout is perched on top of the rock cliff.

Lack of funding forced the closure of Buck Rock Lookout in 1989. The spectacle of the little lookout atop its massive pillar of stone is sure to amaze and delight all comers.

Buck Rock Campground is open June to October. No reservations. No fee.

Big Meadows Campground, Sequoia National Forest *(Hikes 13 and 14).* Although a bit less secluded than Buck Rock Campground, Big Meadows Campground has a more pleasant setting along the banks of Big Meadows Creek. More than 20 sites for tents or RVs attract scores of forest lovers and anglers. You will have to bring drinking water but the campground provides picnic tables, firepits, and non-flush toilets.

To reach Big Meadows Campground, drive east on Highway 180 from Fresno and enter Kings Canyon National Park at the Big Stump Entrance Station. (You will exit the park and enter Sequoia National Forest farther on.) Continue for 1.6 miles and turn right to Sequoia and Giant Grove. Proceed 7 miles and turn left onto Big Meadows Road. Follow the paved road toward Big Meadows for 2.9 miles. At the Buck Rock junction, continue toward Big Meadows. Another 1.2 miles will take you to the campground.

Big Meadows Campground is open June to October. No reservations. No fee.

Stony Creek Campground, Sequoia National Forest *(Hikes 13–17).* This Forest Service campground is an excellent option. Located near the Generals Highway, Stony Creek Campground is tucked into a parcel of Forest Service land between the national park campgrounds of Azalea and Dorst.

To reach the campground, drive east on Highway 180 from Fresno and enter Kings Canyon national park at the Big Stump Entrance Station. Continue for 1.6 miles and turn right to Sequoia and Giant Grove.

Proceed 12.2 miles (passing the turnoff for Big Meadows) to the campground entrance. This pleasantly shaded campground sits on the banks of Stony Creek and comes equipped with a friendly campground host.

Currently, Stony Creek Campground offers some reserved sites through the Forest Service's 800-280-CAMP number (Appendix 1) and some on a first-come, first-served basis. Firepits, picnic tables, drinking water, and flush toilets are standard at the approximately 50 sites for tents or RVs.

The campground is open June to October. Reservations accepted. Moderate fee.

Dorst Campground, Sequoia National Park *(Hikes 15–18)*. Dorst Campground is an excellent accommodation option for the Giant Forest area of Sequoia National Park. If you like camping in style, you will like Dorst Campground. See Appendix 1 to make reservations.

To reach Dorst Campground, enter Sequoia National Park via Highway 180 from Fresno or Highway 198 from Visalia and Three Rivers. You will find Dorst Campground 16.7 miles from the Big Stump Entrance Station (Fresno route) or 12 miles northwest of Giant Forest Village (Visalia route) on the Generals Highway.

Dorst Campground has picnic tables, firepits, piped water, flush toilets, and a bear-proof food storage box for each of its 204 sites. It is located 8 miles from Lodgepole Visitor Center and market, deli, and post office. The campground is situated on Dorst Creek, but you will probably be hard pressed to find the little waterway amid all the asphalt.

Dorst Campground is open June to September. Make reservations. Moderate fee.

Lodgepole Campground, Sequoia National Park *(Hikes 16–20)*. This campground is a bustling testimony to the popularity of Sequoia National Park. It is a hub of activity with reservations nearly mandatory. Unclaimed reserved sites are distributed on a first-come, first-served basis but without reservations your chances of claiming a site are slim.

Situated on the Marble Fork of the Kaweah River (fishing and swimming opportunities abound), Lodgepole Campground has a market, showers, and a laundromat to accommodate its hundreds of daily residents. Its 258 sites for tents and RVs offer picnic tables, firepits, piped water, and flush toilets. Bears are frequent visitors to this grocery-laden corner of the wilderness. Each campsite has a bear-proof box, and patrolling rangers will make sure the boxes are used.

To reach Lodgepole Campground, enter Sequoia National Park via Highway 180 from Fresno or Highway 198 from Visalia and Three Rivers. You will find Lodgepole Campground 4.3 miles northeast of Giant Forest Village on the Generals Highway.

The campground is open all year. Make reservations. Moderate fee.

Atwell Mill Campground, Sequoia National Park, Mineral King *(Hikes 21–26)*. Atwell Mill Campground is a charmer. It's situated in the Atwell Grove of giant sequoias, and these magnificent trees and mighty stumps lend the spot its personality. The campground is seldom crowded and its 23 quiet tent spots are near the banks of Atwell

Creek. One Mineral King hike, Atwell Grove and Paradise Peak (Hike 21), starts just across the road from the camping area. The campground offers drinking water, firepits, picnic tables, non-flush toilets, and a bear-proof food storage box per campsite.

To reach the campground, drive Highway 198 northeast from Visalia and turn off at Hammond (3.6 miles east of Three Rivers) at a sign for Mineral King. Trailers and RVs are not recommended on the narrow, winding Mineral King Road.

It is open May to September. No reservations. Moderate fee.

Cold Springs Campground, Sequoia National Park, Mineral King *(Hikes 21–26).* Cold Springs Campground owns a pleasant spot on the East Fork of the Kaweah River. It's shaded and peaceful. With its proximity to the Mineral King trailheads and ranger station, Cold Springs Campground is usually a hub of activity. Its 37 tent sites are often full, so try to arrive early in the day to claim a spot.

To reach the campground, refer to driving directions for Atwell Mill Campground and continue past Atwell Mill Campground another 4.3 miles.

Cold Springs Campground offers drinking water, non-flush toilets, picnic tables, firepits, and bear-proof food storage boxes.

The campground is open May to September. No reservations. Moderate fee.

9. NORTH GROVE LOOP

Distance ■	1.8-mile loop
Difficulty ■	Easy
Starting point ■	6320 feet
High point ■	6400 feet
Elevation gain ■	400 feet
Trail grade ■	222 feet per mile
Maps ■	USGS Hume 7.5' and USGS General Grant Grove 7.5', or Sequoia and Kings Canyon National Parks Recreation Map (Tom Harrison Maps)
Access road/town ■	Highway 180/Grant Grove Visitor Center

Few visitors to the Grant Grove neglect a stop at the famous General Grant Tree. This massive tree is an impressive sight. Combine a visit to the Grant Tree with this easy walk through the usually quiet North

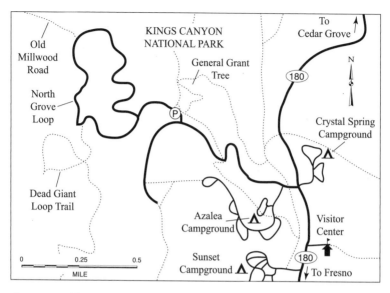

Grove to add some serenity to your sightseeing adventures. This is an ideal hike for families; the distance is short and the grades are easy. If you are staying at the nearby Azalea Campground, take the connecting trail from the campground to the trail.

To reach the General Grant Tree, follow driving directions provided for Azalea Campground at the beginning of this section. After turning off Highway 180 for Azalea Campground and the Grant Tree, continue 0.8 mile to a large parking area beside the much-visited grove. If you want to park near the start of the North Grove loop, drive to the far end of the parking area designated for RV and bus parking.

Proclaimed "the nation's Christmas tree" in 1926, the mighty General Grant Tree has not lost any of its popularity since then. You will certainly get a feel for its sheer size and mass while standing beneath this masterpiece of nature.

Take the 0.5-mile, self-guided loop trail past the Grant Tree, the Robert E. Lee Tree, and the massive Fallen Monarch before starting the North Grove loop.

To start the North Grove Loop, look for a sign at the far end of the RV parking area. The hike begins with a gentle descent on an asphalt roadway. Continue downhill on an old logging road, hiking in the shade of sugar and ponderosa pines, white firs, and incense cedars. Keep an eye out for scattered giant sequoias along the way. They look particularly majestic among the smaller trees.

Giant sequoias (left) and incense cedars grow side by side on the North Grove Loop. Karen & Terry Whitehill

Scan the forest floor for wildflowers. An outburst of Sierra rein orchids can be found in a grassy nook to the right of the trail at the 0.4-mile point. Pass an interesting "twin" sequoia on the left side of the trail at 0.7 mile and continue downhill through a varied forest that's delightfully quiet.

Reach the bottom of the hill and the old Millwood fire road at 0.9 mile. This nearly obliterated roadway leads to the site of Millwood, a busy lumber town in the 1890s. From the town, vanquished giant sequoias were floated down a flume many miles to the town of Sanger, in the San Joaquin Valley near Fresno.

Look for a fire-scarred sequoia on the left side of the trail and start uphill, passing a handful of living sequoias along the way. The presence of sugar pines in this forest offers an ironic study in contrasts. Sugar pinecones are often more than a foot long while the tiny giant sequoia cones, fallen from their towering hosts, nestle comfortably in a child's hand.

The route levels out at 1.2 miles. Regain the paved road at 1.3 miles. Turn left (or go right if you want to lengthen your hike by taking in the Dead Giant Loop Trail) and climb uphill on the asphalt. Reach the parking area at 1.8 miles to complete the short forest loop.

10. BOOLE TREE

Distance	■	2 miles round trip
Difficulty	■	Easy
Starting point	■	6260 feet
High point	■	6750 feet
Elevation gain	■	490 feet
Trail grade	■	490 feet per mile
Maps	■	USGS Hume 7.5' or Sequoia and Kings Canyon National Parks Recreation Map (Tom Harrison Maps)
Access road/town	■	Highway 180/Grant Grove Visitor Center

A journey to the base of the gigantic Boole Tree is markedly different from a visit to the much-publicized General Grant Tree (Hike 9). The Boole Tree is outside the boundaries of Kings Canyon National Park and you won't have to compete with the Grant Grove crowds. You can relax in the solitude and splendor of the Sequoia National Forest even as you absorb the spectacle of a record-sized giant sequoia.

Named for Frank Boole, the general manager of the Sanger Lumber Company, the Boole Tree was discovered, and spared the loggers' saw blades, in 1903. The tree is 269 feet high and holds claim to being the largest sequoia in a national forest.

To reach the trailhead, drive Highway 180 from Fresno and enter Kings Canyon National Park at the Big Stump Entrance Station. Continue 1.6 miles and turn left toward Kings Canyon and Cedar Grove. Drive 5.8 miles, exiting the park along the way, to reach an easy-to-miss turnoff for the Boole Tree. Turn left onto Road 13S55 and follow signs for the Boole Tree Trail. The trailhead parking area

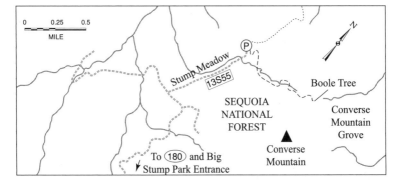

is reached in 2.7 miles. The trail, marked by a sign for the Boole Tree, takes off on the right.

Begin climbing on a footpath lined by fragrant mountain misery. Watch for golden brodiaea and mariposa lily—both are plentiful along the route. It is a steady uphill climb as you traverse a hillside covered

The massive Boole Tree. Karen & Terry Whitehill

with manzanita and bracken ferns. Occasional young sequoias are sprinkled among incense cedars, white firs, and canyon live oaks.

Ascend a series of switchbacks at 0.6 mile and continue up a stairstepped trail to reach the crest of the climb at 0.8 mile. From this point you will get a good look at the battered top of the Boole Tree. Scramble to the top of a burned sequoia stump, on the left side of the trail, for a better view of the canyon of the Middle Fork of Kings River.

A brief descent leads to an informational plaque and an excellent photo opportunity of the Boole Tree at 0.9 mile. Continue your descent and reach the base of this giant at 1 mile. Savor the silence of the spot as you gaze up a seemingly unending tree trunk. Then walk around the giant's base and marvel at this masterpiece of nature before retracing your steps back to the parking area.

11. CEDAR GROVE OVERLOOK

Distance ■	5 miles round trip (Cedar Grove Overlook) / 8-mile loop (Lewis Creek Trail loop)
Difficulty ■	Moderate / Moderate
Starting point ■	4700 feet / 4700 feet
High point ■	6100 feet / 6200 feet
Elevation gain ■	1600 feet / 1800 feet
Trail grade ■	640 feet per mile / 533 feet per mile
Maps ■	USGS Cedar Grove 7.5' or Kings Canyon High Country Trail Map (Tom Harrison Maps)
Access road/town ■	Highway 180/Cedar Grove Visitor Center

This trail will treat you to scenic hiking and an impressive overlook of Kings Canyon and surrounding peaks. An early start is suggested, as the low elevation at the start becomes less enjoyable when the sun is high. Despite the manageable distance, this isn't a great hike for children because of the steep climb. Hike 12, Mist Falls, is a better selection for families with young hikers.

For the more energetic, you can turn this hike into an 8-mile loop by continuing up the Lewis Creek Trail and then descending back to Cedar Grove Village via that route. Dramatic mountain vistas are experienced along the entire loop with views that extend to the Monarch Divide.

The trailhead is located at Cedar Grove just off Highway 180. From Fresno, take Highway 180 east and enter Kings Canyon National Park at the Big Stump Entrance Station. Continue 1.6 miles and turn left for Kings Canyon and Cedar Grove. Drive 30.6 miles on a beautiful but winding road with turnouts to view the deep river canyon. Turn left into Cedar Grove Village and keep to the right following signs to the pack station.

Begin at the Hotel Creek trailhead staying to the right. The trail to the left is the return trail from the Lewis Creek loop. Hike on a sandy footpath, enjoying the shade of incense cedars and ponderosa pines. The aroma of mountain misery blossoms is everywhere.

Pass a footpath veering toward Hotel Creek at 0.3 mile but continue climbing up the main trail. If you are hiking early in the day you may spot deer coming downhill for a drink. Deer tracks are often more numerous than footprints on this path.

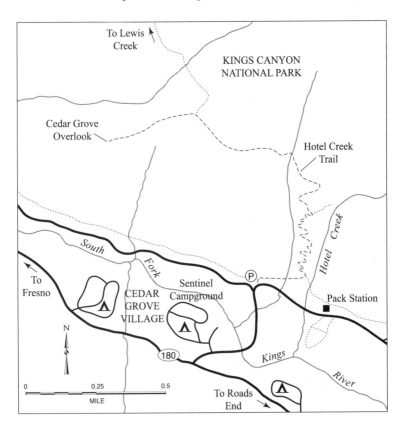

Early morning light on the pinnacles in Sequoia and Kings Canyon National Parks. Paul Richins Jr.

The switchbacks start in earnest at 0.4 mile and you will lose most of the shade as the trail climbs between sun-loving patches of chinquapin, manzanita, and canyon live oaks. *Manzanita* means "little apple" in Spanish. Pretty pinkish white flowers decorate the manzanita branches in the spring. Watch for the plant's small, round berries in August.

Sneak ever-improving views down toward Cedar Grove Village as you continue to ascend. The grade eases slightly at 1.1 miles and another use trail exits toward Hotel Creek.

Continue upward through scattered ponderosa pines and marvel at the multitude of lightning-seared trees. At the 1.7-mile point, a brief downhill leads to more climbing. At 2.1 miles, reach the trail junction for Cedar Grove Overlook and the trail toward Lewis Creek. Descend briefly and catch views of the opposite canyon wall. The trail levels off for a time and then a gentle climb ends abruptly at the rocky knoll overlook at the 2.5-mile point.

Settle down on a comfortable boulder and savor the bird's-eye vista of the canyon floor. You will see Sheep Creek Campground just below and hear the roar of the South Fork of the Kings River filtering up on the breeze. Across the canyon is Sentinel Ridge. Up the canyon, the backcountry of Kings Canyon National Park beckons those with backpacks and strong legs.

If you decide to take the Lewis Creek Trail loop, hustle back 0.4 mile to the trail junction and turn left toward Lewis Creek. Continue north for about 1.5 miles over a gradual trail to the junction of the Lewis Creek Trail. Turn left (south) descending Lewis Creek Trail for 2.1 miles. As you near the South Fork Kings River and Highway 180 turn left (east). In about 1.5 miles you will arrive back at your starting point.

12. MIST FALLS

Distance	▪	8.6-mile loop
Difficulty	▪	Moderate
Starting point	▪	5030 feet
High point	▪	5680 feet
Elevation gain	▪	650 feet
Trail grade	▪	167 feet per mile
Maps	▪	USGS The Sphinx 7.5' or Kings Canyon High Country Trail Map (Tom Harrison Maps)
Access road/town	▪	Highway 180/Cedar Grove Visitor Center

Despite its length, this hike to Mist Falls is a pleasant family outing. The trail is excellent, the ascent is gentle, and the waterfall provides a beautiful destination.

To reach the trailhead from Fresno, take Highway 180 and enter Kings Canyon National Park at the Big Stump Entrance Station. Continue 1.6 miles and turn left toward Kings Canyon Cedar Grove. Drive 36 miles on a scenic but winding paved road to Roads End, where the trail begins. You will pass the turnoff to Cedar Grove and the numerous campgrounds, including Sentinel Campground, about 5 miles before you reach Roads End.

Turn in to the paved parking area and make use of the piped water and toilets before you start. Look for the trailhead sign for Bubbs Creek and Mist Falls at the far end of the parking area (near the information booth) and set out on a level, sandy trail beneath a canopy of black oaks, incense cedars, and ponderosa pines.

Cross a small side stream on a wooden footbridge and walk gently uphill. Views of the canyon walls will attract your eyes even as the murmur of the South Fork Kings River floods your ears. At midday, the sun is warm throughout this section so you will be thankful for a thickening of the trees at 1.5 miles.

Bracken ferns cover the ground beneath an umbrella of green branches. Look for massive boulders among the vegetation, castoffs from the sheer canyon walls. Reach a junction at 1.9 miles and angle to the left toward Mist Falls and Paradise Valley. The Bubbs Creek Trail is to the right and crosses the South Fork Kings River on a long steel bridge.

At the trail junction, the trail starts to gain a bit of elevation. The

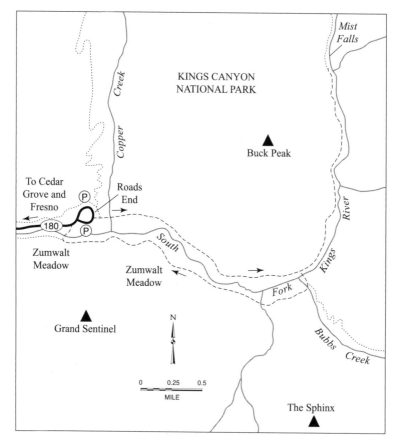

uphill climb is more noticeable as you get a peek at Bubbs Creek joining the South Fork Kings River on the right. Continue along the South Fork, ascending through a proliferation of ferns and thimbleberries.

The river is a beautiful shade of aqua, decorated with a frothy white mane. In June and July the river can be a raging torrent. Your climb intensifies at 3 miles and you will be treated to fine views of the cliffs on both sides of the canyon. Reach a small waterfall at 3.1 miles. The moderate climb continues.

Exchange trees and shade for manzanita and hot granite as you climb. Spectacular views of the south canyon wall will reward your efforts. Arrive at the sign for Mist Falls at 3.9 miles. Veer right onto a short use trail to reach the water's edge. Picnic spots abound beside the waterfall. Choose a place just below the falls and you can enjoy lunch with the mist of the falls cooling your face.

The first 2 miles of the trail to Mist Falls are nearly flat. The scenery along the trail is fantastic, with granite walls towering several thousand feet overhead. Paul Richins Jr.

When you've finished savoring Mist Falls, backtrack 2 miles to the junction beside Bubbs Creek. You can add a scant 0.8 mile to your day and enjoy a return route along the opposite bank of the South Fork of the Kings River by going left at the junction.

Cross the South Fork on a long, steel footbridge and continue to a second junction in 0.2 mile. Turn right toward Roads End. This side of the river has fewer people, more trees to offer shade, and a hefty dose of pleasant scenery. Enjoy gradual downhill walking to a trail junction and another bridge. Turn right and recross the South Fork. Angle upstream to the parking area where you started.

13. WEAVER LAKE

Distance	■	4.2 miles round trip (Fox Meadow trailhead) / 7.2 miles round trip (Big Meadows trailhead)
Difficulty	■	Easy / Moderate
Starting point	■	7900 feet / 7600 feet
High point	■	8710 feet / 8710 feet
Elevation gain	■	810 feet / 1110 feet
Trail grade	■	385 feet per mile / 308 feet per mile
Maps	■	USGS Muir Grove 7.5' or Mount Whitney High Country Trail Map (Tom Harrison Maps)
Access road/town	■	Highway 180/Grant Grove Visitor Center

The pleasant hike to Weaver Lake is a perfect family outing. The trail is good, the inclines are moderate, and the destination pleasing. Carry a fishing pole (if you're in the mood) and a picnic lunch. Weaver

Lake is in the Jeannie Lakes Wilderness and Sequoia National Forest, and is located due west of Kings Canyon National Park.

This hike, as well as Jennie Lake (Hike 14), has two trailheads—one at Big Meadows and the other at Fox Meadow. To reach the trailheads from Fresno, take Highway 180 east and enter Kings Canyon National Park at the Big Stump Entrance Station. Continue for 1.6 miles and turn right toward Sequoia National Park and Giant Grove. Proceed 7 miles and turn left toward Big Meadows. Drive the

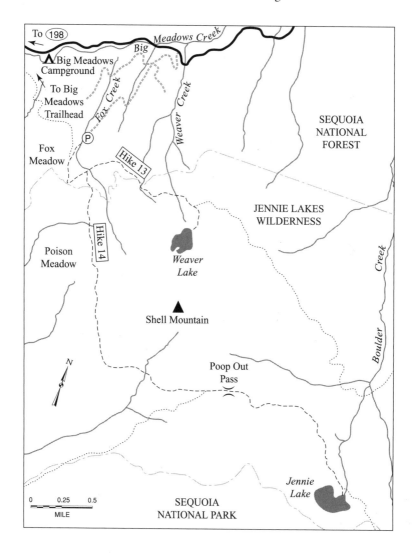

paved road for 2.9 miles to the turnoff to Buck Rock Campground. Continue through the junction toward Big Meadows. You will soon reach the Big Meadows trailhead on the right.

To reach the Fox Meadow trailhead, continue past the Big Meadows trailhead. At the junction to Burton and Heart Meadows stay to your right. Cross Big Meadows Creek and immediately turn right onto the unsigned dirt road, Road 14S16. This turnoff is 1.7 miles from Big Meadows Trailhead and 0.5 mile from the road junction to Heart Meadow. Stay to the left and then to the right when two spur roads (14S16A and 14S16B) branch off the main road. Drive to the end and the trailhead 1.4 miles beyond the paved road.

The Fox Meadow trailhead is unsigned and cuts off about 1.5 miles in each direction. The following description is from the Fox Meadow trailhead.

Start hiking on a trail that skirts the lower edge of a large tree plantation, and then cross over Fox Creek. Look for tiger lily and bistort on the banks of the little waterway. Begin climbing through a shady red fir forest and pass flower-filled Fox Meadow.

The Big Meadows trail comes in from the right at 0.2 mile. Continue to the left, being sure to note the junction so that you don't miss it on your way back. Hike steadily uphill beneath a red fir ceiling, enjoying occasional outbursts of nude buckwheat and mariposa lily.

Arrive at a junction for Weaver and Jennie Lakes at 0.7 mile. Continue to the left for Weaver Lake. Cross a small creek and climb

Weaver Lake is a pleasant hike for young children and offers many fishing opportunities. Paul Richins Jr.

again, negotiating a gentle incline across a hillside carpeted with pinemat manzanita. Pass the entry sign for the Jennie Lakes Wilderness at 0.8 mile.

Granite, trees, and more granite surround you as you walk onward, enjoying open vistas of the mountainous country to the north. The grade eases atop a fir-covered hill at 1 mile. Soon you will reach a lush ravine flooded with ranger buttons, lupine, and Labrador tea at the 1.3-mile point.

Work your way across a boulder-sprinkled hillside. The route levels off at 1.6 miles. Cross a seasonal stream, Weaver Creek, descending from Weaver Lake. Gentle uphill walking follows.

Hike on through red firs and western white and lodgepole pines to arrive at a trail junction at 1.9 miles. Keep to the right and climb gently to reach the shore of Weaver Lake at 2.1 miles.

Although it's fairly shallow, Weaver Lake is attractive, set off by stark granite slopes. A grassy shoreline tempts picnickers and anglers alike. This lake is popular with backpackers as well so you may spot a few tents.

14. JENNIE LAKE

Distance	■	10.4 miles round trip (Fox Meadow trailhead) / 13.4 miles round trip (Big Meadow trailhead)
Difficulty	■	Moderate / Strenuous
Starting point	■	7900 feet / 7600 feet
High point	■	9120 feet / 9120 feet
Elevation gain	■	1400 feet / 1700 feet
Trail grade	■	269 feet per mile / 254 feet per mile
Maps	■	USGS Muir Grove 7.5' or Mount Whitney High Country Trail Map (Tom Harrison Maps)
Access road/town	■	Highway 180/Grant Grove Visitor Center

See map page 77

The trek to Jennie Lake has many features that make this moderately challenging hike worth the effort: the scenery is lovely, the route explores the Jennie Lakes Wilderness, and the trail is much less crowded than routes in the nearby Sequoia and Kings Canyon National Parks.

To reach the trailhead, refer to the driving directions for Hike 13,

Weaver Lake. The trailheads are the same for both hikes. The trail description is from Fox Meadow. Follow the directions for Hike 13 up to the trail junction at the 0.7-mile point. Leave the Weaver Lake route by turning right for Jennie Lake.

The trail gains elevation for a short distance as it enters the Jennie Lakes Wilderness in Sequoia National Forest. The grade mellows slightly as you continue. Cross a small creek at 1.2 miles and enjoy the cheery company of Labrador tea, shooting star, arrowleaf groundsel, and California corn lily. Climb to the edge of Poison Meadow at 1.4 miles, enjoying more level walking.

Soon you will reach a vista to the west at 1.9 miles. The hillside opens up as you traverse a landscape of pinemat manzanita and rock.

Watch for views of peaks to both the south and the east as you begin to angle toward Poop Out Pass at 2.4 miles. If the day is clear you should spot Sequoia National Park's Alta Peak in the distance.

Descend gently and resume climbing at 2.7 miles. The grade intensifies as you traverse a rocky slope. Pass a side trail descending toward Generals Highway at 3.3 miles. Breathe easier as the incline eases once again.

Reach the rather uninspiring Poop Out Pass at 3.7 miles. Unfortunately, the trees obscure the vista from the pass. Begin a steep descent. The trail is rough as it avoids a large slide area.

You will be treated to views of the mountains to the north as you continue across a rocky hillside and then begin the climb toward Jennie Lake at 4.9 miles. Ascend for 0.3 mile over a moderate grade through a forest of red firs, lodgepole pine, and western white pine.

Jennie Lake is a favorite destination for day hikers and backpackers. Paul Richins Jr.

Keep an eye out for Jennie Lake's outlet stream. Leave the main trail by veering right to the outlet of the lake. This short junction is unsigned.

Suddenly, the past few hours of difficult hiking does not seem so bad. This lovely lake is tucked into a semicircle of glaciated white granite. A forested shoreline faces the windswept rocky side, offering shaded camping for backpackers and lunch spots for day hikers.

15. MUIR GROVE

Distance ■	5 miles round trip
Difficulty ■	Easy
Starting point ■	6750 feet
High point ■	6850 feet
Elevation gain ■	450 feet
Trail grade ■	180 feet per mile
Maps ■	USGS Muir Grove 7.5' or Mount Whitney High Country Trail Map (Tom Harrison Maps)
Access road/town ■	Highways 180 or 198/Lodgepole Visitor Center

The hike from Dorst Campground to the Muir Grove is a "don't-miss" trek for anyone staying in a Dorst campsite. The hike offers pleasant walking, enjoyable vistas, and a chance to visit a serene grove of majestic sequoias.

To reach the trailhead, refer to the driving directions for Dorst Campground at the beginning of this section. Enter the campground and follow signs for the amphitheater to a day-use parking area beside the trailhead. If you're camping at Dorst, walk to the trailhead from your campsite.

Set out on the Muir Grove trail by skirting the hillside above Dorst Campground's 204 busy sites. The gentle, undulating trail passes through a shady white fir forest where sunlight-seeking ferns push their fronds skyward. A seasonal stream is crossed at 0.9 mile. Watch for columbine, cow parsnip, and angelica along the banks.

Begin to climb steadily among thick firs and pines. An occasional sugar pinecone will amaze you with its size. Stop and pick up one of these monstrous cones and you will be thankful you weren't underneath it when it fell.

Ascend well-graded switchbacks and gain the summit of a little knoll at 1.3 miles. This knoll will provide the first peek of the tantalizing Muir Grove atop a distant hill. To the right of the trail a granite-covered knob peppered with stout Jeffrey pines makes an excellent vista point.

Continue on the level trail as you begin the detour around the tree-filled ravine that separates you from the sequoia grove. Wild spearmint, spreading dogbane, Indian paintbrush, and nude buckwheat are just a few of the flowers you will find along the trail.

At 2 miles, cross a creek overhung with Pacific dogwood and lush with moisture-loving ferns. Shaded, easy walking follows and you will soon come upon the first of the Muir Grove giants at 2.5 miles.

Even if you've seen sequoias a dozen times before, you will marvel at the grandeur of these giant trees. Something about this setting, hidden away on a forested hilltop miles from parking lots and vending machines, makes the Muir sequoias seem even more magnificent. Wander and wonder, then retrace your steps back to your starting point.

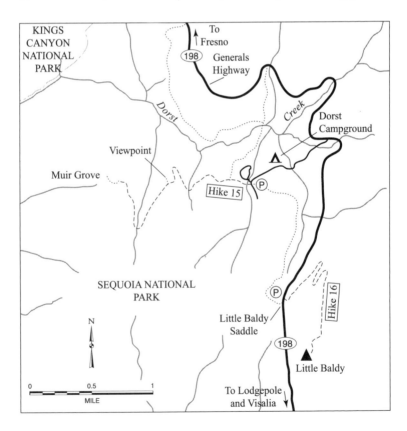

*The Muir Grove rules an unspoiled hilltop in Sequoia National Park. Karen &
Terry Whitehill*

16. LITTLE BALDY

Distance	■	3.4 miles round trip
Difficulty	■	Easy
Starting point	■	7355 feet
High point	■	8040 feet
Elevation gain	■	700 feet
Trail grade	■	412 feet per mile
Maps	■	USGS Giant Forest 7.5' and USGS Muir Grove 7.5', or Mount Whitney High Country Trail (Tom Harrison Maps)
Access road/town	■	Highways 180 or 198/Lodgepole Visitor Center

See map page 82

This easy hike to the top of Little Baldy is a wonderful short hike with
great views to the east into the high country of Sequoia and Kings
Canyon National Parks, as well as to the west and the Central Valley.

Little Baldy is perched immediately above the Sequoia–Kings Canyon Highway. The short hike to the top offers a 360-degree view of Sequoia and Kings Canyon National Parks. Paul Richins Jr.

Due to its commanding views, Little Baldy was used as a fire lookout many years ago. The trek is easy enough for young children. Bring your binoculars and camera.

To reach the Little Baldy trailhead, enter Sequoia National Park from Fresno via Highway 180 or Visalia on Highway 198. The Little Baldy Trail is about 6.7 miles beyond Lodgepole Campground (via Visalia) or 1.6 miles beyond Dorst Campground (via Fresno). Park in the roadside pullout area at Little Baldy Saddle.

Set out on a shaded trail that climbs gently beneath a forest of white firs. Continue up the hill and gain a view of Big Baldy at the 0.4-mile point. You will see this barren, granite dome off to the left, thrust above a dark-green foreground of trees. There is a short trail to Big Baldy, but the hike up Little Baldy is the better choice with superior views.

Ascend a series of rocky switchbacks. The cooling shade is left behind as the trees begin to thin. Scattered Jeffrey pines sweeten the air with the butterscotch scent of their trunks. Top a rise at 1.1 miles and begin a gentle descent through a forest of red firs. A brief climb at 1.3 miles provides a dramatic view of the distant mountains. Hike on as a jagged line of peaks unfolds along the distant horizon.

At 1.5 miles, start into the final uphill push toward Little Baldy's summit. The hike ends atop this treeless, granite dome at 8040 feet. Enjoy the panoramic view from the top. Views of the High Sierra and the wilderness areas of Sequoia and Kings Canyon National Parks to the east can be fantastic on a cloudless day. The view to the west is usually hazy but the sunsets can be special from the dome. If you plan to watch the sunset from the top, bring a flashlight for the easy descent.

17. TOKOPAH FALLS

Distance	▪	3.8 miles round trip
Difficulty	▪	Easy
Starting point	▪	6750 feet
High point	▪	7380 feet
Elevation gain	▪	630 feet
Trail grade	▪	332 feet per mile
Maps	▪	USGS Lodgepole 7.5' or Mount Whitney High Country Trail Map (Tom Harrison Maps)
Access road/town	▪	Highways 180 or 198/Lodgepole Visitor Center

The falls are at their finest in the spring (April, May, and June) when the river is raging with the runoff from the winter snows high above Pear Lake (Hike 18). In the summer the falls almost disappear and the river is reduced to a relative trickle as the last of the snow melts.

The hike offers a scenic walk beside the Marble Fork of the Kaweah River. It is a great opportunity to trade the busy life at Lodgepole Campground for an enjoyable stroll along a shaded stream. In the early morning hours, deer and other wildlife may be spotted along the way.

To reach the trailhead, turn in to Lodgepole Campground from the Generals Highway (Highway 198), and drive 0.7 mile to the

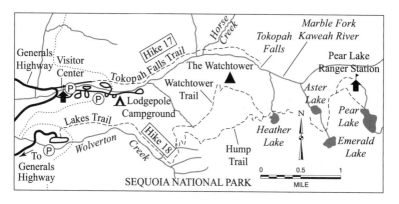

Tokopah Falls trailhead. There is parking just before a log bridge that crosses the Marble Fork. The trail begins on the other side.

Start hiking beside the Marble Fork and take in views across the river to the campsites along the opposite shore. Afternoons bring scores of swimmers to the riverbanks but the crowds begin to thin as you leave the campground.

Climb gently beneath a canopy of red firs, Jeffrey pines, and incense cedars. Keep an eye out for the impressive form of the Watchtower perched high above the river canyon on your right. The trail to Heather and Pear Lakes traverses above the Watchtower. This 1600-foot cliff survived the grinding passage of the Tokopah Glacier, the

The short trail to Tokopah Falls starts near the Lodgepole Campground and Visitor Center. Photo compliments of Sequoia and Kings Canyon National Parks.

massive chisel of moving ice that sculpted this U-shaped canyon millions of years ago.

Pass a small waterfall and a handful of inviting wading pools at 0.6 mile. The Tokopah Falls Trail continues at a gentle incline beside the Marble Fork. Children may require a helping hand through a few brief rocky sections but most of the route is easy. At 1.2 miles, reach a tempting nook where the Marble Fork scoots across a bench of water-smoothed stone. Cross a feeder stream on a footbridge. Views of the Watchtower unfold as you reach a second bridge at 1.3 miles. Above the Watchtower you may be able to glimpse the trail to Heather and Pear Lakes. The forest floor is green with bracken ferns. Cross another bridge at 1.4 miles. Continue on through red firs and Jeffrey pines.

You will get your first peek at Tokopah Falls at 1.6 miles. Early in the season, when the runoff is abundant, Tokopah Falls is a wonderful cascade of gushing water. Later in the summer, it is simply a pretty picture, a score of rivulets trickling across a wall of rock decorated with cheery yellow common monkeyflower.

The landscape becomes increasingly rocky and occasionally passes beneath a large overhanging boulder. The trail ends abruptly near the base of the falls at 1.9 miles.

18. HEATHER LAKE AND PEAR LAKE

Distance	▪	8.2 miles round trip (Heather Lake) / 12.4 miles round trip (Pear Lake)
Difficulty	▪	Moderate / Strenuous
Starting point	▪	7280 feet / 7280 feet
High point	▪	9200 feet / 9510 feet
Elevation gain	▪	2120 feet / 2630 feet
Trail grade	▪	517 feet per mile / 424 feet per mile
Maps	▪	USGS Lodgepole 7.5' or Mount Whitney High Country Trail Map (Tom Harrison Maps)
Access road/town	▪	Highways 180 or 198/Lodgepole Visitor Center

See map page 85

The hike to Heather Lake and on to Emerald and Pear Lakes is perhaps the best of the westside hikes. The scenery is outstanding, the

Heather Lake and Pear Lake are two of the more beautiful destinations described in this guidebook. Paul Richins Jr.

canyon below the Watchtower is spectacular, and the high alpine terrain of Emerald Lake and Pear Lake is superb. Emerald Lake and Pear Lake are about 1 and 2.1 miles beyond Heather Lake and are the gems of this outing. An added bonus is the Pear Lake Ranger Station, the finest backcountry hut in the Sierra Nevada. The hut is occupied by a park ranger in the summer. The trip to Pear Lake is a classic whether taken on foot in the summer and fall or on skis in the winter and spring.

To reach the trailhead, take the Wolverton turnoff from the Generals Highway (2.7 miles northeast of Giant Forest Village) and drive 1.5 miles on paved road to the trailhead parking lot.

Start hiking by climbing through a red fir forest to reach the junction with Lodgepole Campground Trail at 0.1 mile. Stay right following the Lakes Trail (don't take the Long Meadow Trail, which turns sharply to the right) and continue gently up through the forest. The mountainside is dry and relatively open, and is scattered with chinquapin, nude buckwheat, and gayophytum.

At 0.9 mile the environment changes as the trail begins to follow a wildflower-lined creek. Enjoy broadleaf lupine, cow parsnip, leopard lily, and arrowleaf groundsel as you climb. Meander through a spearmint-scented meadow at 1.7 miles. Cross the creek and reach a trail junction at 1.8 miles. Turn left toward Heather Lake.

Cross another flower-lined waterway and climb steadily to the junction of the Hump and Watchtower Trails at 2 miles. The trail via the Watchtower is recommended because it is much more scenic and bypasses the steep climb and descent of the Hump Trail. However, the Hump is a good option for early-season hiking when snow is present. The Watchtower Trail is generally free of snow by the end of June. Check with the park ranger for trail conditions. The Watchtower Trail traverses high above the canyon and provides spectacular views of the Kaweah River's Marble Fork far below. The trail description and mileage of this hike assumes the Watchtower option.

Turning left for the Watchtower Trail, the grade mellows. Cross another creek at 2.5 miles. The flowers are spectacular in July. A series of switchbacks gradually ascends toward the Watchtower as the unfolding view diverts your attention. Pause at the cliffs for an amazing vista down into the canyon cut by the Marble Fork and Tokopah Falls (Hike 17). This massive prow of granite that you are now standing on is the Watchtower, rising 1600 feet above the river below.

The route continues upward along a trail hewn into the face of the cliff above Tokopah Valley at 3.6 miles. You will spot the Tokopah Falls Trail to Tokopah Falls far below. This is one of the best parts of the hike. The trail is as spectacular as the view. Look for Silver Peak and Mount Silliman in the distance.

The trail angles away from the cliffs at 4 miles. The Hump Trail will join in from the right. Gain the shore of Heather Lake at 4.1 miles. From Heather Lake the trail traverses through the Emerald Lake/Aster Lake drainage, around a prominent point to Pear Lake

Ranger Station and Pear Lake. Pear Lake is nestled in a spectacular horseshoe-shaped glacial cirque below Alta Peak. For those planning an overnight backpack trip, there are excellent campsites at Emerald Lake and Pear Lake. A wilderness permit is required (Appendix 1).

The Pear Lake Ranger Station is about 0.3 mile below the lake and is staffed with a ranger in the summer. In the winter the hut makes a wonderful base camp for telemark skiers. The hut can be reserved in the winter, but not the summer, through Sequoia Natural History Association (Appendix 2).

19. BIG TREES

Distance ■	4.3-mile loop
Difficulty ■	Easy
Starting point ■	6900 feet
High point ■	7000 feet
Elevation gain ■	300 feet
Trail grade ■	70 feet per mile
Maps ■	USGS Lodgepole 7.5' and USGS Giant Forest 7.5', or Mount Whitney High Country Trail Map (Tom Harrison Maps)
Access road/town ■	Highways 180 or 198/Lodgepole Visitor Center

This enjoyable family hike begins on the 2-mile Congress Trail, perhaps the most often hiked trail in Sequoia National Park. Despite the crowds, the Congress Trail is worth a visit. It passes the world's most impressive giant sequoias. Combine the Congress Trail with the remainder of this hike and you will have a fine mix of solitude and splendor.

To reach the trailhead, drive the Generals Highway 2.1 miles east of Giant Forest Village and turn off at the General Sherman Tree. There's a vast parking area just off the highway complete with restrooms and tour buses. Informational pamphlets for the Congress Trail are available at the trailhead.

Begin your walk at the trail sign for the Sherman Tree—why not start with the biggest first? A brief climb leads to the base of this forest giant where a sign proclaims the Sherman Tree to be the "largest living thing on earth."

From the General Sherman Tree, turn right and walk to the self-guiding-pamphlet dispenser. Then continue along the sidewalk to a sign for the Congress Trail.

The forest hike starts by crossing shimmering Sherman Creek on a wooden footbridge and then proceeding past the Leaning Tree. Climb gently on an asphalt pathway, passing beneath sequoias and past scores of sheltering firs. Reach a junction at 0.5 mile and keep left on the Congress Trail.

Continue climbing to a junction with the Alta Trail at 0.9 mile. Stay right and descend through a picturesque setting of broadleaf lupine and dozens of towering sequoias. Follow the Congress Trail to

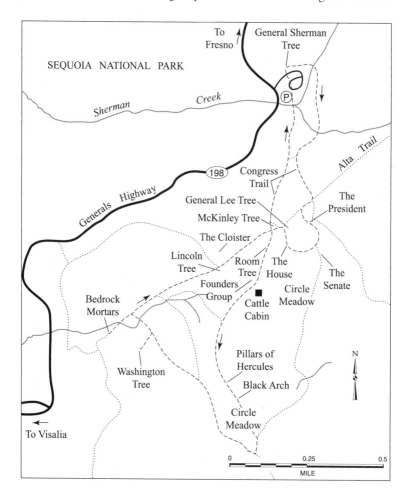

the feet of the President at 1.1 miles and walk on to view the Senate nearby. The group of sequoias known as the Senate is a lovely cluster of closely spaced giants.

Stay on the Congress Trail and descend through a forest awash in broadleaf lupine and bracken ferns to find the House at 1.3 miles. Like its counterpart, the Senate, this group of sequoias is enchanting, especially when the morning sun slants through the ancient trunks in a golden glow.

Soon you will pass the General Lee Tree. Stay left along the Congress Trail to reach a junction beside the McKinley Tree at 1.4 miles. Make your escape from the crowds as you abandon the busy Congress Trail and head left on a pathway for Cattle Cabin.

Descend past the Room Tree on the unpaved trail. The forest floor is spectacular, a canvas painted with sun, trees, and blossoming lupine. Pass through the Founders Group at 1.6 miles and arrive at Circle Meadow. Continue to the right, hiking beside flower-filled Circle Meadow, as you proceed to a junction at 1.8 miles.

Turn left for Crescent Meadow and follow the undulating trail through firs and giant sequoias. Your path will take you between two mighty stumps, called the Pillars of Hercules, at 2.1 miles. Tiptoe through the Black Arch and descend to Circle Meadow.

Pause to enjoy the view along the meadow filled with wildflowers. At the next junction, continue to the right toward Crescent Meadow. In 0.1 mile, turn right again toward the Washington Tree.

Descend to the edge of Circle Meadow. Angle left for the Washington Tree at 2.6 miles. Your undulating route leads to a short spur trail for the Washington Tree at 2.9 miles. Stay right at the junction, following the sign for the Alta Trail.

You will reach a junction with the Alta Trail at 3.1 miles. A short side trip to the left leads to a scattering of bedrock mortars and an interesting glimpse into the daily lives of the Indians who inhabited this forest long before the arrival of the Europeans. Return to the junction and continue on toward the Congress Trail as you begin to close your loop.

Stay with signs for the Congress Trail to reach the Lincoln Tree at 3.6 miles. Continue straight on the Alta Trail, passing the serene group of sequoias known as the Cloister along the way. You will regain the paved and populated Congress Trail at the McKinley Tree (3.7 miles). Go left and return to your starting point at 4.3 miles.

20. CRESCENT MEADOW

Distance	▪	2.3-mile loop
Difficulty	▪	Easy
Starting point	▪	6700 feet
High point	▪	6880 feet
Elevation gain	▪	180 feet
Trail grade	▪	78 feet per mile
Maps	▪	USGS Lodgepole 7.5' or Mount Whitney High Country Trail Map (Tom Harrison Maps)
Access road/town	▪	Highways 180 or 198/Lodgepole Visitor Center

Like the preceding hike, this walk in Crescent Meadow promises a visual overload of forest beauty. Bring along the family, take your camera for the flowers and the big trees, and douse yourself with bug juice for the nasty mosquitoes.

To reach the trailhead, turn off Generals Highway at Giant Forest Village and take the paved road for Moro Rock and Crescent Meadow. Drive 2.7 miles to the large parking area at Crescent Meadow. You will find restrooms and drinking water.

If you have the time pause at Moro Rock before or after your trek through Crescent Meadow (the Moro Rock turnoff is 1.3 miles off

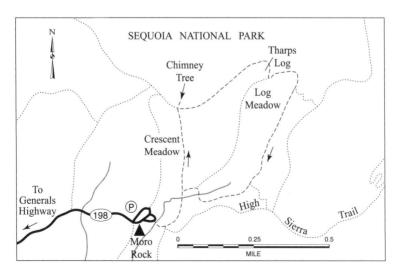

Early morning light illuminates Moro Rock. Take the stairs to the top for a wonderful view. Paul Richins Jr.

the Generals Highway on the road to the Crescent Meadow). Moro Rock provides a spectacular view of the Kaweah River and a vista that encompasses the Great Western Divide to the east and the San Joaquin Valley to the west. Be ready—353 stair steps and a 300-foot climb leads to the top of this impressive rock.

From the parking lot at the Crescent Meadow trailhead, begin walking at a large redwood sign marking the beginning of the High Sierra Trail. This trail ends on the summit of Mount Whitney, about 70 miles to the east, and is one of the most spectacular trails in the entire Sierra Nevada; it tunnels through the mountain in places and is blasted out of vertical cliffs in other areas. Your asphalt pathway skirts the edge of Crescent Meadow, a charming swath of flower-speckled green, immortalized by the writings of John Muir a century ago and guarded by an encircling battalion of giant sequoias today.

At 0.1 mile turn left for Tharps Log. Turn left again at 0.3 mile toward Chimney Tree. Pause often to savor the sweetness of the meadow. Set against a backdrop of dark tree trunks, the glowing green of the sunlight-splattered meadow is a beautiful sight.

Turn in to the forest, along a trail edged with lush ferns and broad-leaf lupine, and reach a junction at 0.7 mile. Go right for Tharps Log but first explore the short side trail to the amazing Chimney Tree. Climb away from the junction on a winding trail and make the short descent to Log Meadow and Tharps Log at 1 mile. Hale Tharp was the first white man to taste the treasures of the Giant Forest. He brought his cattle to this hidden meadow more than 100 years ago, passing the sweltering months of summer living in the cool shadows of the hollowed-out Tharps Log.

Leave Tharps Log and continue toward the High Sierra Trail by skirting the perimeter of Log Meadow. This is a hauntingly beautiful scene, a hymn to the ongoing life of the forest. Massive fallen giants sprawl across the meadow floor, their long-dead trunks impervious to decay, their once-green needles replaced by sprays of living wildflowers.

A junction at 1.2 miles will lead toward the High Sierra Trail. Continue along the edge of Log Meadow to another junction at 1.7 miles. Go right for Crescent Meadow. When you reach the main trail go left. Veer left once more as you regain the edge of Crescent Meadow. Keep right at the next junction and return to the parking lot at 2.3 miles.

21. ATWELL GROVE AND PARADISE PEAK

Distance	■	3.8 miles round trip (Atwell Grove) / 11 miles round trip (Paradise Peak)
Difficulty	■	Easy / Strenuous
Starting point	■	6520 feet / 6520 feet
High point	■	7500 feet / 9362 feet
Elevation gain	■	980 feet / 2842 feet
Trail grade	■	516 feet per mile / 517 feet per mile
Maps	■	USGS Silver City 7.5' or Mount Whitney High Country Trail Map (Tom Harrison Maps)
Access road/town	■	Highway 198 to Mineral King Road/ Silver City Resort

Although the climb to Paradise Peak is a strenuous 11-mile trek, don't let that stop you. This hike has great potential as a family outing, especially for those staying in the adjacent Atwell Mill Campground. Simply walk as far as you like. You will get a look at a wonderful assortment of giant sequoias within the first mile.

To reach the trailhead for Atwell Grove and Paradise Peak refer to the driving directions for Atwell Mill Campground at the beginning of this section. The trailhead is located about 0.3 mile west of the campground entrance on the Mineral King Road. It is signed "Hockett Trailhead Parking."

Begin climbing in the shade of thick incense cedars and white firs following a trail lined by fragrant mountain misery. Deer are common. Ascend steadily in countless switchbacks. Jeffrey pines and sugar pines contribute to the vast variety of trees along the way. You will gain a view across the canyon at 0.6 mile as the grade eases briefly. The first large grouping of giant sequoias is nearby. The trees are beautiful, towering silently above the trail, their trunks glowing red in the filtered sunlight. The giant sequoias hidden away on this forested hillside seem timeless and untouched by tourism.

Ascend through a lush ravine awash in ferns and broadleaf lupine at 1 mile. Fallen sequoias have transformed the hillside into a giants' cemetery. The atmosphere is almost eerie. Climb on across a more open slope with views toward the upper reaches of the East Fork of the Kaweah River.

Manzanita, mountain misery, and assorted brambles threaten to overrun the trail. Continue upward to gain another treat at the 1.8-mile point. More sequoias linger in the shadows, guarding both sides of the path like sentries expecting an enemy attack.

The switchbacks become more serious; if you are making this hike to view the sequoias you may turn back at this point. If you are en route to Paradise Peak, shift to low gear and continue upward.

Arrive at a saddle in Paradise Ridge at 3.2 miles. Unfortunately, there's not much of a view. The trail to the right continues on to Redwood Meadow. Take the route to the left toward Paradise Peak, following a faint trail along the tree-covered ridge.

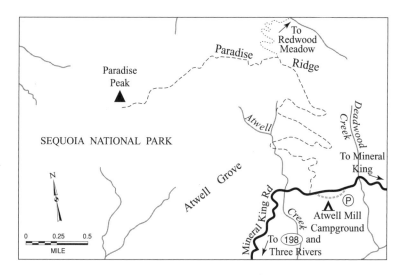

The view from Paradise Peak. Karen & Terry Whitehill

Intermittent rock cairns will help you stay on the trail. The climb picks up momentum and the views improve as you advance along the ridge. Skirt to the right of a granite knoll at 4 miles. The short scramble to its top will provide a view of several peaks above Mineral King Valley. Push on. The Castle Rocks come into view to the north.

Pick your way along an increasingly open, rocky ridge. Suddenly you will arrive, gaining the flat-topped pile of boulders known as Paradise Peak. Congratulations!

A small weather station and a USGS marker identify the spot. It seems rather anticlimactic—until you sample the view. Peer over the edge of the rocky outcropping and hold on. You will be looking down the side of a cliff that drops 6000 feet in one leap, all the way to the banks of Paradise Creek.

Gaze northward at the impressive vista of the Castle Rocks, Moro Rock visible beyond, looking rather uninspiring from this vantage point. The view into the heights of Mineral King is wonderful, encompassing Mineral Peak and White Chief Peak. Pull out your camera and take some photographs of the inspiring scenery.

22. MONARCH LAKES AND SAWTOOTH PASS

Distance ■	9.4 miles round trip (Monarch Lake / 12.2 miles round trip (Sawtooth Pass)
Difficulty ■	Strenuous / Strenuous
Starting point ■	7800 feet / 7800 feet
High point ■	10,380 feet / 11,600 feet
Elevation gain ■	2580 feet / 3800 feet
Trail grade ■	549 feet per mile / 623 feet per mile
Maps ■	USGS Mineral King 7.5' or Mount Whitney High Country Trail Map (Tom Harrison Maps)
Access road/town ■	Highway 198 to Mineral King Road/ Silver City Resort

If you are looking for spectacular scenery you can't do much better than the Mineral King area of Sequoia National Park. This trek to Monarch Lake is among the finest day hikes the region has to offer. Start early in the day, carry plenty of water, and prepare yourself for a visual treat and a physical challenge you will be talking about long afterward.

To reach the trailhead, drive Highway 198 northeast from Visalia and turn off at Hammond (3.6 miles beyond Three Rivers) on Mineral King Road. Follow the narrow, winding road for about 25 miles to the Sawtooth Trail parking area.

The trail begins its steady climb almost immediately as it ascends through sage, manzanita, and scattered junipers. You will spot White Chief Peak on the right and 11,947-foot Vandever Mountain on the left as you near Monarch Creek. Arrive at the trail junction for Timber Gap at 0.6 mile. Continue to the right, toward Monarch Lake, ascending moderately graded switchbacks. At 1 mile, a series of short, steep zigzags ascend the hillside. Climb beside Monarch Creek and enjoy red penstemon, lupine, and yarrow.

Soon you will arrive at Groundhog Meadow at 1.3 miles. The meadow is a wildflower extravaganza in early summer. Tiger lily, corn lily, shooting star, swamp onion, and Indian paintbrush all compete for your attention. Keep to the right. Cross over Monarch Creek as you push onward and upward toward the lake.

A red fir forest offers welcome shade for a time. Then the terrain opens up as the trail continues at a moderate incline. Work your way up a lush hillside by ascending a series of switchbacks. Stay on the main

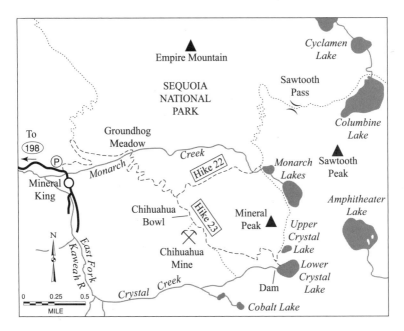

trail. An unmarked use trail heads into the rocky reaches of Monarch Canyon—it's not a recommended shortcut.

At 3.1 miles you will round a bend and be greeted with wonderful views of Vandever Mountain (on the left) and White Chief Peak (on the right). Continue up a lupine-covered hillside and reach the junction for Crystal Lakes (Hike 23) at 3.5 miles. Keep left.

A steady climb leads through Monarch Canyon with spectacular views of rugged Sawtooth Pass and 12,343-foot Sawtooth Peak. Early-season hikers often encounter snow in this area. Footing can be treacherous on the steep hillside.

The trail degenerates into a pathway through loose shale at 4.1 miles. Walking is rougher and slower as you angle into the canyon. Cross over Monarch Creek at 4.6 miles among a flood of alpine shooting star.

Continue climbing to reach Lower Monarch Lake at 4.7 miles. What a scene! The lake is clear and deep, overlooked by the distinctive form of 11,615-foot Mineral Peak and fed by the white-flecked cascade trickling down from Upper Monarch Lake. Wildflowers dot the shoreline.

Although the frigid water of Lower Monarch Lake will probably cool your swimmer's ardor, you will surely want to sample the scenic beauty of the spot. There are a number of possibilities for further exploring if time and energy permits. A short but rocky scramble (with

The marvels of Sawtooth Pass await those who venture beyond Lower Monarch Lake. Karen & Terry Whitehill

no defined trail) leads up to the larger Upper Monarch Lake. Or you can continue on the main trail to Sawtooth Pass.

The climb to Sawtooth Pass involves an additional 1.4 miles and 1200 feet of climbing via a series of tight switchbacks. However, the view from Sawtooth Pass is magnificent, extending north and east to a score of peaks including Mount Whitney about 18 air miles northeast.

23. CRYSTAL LAKES AND CRYSTAL–MONARCH LAKES LOOP

Distance ■	10.8 miles round trip (Crystal Lakes) / 11.1-mile loop (Crystal–Monarch Lakes Loop)
Difficulty ■	Strenuous / Strenuous
Starting point ■	7800 feet / 7800 feet
High point ■	10,850 feet / 11,200 feet
Elevation gain ■	3050 feet / 3400 feet
Trail grade ■	565 feet per mile / 586 feet per mile
Maps ■	USGS Mineral King 7.5' or Mount Whitney High Country Trail Map (Tom Harrison Maps)
Access road/town ■	Highway 198 to Mineral King Road / Silver City Resort

See map page 99

Set into a lofty cirque of granite just below Mineral Peak, Lower Crystal Lake is a pristine gem. The steep rock walls around the lake

100

provide a spectacular backdrop. The lake's cold, clear water holds hungry fish for those who enjoy the sport. The hike to Crystal Lakes is enjoyable but challenging.

The trail to Monarch Lake (Hike 22) and Crystal Lakes share the same trail for the first 3.5 miles. If you have time for only one hike, the trail to Monarch Lake is more scenic and less difficult. However, if you desire a more isolated experience and want to avoid the many backpackers heading for Sawtooth Pass, check out Crystal Lakes. Another option is to ascend the trail to Crystal Lakes, scramble over the divide to Monarch Lakes, and return to the trailhead via Hike 22 for a dramatic Crystal Lakes to Monarch Lake loop.

To begin the trek to Crystal Lakes, refer to Hike 22. From the junction at the 3.5-mile point, turn right toward Crystal Lakes. The climb quickly gains intensity. Pass a use trail descending to the right and continue climbing through an open basin dotted with scrubby white-bark pines. Behind you is a spectacular view of the mountains across the Kaweah Canyon.

The climb eases slightly at 3.8 miles as you traverse the Chihuahua Bowl, site of the old Chihuahua Mine. Look for the mine site off to the right. It's marked by stone foundations, discarded lumber, and piled tailings.

This lofty basin was the origin of a large avalanche that demolished a building on the valley floor in 1969, but winter snows seem far away

Lower Crystal Lake sparkles with alpine beauty. Karen & Terry Whitehill

when you climb past an abundance of wildflowers on the rugged trail. Actually, the steep terrain of the Mineral King area contains many excellent spring skiing and snowboarding opportunities. *50 Classic Backcountry Ski and Snowboard Summits in California: Mount Shasta to Mount Whitney* features numerous ski/snowboard ascents in the area, including two that follow the summer routes described in this book for Hike 22 (Lower Monarch Lake) and Hike 26 (White Chief Canyon).

The trail soon begins a steep climb to the ridge. Hike past sulfur flower, meadow penstemon, and mountain heather. The climb tops out on the ridge (10,400 feet) at 4.1 miles. The view from the lofty ridgeline notch is magnificent. The trail traverses the hillside, descending slightly. Little Cobalt Lake is directly below. Its outlet stream feeds into the chilly waters of Crystal Creek and together they tumble down the mountain to the East Fork Kaweah River.

Keep a sharp eye out for a trail junction at 4.2 miles. A piled-stone cairn identifies the spot where the trail splits. A well-defined trail descends to Cobalt Lake, luring many would-be visitors to Crystal Lakes into an unplanned detour. Stay left at the junction and follow the fainter trail that traverses the hillside.

Enjoy level walking through ferns and manzanita. Above is a notch where a lovely waterway spills out of the basin that cradles Lower Crystal Lake. That defines the final climb to the lake.

Shift into low gear as the ascent kicks in again at 4.5 miles. Alpine shooting star, purple gentian, Bigelow's sneezeweed, and swamp onion line the trail as you continue upward.

Ascend a series of steep and rocky switchbacks. Pass a rock duck and the cutoff trail to Upper Crystal Lake. (It is a short side trip to the upper lake and well worth the detour.) Continue straight toward Lower Crystal Lake and gain the dam at the lake's outlet at 5.2 miles.

Pause on the dam built by the Mount Whitney Power Company in 1903 and reward your efforts with a vista you will long remember. There are wonderful views of Mineral Peak, looming above the trail. The panorama of the entire Mineral King area from the dam is exquisite.

Savor the spot and then make the 0.2-mile jaunt to the smaller Upper Crystal Lake before you head back. Experienced scramblers may be tempted to climb 350 feet to the ridgeline above Upper Crystal Lake and descend to Monarch Lakes from this saddle east of Mineral Peak, converting this hike into a challenging but extremely scenic loop from Crystal Lakes to Monarch Lakes.

24. FRANKLIN LAKES

Distance	■	10.8 miles round trip
Difficulty	■	Strenuous
Starting point	■	7800 feet
High point	■	10,331 feet
Elevation gain	■	2531 feet
Trail grade	■	469 feet per mile
Maps	■	USGS Mineral King 7.5' or Mount Whitney High Country Trail Map (Tom Harrison Maps)
Access road/town	■	Highway 198 to Mineral King Road/ Silver City Resort

Franklin Lakes lie in a spectacular granite cirque ringed by Tulare Peak, the great north face of Florence Peak, Franklin Pass, and Rainbow Mountain. The hike to Franklin Lakes is an exceptional hike among a group of hikes originating in Mineral King Valley. You can't go wrong selecting any of these five hikes. However, this one, Monarch Lake (Hike 22), and White Chief Canyon (Hike 26) are favorites in the area.

In the 1870s, miners flooded into Mineral King Valley on the wave of a silver rush. Several mines, including the Empire, White Chief, and Lady Franklin, were partially developed. However, by the end of the 1880s the silver rush and mining activity faded. One of the obvious results of the mining was Mineral King Road, which was completed in

The lush green meadows and ample water in Mineral King Valley attract deer and other wildlife. Paul Richins Jr.

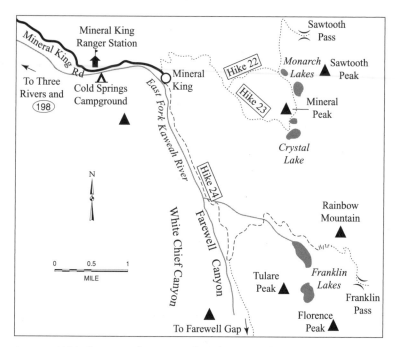

August 1879. Someone has painstakingly counted the 698 curves in the 25-mile road.

The Mineral King Valley is an isolated, unique, and exceptional part of Sequoia National Park. In the summer, wildlife and flowers are abundant. The wildlife is plentiful and evident: deer, mountain lions, coyotes, pine martens, wolverines, black bears, marmots, gray foxes, bobcats, and trout in the lakes and streams. High alpine lakes, meadows, streams, and waterfalls abound. Numerous peaks and high passes ring the valley, providing countless hiking, camping, fishing, and backcountry skiing (in April and May) opportunities.

This hike starts near the end of Mineral King Road. To reach the trailhead, drive 36 miles south of Fresno on Highway 99 to Highway 198. Turn east on Highway 198 to Visalia and proceed through the town of Three Rivers. Beyond Three Rivers and about 2 miles before the entrance to Sequoia National Park, turn right onto Mineral King Road, a long, narrow, winding road to Silver City and Mineral King Valley. Allow at least 90 minutes to drive the 25 miles to the trailhead.

The abundant wildlife in the area includes many marmots. Marmots have been known to damage cars by climbing into the engine compartments and eating hoses and wires. If parking your car for any length of time, consider placing chicken wire or mesh completely around the car to keep the marmots out. Check with the park ranger for suggestions.

The Franklin Pass–Farewell Gap Trail heads south from near the end of the road past the pack station and horse corrals that are within sight of the road. Over the first 2 miles, the gentle trail follows the East Fork Kaweah River as it ascends Farewell Canyon. Wildlife and wildflowers are abundant in this lush valley. Florence Peak, Vandever Mountain, White Chief Mountain, and many other summits ring the canyon.

After 2 miles, the trail steepens and over the next 1.4 miles crosses Franklin Creek and ascends several switchbacks to the junction of the Farewell Gap Trail and the Franklin Pass Trail. Turn left on the Franklin Pass Trail as it leaves the valley floor and ascends to the Franklin Lakes basin and on to Franklin Pass. The Franklin Lakes basin is impressive; the north face of Florence Peak (the highest summit in the Mineral King area) and Tulare Peak tower over the lake basin. If you plan an overnight hike, three bear-proof food storage boxes have been placed at Franklin Lakes.

The 5.4-mile trek to the first lake is not particularly long but the 2500-foot gain in elevation makes this a moderately strenuous hike well worth the effort. For the ambitious, Franklin Pass is nearby, requiring a 1300-foot climb over a couple of miles on an excellent trail. The view from the pass of the Kern Canyon, Mount Whitney, and miles upon miles of mountains is inspiring.

25. EAGLE LAKE

Distance	■	6.8 miles round trip
Difficulty	■	Moderate
Starting point	■	7800 feet
High point	■	10,010 feet
Elevation gain	■	2210 feet
Trail grade	■	650 feet per mile
Maps	■	USGS Mineral King 7.5' or Mount Whitney High Country Trail Map (Tom Harrison Maps)
Access road/town	■	Highway 198 to Mineral King Road/ Silver City Resort

The scenic trek to Eagle Lake is one of the easier hikes in the Mineral King area. Even so, it is still challenging. If you are planning several hikes in the area this is a good warmup trip.

To reach the trailhead, drive 36 miles south of Fresno on Highway 99 to Highway 198. Turn east on Highway 198 to Visalia and proceed through the town of Three Rivers. Beyond Three Rivers and about 2 miles before the entrance to Sequoia National Park, turn right onto Mineral King Road, a long, narrow, winding road to Silver City and Mineral King Valley. Allow at least 90 minutes to drive the 25 miles to the trailhead. The Eagle Lake–White Chief Canyon Trail takes off at the far end of the parking lot.

Begin climbing on a sage-lined trail along the East Fork Kaweah River. Admire the 11,947-foot Vandever Mountain and Farewell Gap up ahead. Cross columbine-edged Spring Creek on a wooden footbridge at 0.3 mile.

Continue along the East Fork, passing an unmarked side trail descending toward the pack station. Ascend an open hillside decorated with the blossoms of mariposa lily, red penstemon, Indian paintbrush, and nude buckwheat. If you gaze directly across the Kaweah River canyon, you will spot lovely Crystal Creek (see Hike 23) trailing down the canyon wall.

The grade intensifies at 1 mile. Climb steeply through red fir shade to reach a junction at 1.1 miles. Go right for Eagle Lake and ascend challenging switchbacks for a short distance. A meadowy hillside flanks

Eagle Lake is a picture-perfect Sierra destination. Karen & Terry Whitehill

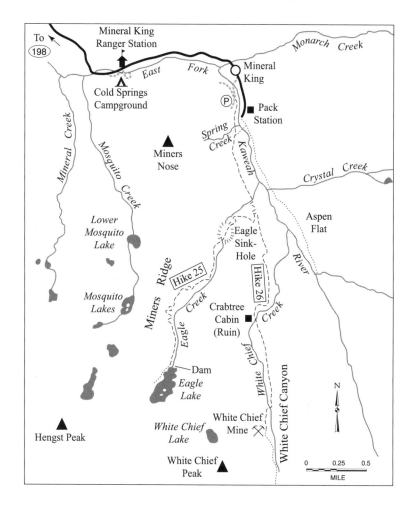

the trail at 1.4 miles. The alpine beauty of larkspur, tiger lily, bistort, arrowleaf groundsel, and monkeyflower will add enjoyment to the hike.

The incline mellows at 1.7 miles as you will reach the shaded banks of Eagle Creek. Watch for the mysterious sinkhole where Eagle Creek dives into oblivion. No one is certain where the water reappears.

At 2 miles, the trail forks. Take the left branch to Eagle Lake. A short stretch of level walking provides a breather before another climb begins at 2.2 miles. Ascend on a steep and rocky trail and admire the expanding views of Sawtooth Pass and Mineral Peak. The incline eases briefly at 2.6 miles but this is just the introduction to another challenging assault on the seemingly unending hill.

The rocky trail and steep ascent will slow your progress. By mile 3 the worst of the terrain will have passed. Soon you will arrive at the lofty shores of Eagle Lake.

The headwall behind the lake is a fortress of shining granite dotted with tenacious patches of snow, even in late July. Walk out onto the dam at the close end of the lake to gain a perfect photo. The views are great.

You will probably see a few anglers and backpackers camping at Eagle Lake. But this lovely corner of the wilderness is usually not crowded and it invites you to enjoy a leisurely afternoon.

26. WHITE CHIEF CANYON

Distance	■	7 miles round trip
Difficulty	■	Moderate
Starting point	■	7800 feet
High point	■	9600 feet
Elevation gain	■	1800 feet
Trail grade	■	514 feet per mile
Maps	■	USGS Mineral King 7.5' or Mount Whitney High Country Trail Map (Tom Harrison Maps)
Access road/town	■	Highway 198 to Mineral King Road/ Silver City Resort
		See map page 107

Like the trek to Eagle Lake (Hike 25), the walk up White Chief Canyon is one of the less demanding hikes in the Mineral King area. If you are looking for a pleasant family outing, consider putting White Chief Canyon at the top of your list. Wildflower admirers will be delighted with the canyon's meadow finery early in the season and would-be spelunkers will find the canyon's array of abandoned mine shafts tantalizing. Be sure to carry a strong flashlight if you plan to do any exploring, and exercise caution.

To begin your White Chief Canyon outing, refer to the driving directions and the beginning of Hike 25 to Eagle Lake. From the junction at the 1.1-mile point, keep to the left for White Chief Canyon. You will climb steadily, as the trail gains elevation rapidly with every step. Wonderful views of the Kaweah Canyon and the sheer beauty of the area will liven your step. The climb continues but large red firs offer much-needed shade as you ascend. Gain sight of the

A lone Sierra juniper is silhouetted against the morning sky. Paul Richins Jr.

little waterway coming out of the White Chief Basin just before a short switchback offers some respite from the climb.

Peaks begin to appear everywhere as you gain altitude. Continue up a rocky trail amid the haunting shapes of twisted Sierra junipers among the boulders. You will soon pick up the company of foxtail pines, a testimony to the lofty elevation. Pause for a postcard view back toward Mineral King. The scene encompasses Mineral Peak and the rugged Sawtooth Ridge.

Press on into an open, rocky bowl ringed by mountains. This is the start of the White Chief Basin, famed in Mineral King history as the site of the Crabtree Cabin and the White Chief Mine. James Crabtree claimed the White Chief Mine in 1873, and the news that silver had been discovered soon transformed this area into a miners' paradise.

Devastating winters and disappointing yields turned the mining boom into a major bust, leaving broken dreams and abandoned mine shafts in its wake. You will find the ruins of the Crabtree Cabin 20 yards to the right of the trail just before you cross the rocky creekbed that holds White Chief Creek. Stand beside the decaying timbers and toppled stovepipe of James Crabtree's home, its walls long fallen.

Return to the trail and cross the creek at 2.4 miles. Cruise on across the basin. Wildflowers are abundant early in the hiking season and the chorus of blossoms blends the colors of alpine shooting star, cinquefoil, yarrow, and lupine.

Continue over gentle terrain through the beautiful basin. Weathered tree trunks lie like scattered matchsticks on the meadow floor, long-dead victims of the avalanches that roar down from the heights each winter. Ease into a mellow ascent along a ridgeline containing red firs and foxtail pines. The views begin to open up as you press onward.

Below on the right, look for the often-waterless gully cut by White Chief Creek, its water swallowed by the marble-riddled bed of stone it travels. The meadow flowers return with new variety as you continue higher.

Approach the waterfall-decorated headwall of the basin at 3.4 miles. The trail makes a 90-degree turn to the right, diving steeply downhill to cross the creek. A use trail continues straight ahead but fades into confusion not long afterward.

This is a good spot to pause and savor your surroundings. If you have the time and energy, the brief climb up the opposite hillside to the White Chief Mine is well worth it. The shaft opening is visible from the trail, marked by a pile of glowing white tailings. Scramble up the steep incline to gain the mine opening at 3.5 miles.

A cool blast of air will meet you at the entrance. Click on your flashlight and probe the darkness. The walls of the shaft hold the marks of tools that fought the stone more than 100 years ago, and park rangers talk of graffiti dating back to 1900 that's hidden in the shadows. The shaft ends at a wall of solid stone after less than 300 feet.

Return to the basin to savor the sweetness of the meadow flowers or press onward along the trail as it climbs steeply from the White Chief Mine. The upper reaches of the canyon will repay your efforts with increasing alpine beauty, but the trail becomes faint.

Opposite: *Quaking aspen silhouetted against the rich blue sky. In the fall, the trees' leaves turn a bright yellow and gold. Paul Richins Jr.*

EASTSIDE
TRAILHEADS

If you have not visited the east side of the Sierra Nevada, the drive along Highway 395 will be a wonderful and surprising discovery for you; the area is replete with natural wonders and scenic vistas. From Lake Tahoe in the north to Mount Whitney in the south, the rugged east-face escarpment of the Sierra Nevada gradually increases in height and grandeur, culminating atop Mount Whitney, whose spectacular summit rises nearly 10,000 feet above the surrounding terrain. The popular summit of Mount Whitney, the highest peak in the Lower 48, is attempted by more than 30,000 hikers and would-be summiteers each year. Hike 32 provides a thorough description of a single day hike of this highly coveted summit.

In addition to Lake Tahoe and Mount Whitney, the east side of the Sierra Nevada includes many outstanding geographic features: Mono Lake, Mono Craters, the Minarets, Devils Postpile National Monument, Little Lakes Valley, Mount Humphrey, Piute Pass, Bishop Pass, South Lake, Lake Sabrina, the Palisades, Kearsarge Pass, University Peak, and Mount Williamson.

The small communities of Lone Pine, Independence, Big Pine, Bishop, Toms Place, Mammoth Lakes, June Lake, and Lee Vining, spread over 120 miles along Highway 395, serve as gateways to the various eastside trailheads. The short drives from these gateway communities reveal dramatic viewscapes of the Sierra Nevada. However, to fully appreciate all that the mountains have to offer, experience the wilderness firsthand: hike the wilderness trails, explore the lush meadows and streams, camp alongside alpine lakes, and scramble up nearby peaks. You will come away from the experience refreshed and invigorated.

Generally, the hikes originating on the east side of the Sierra Nevada start higher and are steeper than their counterparts originating on the west side. Because of the topography of the Sierra Nevada, the east side is steep, with short approaches in a dry climate created by the rain and snow shadow of the Sierra Nevada. This is in stark contrast to the west side of the range, where the terrain is more gentle and the heavily timbered mountains receive abundant rain and snow each year.

Forty hikes (Hikes 27–66) begin on the east side of the range. Whitney Portal Road (starting in Lone Pine), Onion Valley Road (Independence), Big Pine Creek Road (Big Pine), Highway 168 (Bishop), Rock Creek Road (Toms Place), Convict Lake Road (near the Mammoth Lake Airport), Highway 203 (Mammoth Lakes), and Highway 158 (June Lake) provide east–west access from Highway 395 to these trailheads.

MOUNT WHITNEY AREA

Trails in the Mount Whitney area offer spectacular hiking for those who wish to explore this outstanding area. Within a 6-mile radius of Mount Whitney, five other majestic peaks (Mounts Tyndall, Williamson, Russell, Muir, and Langley) tower above the magical 14,000-foot level. The area is characterized by not only the highest peaks in California, but many other summits nearing 14,000 feet. Deep gorges, glaciated cirques, hanging valleys, serrated ridges, and lofty summits provide a spectacular backdrop for the hikes in this region. From the high passes and marvelous summits, the grandeur of the Sierra Nevada stretches as far as the eye can see, miles and miles of rock on rock, mountain on mountain.

All trailheads on the east side are accessed via Highway 395, which runs along Owens Valley. The Owens Valley is the deepest valley in North America (based on the difference in elevation between the 14,491-foot summit of Mount Whitney and the valley floor). Provisions, gasoline, lodgings, and information are available in the towns of Independence and Lone Pine.

The trails in this area begin from three separate trailheads. At 10,000 feet, Horseshoe Meadow is the highest start of any hike in this

Mount Whitney's east face as viewed from the Whitney Portal Road near Lone Pine. Paul Richins Jr.

113

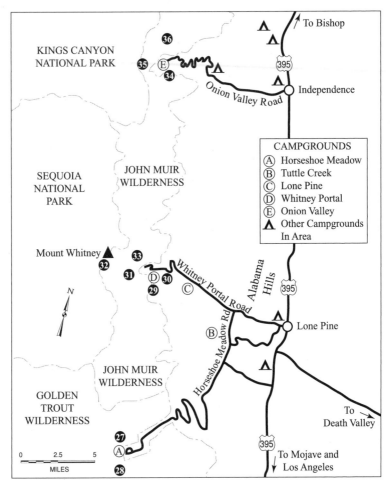

guidebook and is likely the highest start to any trail in the Sierra Nevada. Horseshoe Meadow Campground is on the edge of this expansive meadow and Hikes 27 and 28 begin there. The campground is also close enough to the Mount Whitney trailhead that the campground can serve as an ideal spot to acclimate for Hikes 29–33.

The second trailhead in the area is Whitney Portal, with a campground, fishing pond, store, and restaurant. It is the busiest trailhead in the state, with 30,000 hikers seeking to claim the summit of Whitney. At 8300 feet it is the lowest of the trailheads in the region and provides access for Hikes 29–33.

Lastly, Onion Valley (9200 feet) includes a campground and trailhead access for Hikes 34–36. Onion Valley is west of Independence, whereas Horseshoe Meadow and Whitney Portal are west of Lone Pine.

The automobile ascent from Owens Valley to these trailheads is a climb of 4000 to 6000 feet. From the various trailheads, your route on foot will ascend to lofty passes on the crest of the Sierra Nevada, beautiful alpine lakes, and perhaps the summit of Mount Whitney.

Altitude sickness is a potential concern, as the trails on the eastside of the crest begin above 8000 feet. The rapid gain in elevation by automobile to reach these trailheads may cause some to experience minor symptoms of altitude sickness. See the discussion on mountain sickness at the beginning of the book.

It may be beneficial to allow some time to become acclimated before attempting one of the more strenuous outings. The best way to acclimate is to spend a night or two with light hiking or activity during the day at the trailhead campgrounds between 8000 and 10,000 feet.

A stop at the Mount Whitney Ranger Station in Lone Pine is a good way to begin your exploration of the area. They can provide maps, guidebooks, wilderness permits (for overnight visits), and campground and trail information. They also have a wilderness office help line and a website to answer your questions when planning your trip (see Appendix 1).

CAMPGROUNDS

Horseshoe Meadow Campground (*Hikes 27–33*). This isolated walk-in campground is designed for the convenience of hikers using the Cottonwood Lakes and Cottonwood Pass Trails. It is a short walk from the parking area to each site. The campground's lofty elevation (10,000 feet) makes it a cool escape from the Owens Valley heat, and an ideal campsite to acclimate and relax. This 10-site campground is an alternative to the crowded Whitney Portal Campground and provides several nice options for relaxing acclimation hikes.

To find the campground, turn west off Highway 395 in Lone Pine for Whitney Portal. Drive 3.2 miles on Whitney Portal Road and turn left on Horseshoe Meadow Road. Travel the paved Horseshoe Meadow Road 19.3 miles. There are actually two trailheads at Horseshoe Meadow: a trailhead for Cottonwood Lakes and New Army Pass (Hike 27) and a second about 0.5 mile away for Cottonwood Pass (Hike 28). Both have similar walk-in campsites, water and toilets.

Horseshoe Meadow Campground is open June to October. No reservations. Moderate fee.

Tuttle Creek Campground *(Hikes 27–33)*. This Bureau of Land Management campground is an option for those who want to avoid the overnight crowds around the Mount Whitney trailhead. However, Tuttle Creek Campground is definitely not a spot for those who want to linger around camp during the day—it is on the valley floor and hot when the sun is high.

Spend your days hiking in the mountains and return to Tuttle Creek Campground to watch the sun set behind picturesque Lone Pine Peak. If an early riser, you will be awed by the beauty of the sunrise. The surrounding Alabama Hills are stark and lovely against the scenery of the Sierra crest. These ancient rock formations look exactly like the rugged backdrop for TV westerns—indeed, many movies and commercials have been filmed in the area.

To find the campground, turn west off Highway 395 in Lone Pine for Whitney Portal. Drive 3.2 miles on Whitney Portal Road and turn left at a sign for Horseshoe Meadow and Tuttle Creek Campground. Continue 1.6 miles on this paved road and go right toward Tuttle Creek Campground. In an additional mile you will reach the campground.

Tuttle Creek Campground's 85 sites for tents and RVs offer picnic tables, firepits, and non-flush toilets. There is no drinking water and the only shade will be underneath your picnic table.

Tuttle Creek Campground is open April to October. No reservations.

Lone Pine Campground *(Hikes 27–33)*. Lone Pine Campground is another lowland camping alternative. Its 44 sites for tents and RVs are situated along Lone Pine Creek. In addition to a bit of shade, sites offer drinking water (available May through October only), firepits, picnic tables, and non-flush toilets.

To find Lone Pine Campground, turn west off Highway 395 in Lone Pine for Whitney Portal, and drive 6.7 miles on Whitney Portal Road to Lone Pine Campground.

Lone Pine Campground is open all year. Reservations accepted. Moderate fee.

Whitney Portal Campground *(Hikes 29–33)*. What this popular campground lacks in solitude and serenity, it makes up for in convenience and scenic beauty. The campground has views of Mount Whitney, and it is a great jumping-off spot for the nearby trailheads. Unfortunately, it's often difficult to find an available campsite without a reservation.

The campground has 44 shaded campsites for tents and RVs at the 8000-foot level. Lone Pine Creek runs through the middle of the campground. Campsites offer firepits, picnic tables, drinking water, flush toilets, and a campground host. Whitney Portal's store, restaurant, and fishing pond are located a mile away at the Mount Whitney trailhead.

To reach the campground, turn west off Highway 395 in Lone Pine onto Whitney Portal Road and drive 12 miles. The campground is on the left side of the road, one mile east of Whitney Portal and the trailhead for Mount Whitney.

Whitney Portal Campground is open May to October. Reservations accepted. Moderate fee.

Onion Valley Campground *(Hikes 34–36)*. With a spectacular setting and superior trailhead access, Onion Valley Campground has just about everything going for it—and everyone going to it. You will really have to scramble to find a weekend campsite. Weekdays can also be busy so come as early as possible.

The campground's 29 tent sites are tucked in a beautiful mountain canyon at an elevation of 9200 feet. Picnic tables, firepits, drinking water, and flush toilets are provided. Bears are frequent campground raiders, so use the bear-proof food boxes provided by the Forest Service.

To find the campground, turn west off Highway 395 in Independence onto Onion Valley Road. Drive 13 miles on the paved road. The campground is at the end of the road.

Onion Valley Campground is open June to September. Reservations accepted. Moderate fee.

27. COTTONWOOD LAKES AND NEW ARMY PASS

Distance	▪	11.5 miles (Cottonwood Lakes loop) / 14 miles (New Army Pass)
Difficulty	▪	Moderate / Strenuous
Starting point	▪	10,040 feet / 10,040 feet
High point	▪	11,186 feet / 12,320 feet
Elevation gain	▪	1260 feet / 2400 feet
Trail grade	▪	229 feet per mile / 343 feet per mile
Maps	▪	USGS Cirque Peak 7.5' or Mount Whitney High Country Trail Map (Tom Harrison Maps)
Access road/town	▪	Highway 395 to Whitney Portal Road / Lone Pine

This is a popular trail with anglers as the Cottonwood Lakes Basin is home of the golden trout, California's state fish. The sheer beauty of the rugged mountains forming the basin makes this an excellent outing for day hikers and backpackers. The Cottonwood Lakes basin lies in a high granite amphitheater ringed by Cirque Peak, New Army Pass, Old Army Pass, and the 14,000-foot Mount Langley. The alpine lake basin contains six numbered Cottonwood Lakes plus ten or more other lakes. The route also provides for a side trip past Long Lake and High Lake to New Army Pass with incredible views of Mount Langley and Cirque Peak. With an early start the hike to Cottonwood

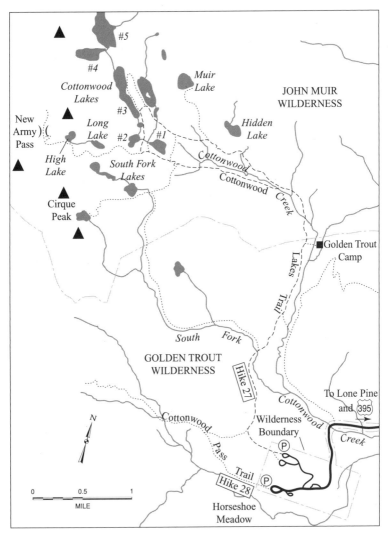

Lakes is manageable even for an average hiker; the side trip to New Army Pass is for the ambitious.

To reach the trailhead, turn west off Highway 395 in Lone Pine (60 miles south of Bishop) toward Whitney Portal. Drive 3.2 miles on the Whitney Portal Road and turn left on the road to Horseshoe Meadow. Travel 19.3 miles on paved Horseshoe Meadow Road as the road climbs to the 10,000-foot, subalpine Horseshoe Meadow. At the edge of the large meadow, turn right toward the Cottonwood Lakes/New Army Pass trailhead (do not confuse this trailhead with the trailhead to Cottonwood Pass (Hike 28). Continue 0.6 mile to a large paved parking area complete with drinking water, toilets, and a camping area.

Begin at the Forest Service information boards and the trail sign for Cottonwood Lakes. The sandy trail passes through a scattering of foxtail pines to arrive at the boundary of the Golden Trout Wilderness at 0.2 mile. Continue on the mostly level route, traversing an open landscape through foxtail and lodgepole pines. The red-hued trunks of the foxtails are particularly impressive in the early-morning light.

Cross the South Fork Cottonwood Creek at 1.5 miles and wander through platoons of pines. You will begin to hear the murmur of Cottonwood Creek as it rushes through a willow-filled gully at 2.3 miles. Climb gently beside a creek-fed meadow.

Arrive at an entry sign for the John Muir Wilderness at 3.1 miles. The surrounding meadow will be aflame with Indian paintbrush, yampah, little elephant heads, and cinquefoil in early summer. Cross Cottonwood Creek at 3.2 miles and begin climbing more noticeably, ascending to a trail junction at 3.7 miles. The trail to the right (signed for Cottonwood Lakes) will be your return route if you're making a loop. Veer left toward South Fork Lakes and New Army Pass.

Some nifty rock hopping will keep your feet dry as you cross Cottonwood Creek. Continue climbing gently, enjoying meadow views and glimpses of anglers working the banks of the little waterway. The grade intensifies at 4.5 miles as you climb toward a canyon headwall decorated with trickling waterfalls.

Reach a junction at 5 miles and angle right for New Army Pass (the route to the left leads to South Fork Lakes). Continue steadily uphill through trees and rocks and gain sight of Cottonwood Lake 1 at 5.2 miles. At the next junction in the trail, stay to the left and head toward New Army Pass. Enjoy level walking past the open, meadow shore of Cottonwood Lake 1.

Explore deeper into this vast windswept alpine lake basin, savoring vistas of surrounding granite slopes and guardian peaks. Watch carefully for a faint use trail on the right as you approach Cottonwood Lake 2 at 5.5 miles. The use trail cuts off the main trail just before a little knoll.

At this trail junction consider taking a brief side trip to Long Lake and High Lake. This will add about 2 miles to the hike. High Lake is ringed by sheer granite walls that appear to glow at sunrise and sunset. Visiting the impressive cirque, located directly below New Army Pass, makes the side trip worth the added effort. Turn around at High Lake or ascend the trail's numerous switchbacks to New Army Pass (about 2 miles and a climb of about 850 feet above High Lake) for great vistas of Cirque Peak and Mount Langley.

Now return to the trail junction between lakes 1 and 2, and follow it across the meadow, fording the stream between lakes 1 and 2. Be careful to stay on the trail as you wander through this pristine meadow. The delicate primrose monkeyflower, meadow penstemon, and hikers gentian that make the meadow so enchanting will thank you for your careful footsteps.

Keep Cottonwood Lake 2 on your left as you head for a low jumble of boulders sprinkled with foxtail pines. Just beyond the little mound is the small pothole that marks the lower reaches of Cottonwood Lake 3. Follow the footpath along the right shore and reach the lake proper at 5.9 miles. Cottonwood Lake 3 is long and lovely, set against a breathtaking backdrop of cliffs. The shoreline includes an assortment of alpine wildflowers and grasses. If you're still looking for a lunch spot, this is it.

Proceed to the upper end of Cottonwood Lake 3 and the junction of the main Cottonwood Lakes Trail. You can continue another half mile to lakes 4 and 5.

Hikers follow the scenic trail through the Cottonwood Lakes Basin. Karen & Terry Whitehill

Or, at the trail junction turn right and head back. Enjoy a gentle descent toward the lower reaches of the lake basin.

You will get another peek at Cottonwood Lake 1 as you continue. Turn back for a view of Cirque Peak and the impressive granite basin. Pass a cutoff trail for Muir Lake at 6.8 miles and bid a regretful farewell to the Cottonwood Lakes Basin.

A fistful of rocky switchbacks evolves into a mellower downhill at 7.2 miles. You will regain sight of Cottonwood Creek less than 0.5 mile later. Reach the trail junction to South Fork Lakes at 7.8 miles. Continue straight and backtrack to your starting point at 11.5 miles. (Be sure to follow signs for hiker parking—not the pack station—as you near the finish.)

28. CHICKEN SPRING LAKE AND COTTONWOOD PASS LOOP

Distance ■	9.6 miles round trip (Chicken Spring Lake) / 11.4 miles (Cottonwood Pass)
Difficulty ■	Moderate / Moderate
Starting point ■	9950 feet / 9950 feet
High point ■	11,242 feet / 11,250 feet
Elevation gain ■	1292 feet / 1400 feet
Trail grade ■	270 feet per mile / 325 feet per mile
Maps ■	USGS Cirque Peak 7.5' or Mount Whitney High Country Trail Map (Tom Harrison Maps)
Access road/town ■	Highway 395 to Whitney Portal Road / Lone Pine

This hike lacks the stunning scenery of the Cottonwood Lakes Basin (Hike 27), but it is an enjoyable and relaxing outing with considerably less foot traffic. From this trailhead, you have two choices. Select a loop hike over Cottonwood Pass and Trail Pass; or once Cottonwood Pass is reached continue on to Chicken Spring Lake less than a mile away for swimming, fishing, and relaxation.

To reach the trailhead, turn west off Highway 395 in Lone Pine on Whitney Portal Road. Drive 3.2 miles and turn left at a sign for Horseshoe Meadow. Travel the paved Horseshoe Meadow Road 19.6 miles to the end and the parking area for Cottonwood Pass. Do not confuse this trailhead with the trailhead to Cottonwood Lakes and

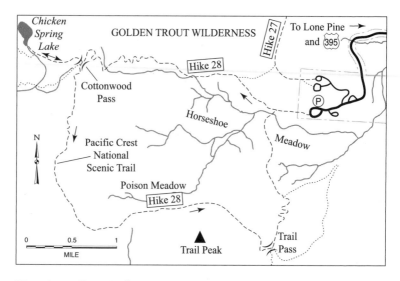

New Army Pass (Hike 27). Pass the junction to Cottonwood Lakes Basin and drive straight ahead for about 0.3 mile to the Cottonwood Pass parking area and walk-in campground. The area has drinking water and toilets to accommodate visitors.

Start at a sign for Cottonwood Pass. The wide, flat trail leads to an entry sign for the Golden Trout Wilderness at 0.1 mile. Continue past scattered lodgepole pines and purple-hued patches of mat lupine. You will arrive at a trail junction at 0.3 mile (the trail to the left is your return route). Continue right along the sandy trail toward Cottonwood Pass. Climb gently along the edge of vast Horseshoe Meadow. Enter a more concentrated stand of lodgepole pines at 1 mile. The walking along the edge of Horseshoe Meadow is level and easy. A small creek is crossed at 1.4 miles. Look for yampah, shooting star, little elephant heads, meadow penstemon, and ranger buttons.

The climb gains momentum at 1.9 miles as you approach the base of a foxtail-sprinkled hill. Your zigzag ascent to Cottonwood Pass begins in earnest at 2.1 miles. Ascend a series of switchbacks that traverse a hillside characterized by chinquapin, rocks, and pines. Views expand to take in Horseshoe Meadow and the Inyo Mountains east of the Owens Valley.

The switchbacks cease at 2.9 miles. Walk through a willow-filled meadow, delighting in the blossoms of mountain pennyroyal, fireweed, nude buckwheat, spreading dogbane, larkspur, and California corn lily. Leave the meadow at 3.1 miles and climb several more switchbacks before a final uphill push leads to the 11,180-foot crest of Cotton-wood Pass.

Turn east to look back on the 4 miles of trail behind you. The view extends to the dark faces of the distant Inyo Mountains. Gaze westward from the pass and you will see the peaks of the Great Western Divide as well as the hidden reaches of the Golden Trout Wilderness and Sequoia National Park.

If you prefer to hike to a lake, Chicken Spring Lake lies less than a mile west of Cottonwood Pass. This is a picturesque lake at the base of Cirque Peak. To reach the lake, take the right fork of the four-way intersection just west of Cottonwood Pass. The lake is at 11,242 feet so little elevation gain is required, and you will soon arrive by following the Pacific Crest Trail to the northwest. The lake lies uphill from the trail; follow the outlet stream through a small meadow to its shore. Campsites abound at the lake.

To continue to Trail Pass from Cottonwood Pass, turn left at the four-way trail junction and follow the Pacific Crest Trail south toward Trail Pass. Pick up a view of 12,900-foot Cirque Peak to the north as you skirt along a rocky slope, enjoying level walking and

Cirque Peak as seen from Chicken Spring Lake. Paul Richins Jr.

expanding mountain vistas. Angle left along the trail to cross a ridgeline at 4.7 miles and then descend into a meadow basin with fine views of surrounding peaks.

A mostly level trail leads to a brief climb at 5.9 miles. Watch for a rocky outcropping to the right. From here, you will get a look into the heart of the Golden Trout Wilderness with views of Olancha Peak, Templeton Meadow, and Kern Peak.

You will gain your first view of Poison Meadow at 7.2 miles. The "poison" doesn't seem to bother the scores of cattle that graze the area in the summer. Horseshoe Meadow appears in the distance and Mount Langley dominates the view to the north.

Abandon the Pacific Crest Trail at 9.2 miles and turn left toward Horseshoe Meadow. Continue steeply down on a sandy trail. At 9.8 miles, turn left at the sign for "Trailhead-pack station." Your descent becomes more gradual as you head across the level expanse of Horseshoe Meadow. Once across the meadow, regain your entry route as you go right at a sign for "Hiker parking" at 11.1 miles. The final 0.3 mile is an easy retreat to the parking lot.

29. CAMP LAKE AND MEYSAN LAKE

Distance ▪	10.2 miles round trip (Camp Lake) / 11.2 miles round trip (Meysan Lake)
Difficulty ▪	Strenuous / Strenuous
Starting point ▪	8000 feet / 8000 feet
High point ▪	11,200 feet / 11,500 feet
Elevation gain ▪	3200 feet / 3500 feet
Trail grade ▪	627 feet per mile/625 feet per mile
Maps ▪	USGS Mount Langley 7.5' and USGS Mount Whitney 7.5', or Mount Whitney High Country Trail Map (Tom Harrison Maps)
Access road/town ▪	Highway 395 to Whitney Portal Road / Lone Pine

The climb to Camp Lake or Meysan Lake is wonderful trip but the continuous elevation gain along the trail is a challenge. Hikers in good shape will enjoy this hike—the scenery is superb. As one ascends the trail, the northwest face of Lone Pine Peak towers over the canyon on the left and a sheer granite wall rises on the right.

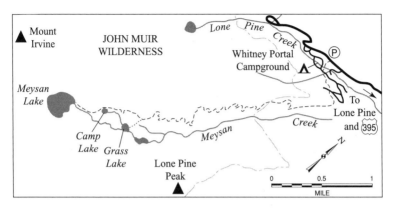

If you are staying at the Whitney Portal Campground, the trek to Camp Lake and Meysan Lake will begin from your campsite. To drive to the trailhead from Lone Pine, turn west off Highway 395 onto Whitney Portal Road and proceed 11.2 miles. Look for a sign for Meysan Lake parking. Park your vehicle on the left shoulder of the road at the Whitney Portal Campground.

Be sure to bring extra clothes, water, and food. The hike begins at 8000 feet and finishes well above 11,000 feet. Also, start as early in the day as possible. This will ensure that you beat the heat as you ascend the south-facing canyon. An early morning start will provide early morning light with various hues of red alpenglow on the mountains.

Begin at the gated asphalt road that descends from the Whitney Portal Road to Whitney Portal Campground. You will need to keep a sharp eye out for trail signs as you traverse the camping area, crossing the campground's lively Lone Pine Creek and gaining the trail proper at 0.2 mile.

Start uphill through a rock- and sage-sprinkled landscape and enjoy the first of many views toward the Alabama Hills, the Owens Valley, and the Inyo Mountains. Join an asphalt road through a handful of summer cabins at 0.4 mile. Then quickly abandon the asphalt by turning onto the footpath.

Climb steadily (the story of this hike) with a vista of 12,943-foot Lone Pine Peak. Ascend a series of switchbacks to arrive at an entry sign for the John Muir Wilderness at 0.9 mile. Intermittent sets of switchbacks ascend the gorge toward the canyon headwall. The steady climb takes you past scattered white firs, Jeffrey pines, and an abundance of chinquapin.

Cross a seasonal creek at 1.9 miles and gain sight of Meysan Creek.

Meysan Creek tumbles downward through the deep gorge. There's an unmarked side trail leading toward the creek but it is an ill-advised, lengthy detour.

Climb more switchbacks, enjoying a cooling breeze and the presence of foxtail pines as you gain more elevation. The roar of Meysan Creek intensifies as the trail leads into a small basin at 3.6 miles.

Leave the basin by climbing several switchbacks on a markedly deteriorating trail. The way is difficult to follow so pay close attention. Reach open ground and continue by ascending a sandy slope.

The trail grade abates at 4.5 miles and you will ascend more gently to reach a breathtaking vista of the valley floor. Arrive at a fork in the trail at 4.7 miles. To the left, a 0.3-mile jog leads to Grass Lake. If you're feeling the strain of this difficult trek, Grass Lake makes a worthy early stopping point. However, pushing on to Camp Lake is a better option as it is only 0.4 mile ahead.

To continue, make a sharp right turn with the trail (signed for Camp and Meysan Lakes). Climb steadily to an exquisite amphitheater of peaks. From left to right, look for Mount LeConte, Mount Mallory, and Mount Irvine, all above 13,500 feet. And look for serene Grass Lake in the basin below the trail.

A passage by weather-sculpted foxtail pines leads to meadow-surrounded Camp Lake at 5.1 miles. This petite beauty is nearly overwhelmed by the avalanche of alpine shooting star and mountain heather

Camp Lake is situated in a beautiful alpine meadow directly below Meysan Lake. Paul Richins Jr.

that covers its shores. Pause to enjoy the wildflowers. This is a good place to eat a snack or lunch before pressing on to Meysan Lake.

The trail from here is difficult to follow, but it is only 0.5 mile. Skirt the west shore of Camp Lake and ascend the creek to Meysan Lake. This is the route of an old 1940s or 1950s trail that is no longer visible. An ancient wood sign marking the old trail may be seen as you quickly ascend to Meysan Lake. Since you are following the outlet stream of Meysan you will not gain any extra elevation. The large and beautiful lake comes suddenly into view.

The lofty Meysan Lake basin is a harsh and rugged saucer set in the shadow of the mountain headwall. The lake basin is ringed, left to right, by the four previously noted summits of Lone Pine Peak, Mount LeConte, Mount Mallory, and Mount Irvine. On the right, the base of the near-vertical granite face of Mount Irvine rises from the shore of Meysan Lake. In the center, the large glacial basin above the lake is split by the rugged east ridge of Mount Mallory. And to the left of this ridge are four steep couloirs ascending the LeConte-Mallory plateau high above. Before heading back, pause to absorb and enjoy the beauty of the surrounding mountains.

30. WHITNEY PORTAL NATIONAL RECREATION TRAIL

Distance ■	1 mile one way (Whitney Portal to Whitney Portal Campground) / 4 miles one way (Whitney Portal to Lone Pine Campground)
Difficulty ■	Easy / Moderate
Starting point ■	8360 feet / 8360 feet
Ending point ■	8000 feet / 5640 feet
Elevation gain ■	-360 feet / -2720 feet
Trail grade ■	-360 feet per mile / -680 feet per mile
Maps ■	USGS Mount Langley 7.5' or Mount Whitney High Country Trail Map (Tom Harrison Maps)
Access road/town ■	Highway 395 to Whitney Portal Road / Lone Pine

The trail from Lone Pine Campground to Whitney Portal has been designated a National Recreation Trail (NRT) due to its beauty, character, unique environmental setting, and historical significance. Portions of the trail follow the original route from Lone Pine to the summit of Mount Whitney. In 1881 a crude trail was dug from the mountainside. Samuel P. Langley and his scientific expedition used it to haul supplies and wood. The horse and walking trail was improved in 1904 with funds and labor contributed by the residents of Lone Pine. Eventually this lower portion of the trail gave way to the Whitney Portal Road as main access to Whitney Portal and the present-day Mount Whitney Trail.

This trail has two trailheads. The lower trailhead is at Lone Pine Campground and the upper one at Whitney Portal, near the fishing pond. From the town of Lone Pine on Highway 395, turn west onto Whitney Portal Road and proceed 6.7 miles to Lone Pine Campground and the trailhead. To reach the upper trailhead, continue driving up the Whitney Portal Road for another 6.3 miles to its end at Whitney Portal. Find a parking spot in the large day-use or overnight parking areas.

The trail is about 4 miles long and follows the south side of Lone Pine Creek for most of its length. To enjoy the sights and special features of the upper trail, one does not need to hike the entire 4 miles. A leisurely walk of about 1 mile, from the fishing pond to the Whitney Portal Campground, is enjoyable and recommended for all ages.

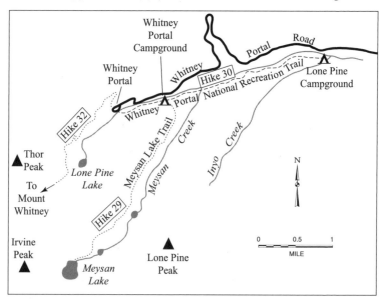

The view of Mount Whitney near the Whitney Portal. Whitney Portal National Recreation Trail begins near the fishing pond at Whitney Portal. Paul Richins Jr.

A short car shuttle eliminates the need to hike the trail in both directions, up and back. Hitching a ride back to your starting point is another option, given the traffic on the Whitney Portal Road. Also, give consideration to the direction of your hike. Starting at the Lone Pine Campground provides continuous views of the crest of the Sierra Nevada and spectacular views of the peaks around Mount Whitney, but you will have to ascend more than 2700 feet in elevation. A less demanding option is to begin at the Whitney Portal fishing pond and descend the trail to Lone Pine Campground. The trail will be described from the top down as this is the direction most people prefer.

From the Whitney Portal pond, cross Lone Pine Creek on a footbridge located near the restroom. The trail gradually descends along the south side of the creek in a dense and beautiful forest. Rainbow, eastern brook, and brown trout are present in the stream. The upper portion of the trail passes through a rock grotto before reaching Whitney Portal Campground. There are many unique rock formations and views of the stream as it cascades through the canyon.

Cross the creek on a wooden bridge and enter Whitney Portal Campground. The trail continues on the north side of the creek for a short distance in the campground. Cross back over to the south side on a car bridge and follow the trail along the creek in the campground.

The campground is a good place to stop for an easy 1-mile walk, or to turn around and retrace your steps to your starting point.

The Meysan Lake Trail (Hike 29) is to the right as you descend along the beautiful stream. The far end of the campground includes a number of impressive and well-maintained summer cabins, some perched on the steep mountainside. Leaving the cabins and campground behind, the trail becomes steeper and more difficult. The trail drops rapidly into the canyon via several switchbacks. There is a log bridge at Meysan Creek where it flows into Lone Pine Creek.

From Meysan Creek, it is all downhill to the Lone Pine Campground. This portion of the trail is more open and is best hiked when the temperatures are cool.

31. LONE PINE LAKE

Distance ■	5.8 miles round trip
Difficulty ■	Moderate
Starting point ■	8365 feet
High point ■	9960 feet
Elevation gain ■	1595 feet
Trail grade ■	570 feet per mile
Maps ■	USGS Mount Langley 7.5' and USGS Mount Whitney 7.5', or Mount Whitney High Country Trail Map (Tom Harrison Maps)
Access road/town ■	Highway 395 to Whitney Portal Road / Lone Pine

This trail attracts thousands of people during the hiking season, as it is the main thoroughfare to the summit of Mount Whitney. It is perhaps the busiest wilderness trail in California, if not the United States. More than 30,000 attempt the summit of the highest peak in the Lower 48 each year. Some might say it's not a trail at all—it's a superhighway. Despite the popularity of the trail, the outstanding scenery in the area is worth exploring.

For a taste of Mount Whitney without the demands of a 22-mile round trip to the summit, this pleasant hike covers the first 2.8 miles of the Mount Whitney Trail. Pack a lunch and make a day of it.

From the traffic light in Lone Pine, turn west on Whitney Portal Road and drive 13 miles to its end. There are a number of large parking

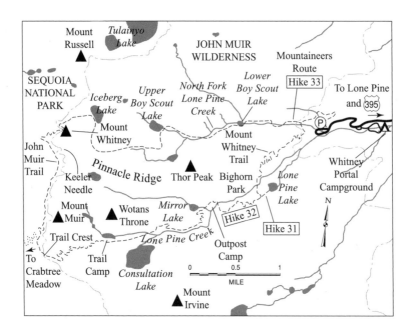

areas complete with a walk-in campground (10 sites), drinking water, and several non-flush toilets. The Whitney Portal Store (immediately west of the trailhead) supplies basic meals, souvenirs, tee shirts, sweatshirts, books, maps, postcards, bear-proof canisters, and showers. The nearby picnic area includes barbecue grills, tables, and a fishing pond.

Day trips up the Mount Whitney Trail beyond Lone Pine Lake require a wilderness permit. Since you will be stopping at Lone Pine Lake, no permit is required. If you plan to head to Mirror Lake (an additional 1.5 miles) or venture to Trail Camp (2.5 miles beyond Lone Pine Lake), a wilderness permit will be required (see Hike 32 and Appendix 1).

The trail begins just east of the Whitney Portal Store by a number of Forest Service display signs. The trail is in excellent condition, well-graded, and never steep even though switchbacks quickly ascend the chinquapin oak-, mountain mahogany-, and manzanita-covered slopes.

The jagged outline of the Sierra Nevada crest and the surrounding sheer granite faces will draw your attention as you ascend. Cross a small creek awash in fireweed, yarrow, and Indian paintbrush at 0.6 mile. Continue up a hillside dotted with Jeffrey pine and single-leaf pinyon pine. There is a second stream crossing at 0.8 mile. Large

rocks have been placed across the stream so that you need not get your feet wet.

Reach the entry sign for the John Muir Wilderness at 0.9 mile. The subsequent switchbacks provide a lovely view east toward the Alabama Hills, the Owens Valley floor, and the distant White Mountains. The grade increases at 1.3 miles and you will get a glimpse of Lone Pine Creek tumbling off the mountain in a white cascade.

Continue beneath white firs, Jeffrey pines, and foxtail pines. Ascend several more switchbacks. Your steady uphill trek will lead to the banks of Lone Pine Creek at 2.6 miles. Cross the creek and arrive at the trail junction for Lone Pine Lake at 2.8 miles. The main trail continues to Mirror Lake, Trail Camp, and the summit of Mount Whitney. Turn left to take the short side trail to the shore of Lone Pine Lake.

Lone Pine Lake does a watery balancing act on the lip of the canyon, clinging to the precipice like some vista-seeking daredevil. This is a great spot for a midday picnic and a cooling splash.

32. TRAIL CAMP AND MOUNT WHITNEY

Distance	▪	12.6 miles round trip (Trail Camp) / 22 miles round trip (Mount Whitney)
Difficulty	▪	Strenuous / Strenuous
Starting point	▪	8365 feet / 8365 feet
High point	▪	12,040 feet / 14,491 feet
Elevation gain	▪	3675 feet / 6306 feet
Trail grade	▪	583 feet per mile / 573 feet per mile
Maps	▪	USGS Mount Langley 7.5' and USGS Mount Whitney 7.5', or Mount Whitney High Country Trail Map (Tom Harrison Maps)
Access road/town	▪	Highway 395 to Whitney Portal Road / Lone Pine
		See map page 131

To stand on the summit of Mount Whitney, the highest peak in the Lower 48, is a highly coveted goal. More than 30,000 hikers attempt this feat each year. Just about any motivated person, in good physical

Opposite: *Hiking the Mount Whitney Trail below Lone Pine Lake. Paul Richins Jr.*

condition, can complete the hike up Mount Whitney. Although a single-day ascent may be out of the question for many, a 2- or 3-day trip can be accomplished by most healthy hikers.

Altitude sickness brought on by a rapid rise in elevation is a serious deterrent for would-be summiteers. Driving from near sea level to Whitney Portal at 8365 feet and then ascending to 12,000 feet or to the summit in a day or two may be too rapid an ascent for many hikers. This can usually be overcome by spending a night or two at Whitney Portal Campground (8000 feet) or, better yet, the Horseshoe Meadow Campground (10,000 feet) before the climb and then spending a night at Outpost Camp (10,360) and second night at Trail Camp (12,000 feet). Taking a few extra days on the approach will allow your body to adjust to the altitude and the lack of oxygen at these higher elevations. Based on records from Sequoia National Park and Inyo National Forest, only about one-third of those attempting Whitney are successful. Altitude sickness, poor planning, and lack of conditioning are the primary factors contributing to this high failure rate.

The Mount Whitney Trail winds through amazing rock towers for the last 2 miles before reaching the summit of the highest peak in the Lower 48. Paul Richins Jr.

A wilderness permit is required whether you plan a single-day assault on the summit or plan a multi-day excursion. Permits can be difficult to obtain, as few unreserved permits are available after the lottery. Refer to Appendix 1 for the details on securing a permit. There are many trails and hiking routes to the summit of Whitney but the one described below is the most popular and direct. Refer to Appendix 6 for books detailing the other twelve routes.

If you plan a single-day ascent, a pre-dawn start is essential to a summit-seeker's success. Be on the trail by 4:00 A.M., as the round trip may take 12–18 hours. Carry plenty of fluids or water-purification tablets (or a water filter). You will need the Ten Essentials—especially sunscreen, warm clothes, a jacket, and a flashlight. Bring a variety of munchies containing a balance of protein and carbohydrates.

Remember one more thing before you try this hike: safety and enjoyment are more important than reaching Mount Whitney's summit. Listen to your body and use common sense. If the distance or the altitude begin to take a toll, slow down and enjoy the scenery. The trail is beautiful all along the way—Lone Pine Lake, Outpost Camp, Mirror Lake, Trailside Meadow, Consultation Lake, Trail Camp, the ninety-seven switchbacks above Trail Camp, Mount Muir, and Mount Whitney's summit. Your day won't be wasted with a premature turn-around.

Refer to Hike 31, Lone Pine Lake, for driving directions and the start of the Mount Whitney Trail. From the trail junction leading to Lone Pine Lake at 2.8 miles, remain on the main Mount Whitney Trail. A series of switchbacks carved into the cliff will lead you onward and upward.

At 3.6 miles, emerge into the meadow known as Bighorn Park. The trail levels off, and you will enjoy an abundance of early-season shooting star as you walk along the edge of the willow-filled meadow. You will arrive at Outpost Camp at 3.8 miles. Campsites and a solar toilet make this an ideal campsite for backpackers planning to spend one or two nights before attempting the summit. The second night can be spent at Trail Camp 2.5 miles ahead.

From Outpost Camp, the climb resumes with a series of short switchbacks leading to quiet Mirror Lake at 4.5 miles. This petite lake has a shaded shoreline, surrounded by lodgepole pine and foxtail pine. Camping is not allowed at Mirror Lake so it is a refreshing and secluded spot to take a breather. Thor Peak rises directly from the lake's shore and its sheer granite face contains many technical rock-climbing routes.

Leave Mirror Lake behind and climb more switchbacks while savoring the terrific views back down to Bighorn Park and Lone Pine Lake. Arrive at the tiny Trailside Meadow at 5.3 miles. This beautiful pocket of alpine extravagance is ankle-deep in shooting star and crimson columbine and is a great spot to take a short rest. After resting, push onward through a series of short switchbacks to gain your first look at Consultation Lake at 5.8 miles.

You will soon reach Trail Camp at 6.3 miles. Trail Camp is the spot where scores of backpackers camp for the night before making their final assault on the summit. This is a good place to take a break and assess your physical condition. For those who planned the shorter hike to Trail Camp, this is your turnaround point. Relax and enjoy the scenery and the rugged east-face escarpment of the Sierra Nevada as it rises to the summits of Mount Muir (14,012 feet) and Mount Whitney. Mount Muir is the high summit above Trail Camp. Mount Whitney is not visible unless you hike to the upper end of Trail Camp and look to the right. It is barely visible.

From Trail Camp, ninety-seven switchbacks ascend from 12,000 feet to 13,660 feet at Trail Crest. The trail is an amazing tribute to the men and women who chiseled and blasted a trail platform out of the granite cliff. You will have fantastic views east into Owens Valley, Lone Pine, Owens Lake, and the White Mountains as you climb the switchbacks to Trail Crest.

The trail tops out at 13,660 feet and 8.5 miles from Whitney Portal. The view is awesome, extending for countless miles to both the east and west. A trail sign marks the eastern boundary of Sequoia National Park.

A brief descent leads to a junction with the John Muir Trail at 9 miles. Continue to the right, following the famous John Muir Trail—the highest trail in the United States—toward its finish at the top. This 212-mile trail begins in Yosemite Valley and winds its way along the scenic Sierra Nevada crest before terminating on Whitney's famous summit. Looking to the west, the John Muir Trail passes Crabtree Lakes, the aptly-named Guitar Lake, and Crabtree Meadow.

From the junction with the John Muir Trail, the summit is only 2 miles away and a little more than 1000 feet of elevation gain. If you are not suffering from the altitude, the next 2 miles will be extremely rewarding. However, this may be the most strenuous portion of the trip—the altitude may have sucked the strength, energy, and desire to continue from your body.

This section of trail provides excellent access for those seeking to climb Mount Muir as well as Whitney. Beyond the trail junction ascend two switchbacks. As the trail levels off, a large rock cairn marks the spot to leave the trail and scramble to the summit of Mount Muir. Muir's summit block is exposed and there is room for only a couple of carefully placed climbers (it is a non-technical scramble but exposed).

The John Muir Trail is a remarkable feat of construction—it snakes its way through towers of granite. Traverse several small gaps between the jagged pinnacles. These windows in the Sierra Nevada crest provide breathtaking views of Trail Camp, the Mount Whitney Trail, and Owens Valley far below.

Back on the Mount Whitney Trail, the path steepens as you near the summit. Several switchbacks seem to go on far too long. Finally, you will suddenly reach Whitney's flat summit and the rock hut built in 1909. Congratulations: you've made it to the top of California and the highest point in the Lower 48.

There is a summit register to sign near the stone shelter. Enjoy your superb accomplishment and take photographs of your success.

Moonlight Ascent of Mount Whitney

A moonlight ascent is a rewarding way to experience Mount Whitney as well. Because this is a single-day/night endeavor, it should only be attempted by hikers in excellent physical condition. Arriving on the summit to view the awakening of a new day and the golden hues of the sunrise alpenglow is extremely gratifying.

Select a cloudless night with a full moon and wait a couple of hours after moonrise before starting. This will provide a moon-illuminated trail on the eastern slopes at the start of the hike. Later on, the moonlight will touch the western slopes in time to light your crossing from the east to the west side of the divide at Trail Crest.

The nights can be cold, especially if a light breeze is blowing. Plan for freezing temperatures above 11,000 feet. The coldest time of the night is just before sunrise. If you are on schedule, you will be on or near the summit, the coldest place on the mountain, at the coldest time of the night. Take gloves, a wind parka, wind pants, and a fleece jacket with hood. Carry a flashlight or headlamp and bring extra batteries.

If you start your hike before midnight you will need a permit for 2 days; if you depart after midnight, a single-day permit is adequate.

33. MOUNTAINEERS ROUTE

Distance ■	9.4 miles round trip
Difficulty ■	Strenuous
Starting point ■	8365 feet
High point ■	14,491 feet
Elevation gain ■	6126 feet
Trail grade ■	1303 feet per mile
Maps ■	USGS Mount Langley 7.5' and USGS Mount Whitney 7.5', or Mount Whitney High Country Trail Map (Tom Harrison Maps)
Access road/town ■	Highway 395 to Whitney Portal Road / Lone Pine
	See map page 131

The Mountaineers Route is the distinctive couloir bisecting the northeast face of Mount Whitney. This prominent feature is readily seen from Highway 395 and the town of Lone Pine as well as from the Whitney Portal Road. In the winter and spring it is a challenging snow couloir for ski mountaineers and backcountry snowboarders. In the summer and fall it is a rock scramble used by many climbers.

John Muir made the fifth ascent of Mount Whitney and the first ascent of what is today known as the Mountaineers Route in the fall of 1873. On foot, without a sleeping bag or modern equipment, Muir completed the round trip from Independence (not Lone Pine) to the summit of Whitney and back in just 4 days. Two years later he made another first ascent, that of Whitney's north slopes via the Whitney–Russell Col. After completing these climbs, Muir wrote, "For climbers there is a canyon which comes down from the north shoulder of the Whitney peak. Well-seasoned limbs will enjoy the climb of 9,000 feet required for this direct route, but soft, succulent people should go the mule way." (In the 1800s the standard route up Whitney was from the west, i.e., the mule way.)

This is the most direct route to the summit of Whitney. It is also the most technically difficult route included in this guidebook. The route includes 0.8 mile of the Whitney Trail, 3.1 miles over an unmaintained climbers' trail, and 0.8 mile of scrambling/rock climbing up the Mountaineers Couloir to reach the summit. It is rugged and strenuous and should not be attempted by inexperienced hikers. Hikers attempting this route should be experienced cross-country climbers proficient with map and compass and the use of ice ax and crampons. The route may contain snow or ice throughout the summer and fall, so it is wise to take an ice ax and crampons at all times. Each year accidents occur on this route and several climbers have been killed on the upper portions of the mountain. Only experienced climbers should attempt this route.

Many complete this route in a single day, but it also makes a wonderful 2- or 3-day trip with an opportunity for a summit bid of Mount Russell as well. This route provides excellent views of the sheer granite east face of Whitney and the Fishhook Arete on Mount Russell. (See Appendix 6 for further reading.)

A wilderness permit is required for an overnight backpack but if the summit is climbed in a single day, no permit is currently required. Refer to Appendix 1 for details on securing a wilderness permit.

At the base of the Mountaineers Route near Iceberg Lake. The route is up the deep couloir to the right of the summit. Paul Richins Jr.

This route also provides an excellent opportunity to traverse Mount Whitney by ascending the Mountaineers Route and descending the Mount Whitney Trail. However, a wilderness permit is required to descend the Whitney Trail.

From the traffic light in Lone Pine on Highway 395, drive 13 miles west on the Whitney Portal Road to its end. The Mount Whitney Trail starts immediately east of the Whitney Portal Store near several large Forest Service display signs. The first 0.8 mile follows the Mount Whitney Trail (refer to Hike 31). The trail begins by heading northeast, away from Mount Whitney, but soon switchbacks toward the west and the crest of the Sierra Nevada. After about 0.6 mile, the trail crosses a small, unnamed stream. Continue up the trail to the next stream, the North Fork of Lone Pine Creek.

Leave the Whitney Trail before crossing the North Fork Lone Pine Creek. A frequently used but unmaintained climbers' trail ascends the steep canyon on the north side of the creek. (Over the next mile the trail gains 1600 feet until it reaches Lower Boy Scout Lake. The climbers' trail is easily followed in most areas, but it occasionally disappears into thick brush or rocky talus slopes.)

From the Whitney Trail, follow the climbers' trail for about 0.25 mile as it ascends the north side of the North Fork Lone Pine Creek. Cross the creek to its south side (near 9000 feet) and follow the use trail through brush and talus for another 0.25 mile before crossing the stream a second time. As you ascend the south side of the stream you will see a Matterhorn-shaped rock in the streambed mostly hidden by willows and water birch. Cross back to the north side of the stream just below this distinctive rock. Reach the base of the main granite wall on the north side and work your way up to the Matterhorn-shaped rock by staying next to the granite cliff on your right. A thicket of willows and water birch will be on your left. Continue another 60 feet above the rock to a wide gully. Leave the stream by turning right at this point and climb up the gully to a large tree about 40 feet above the stream.

Traverse east across rock ledges on the north side of the creek. These ledges are known as the Ebersbacher Ledges. Continue traversing east along these rock ledges until it is possible to climb up to the next level of ledges by turning left (west). Work your way up the ledges in a high traverse as you skirt just below the upper wall. It is advisable to stay high on these ledges where there is less exposure. From high on the Ebersbacher Ledges, the route stays on the north side (climbers' right) of the creek.

From Lower Boy Scout Lake, the rough use trail continues on the south side of the creek through talus, large boulders, and an occasional brush field. Between Lower Boy Scout Lake and Upper Boy Scout Lake the route gains another 1000 feet over 0.9 mile. The route is steep but not nearly as steep as the segment below Lower Boy Scout Lake. From the upper end of Lower Boy Scout Lake, locate a gigantic boulder in the middle of a talus field several hundred feet above. Head for the boulder and cross under it and above the smaller boulder located just below. From this point, traverse right toward the creek through some brush. Near the creek, ascend smooth granite slabs situated between the brush fields and the creek. Climb several hundred feet on these granite slabs and then cross to the north side of the creek. Follow the climbers' trail to Upper Boy Scout Lake, avoiding the willows and brush along the way.

If you have planned an overnight trip, Upper Boy Scout Lake makes an excellent place to camp as does Iceberg Lake another 1300 feet higher. If you plan to climb Mount Russell (14,086 feet) or Mount Carillon, leave from the lower end of the lake and head northeast before ascending to the Russell–Carillon Col.

Above Upper Boy Scout Lake the views of the great east face of Whitney and the four needles to the south of Whitney are magnificent. The route to Iceberg Lake passes below the near-vertical east face of Aiguille Extra (14,042 feet), Third Needle (14,107 feet), Crooks Peak, also known as Day Needle (14,173 feet), Keeler Needle (14,240 feet), and Mount Whitney (14,491 feet).

From the lower end of Upper Boy Scout Lake, hike south for about 0.25 mile, skirting the rock buttress, and then turn west, staying high above the unnamed lake to the south. There are numerous use trails in the area that wander high above the creek. The preferred route is to follow the lower trail that meets the creek near 11,900 feet. There are several excellent campsites along this route. Follow the creek drainage past a waterfall and the main Iceberg Lake outlet creek (on your right).

Continue beyond this waterfall and pass a wall of weeping water. Ascend easy ledges to the left of the last water. This will take you to the lower end of Iceberg Lake, located at the base of Whitney's sheer east face and the Mountaineers Route, the steep couloir to the right of the summit.

Iceberg Lake is an impressive place to camp, relax, explore, and take photographs. From Iceberg Lake, rock climbers ascend various technical routes on the east and southeast faces of Whitney. You may be able to see some roped climbers high on the rock face or others scrambling up the Mountaineers Route.

The Mountaineers Route is the obvious couloir ascending the right shoulder of the east face of Whitney. In spring and early summer it is filled with snow. Crampons and an ice ax may be needed at any time of the year. Scramble to the top of the couloir that ends in a notch near 14,200 feet. The east ridge and east face of Mount Russell are impressive from the top of the couloir. Angle west, descending slightly, and then turn left toward the summit, climbing a gully that is extremely steep near the top. This gully can also be icy any time of year. The gully crests the ridge near the Mount Whitney summit latrine. Hike past the latrine to reach the stone hut and the actual summit.

Congratulations. You have summited Mount Whitney, the highest peak in the Lower 48, by an impressive route.

After relaxing on the summit and photographing your success, retrace your steps down the Mountaineers Couloir; or if you did not leave any equipment or a camp below, you have the option of hiking out the Mount Whitney Trail. However, the route is twice as long and requires a wilderness permit. Refer to Hike 32 for a complete description of the Mount Whitney Trail.

34. ROBINSON LAKE

Distance ■	3.4 miles round trip
Difficulty ■	Moderate
Starting point ■	9200 feet
High point ■	10,500 feet
Elevation gain ■	1300 feet
Trail grade ■	765 feet per mile
Maps ■	USGS Kearsarge Peak 7.5', or Mount Whitney High Country Trail Map (Tom Harrison Maps)
Access road/town ■	Highway 395 to Onion Valley Road / Independence

The Robinson Lake Trail has not been maintained for many years, and there is some brush, but the trail is easy to follow because numerous rock cairns mark the way. From the eastern end of the Onion

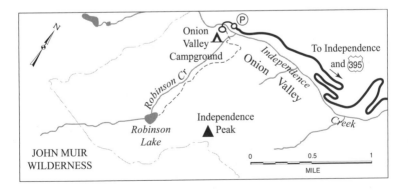

University Peak is located between Robinson Lake and Kearsarge Pass. Paul Richins Jr.

Valley Campground, the trail heads south to Robinson Lake and a large hanging valley. The trail climbs steeply to the lake, gaining 1300 feet. This short, steep trail passes through large stands of virgin timber and groves of aspen trees. Deer are common in the area and may be seen early in the morning. The trail ascends the glacial moraine far to the left of the lake's outlet stream. At the top of the moraine, many large trees have been uprooted by powerful avalanches that have swept down the steep slopes of Independence Peak.

From the town of Independence (45 miles south of Bishop), turn west onto Onion Valley Road and drive 13 miles to its end. This paved road usually is open from May to early November.

The start of the trail is not well signed and begins inside the Onion Valley Campground, next to campsite 8. A sign to Robinson Lake marks the spot.

Begin by crossing rambunctious Robinson Creek. The creek ravine is filled with flowers. Look for fireweed, lupine, ranger buttons, monkshood, angelica, and Indian paintbrush.

The gradual climb quickly escalates into a steady uphill ascent.

Climb across a rocky hillside characterized by sage and wildflowers. Whitebark and foxtail pines offer occasional patches of shade. The steady uphill trail is punctuated by several steep segments. The incline mellows slightly at 0.5 mile as you walk across an avalanche-blighted hillside strewn with uprooted trees. In the early 1980s, a large avalanche broke loose high on the steep face of Independence Peak and swept down the mountain, destroying everything in its path. It terminated in Onion Valley and demolished the ranger cabin at the bottom.

Cross a small feeder creek at 0.7 mile and continue alongside another larger creek. The ascent picks up momentum as you weave through the willows. Climb across a rocky, open slope strewn with massive boulders at 1 mile. Delicate Sierra primrose is tucked in the rocks and crevices. The incline abates at 1.4 miles. Continue on a level path to reach the shore of Robinson Lake. This shallow, alpine lake is guarded by a battalion of encircling peaks. A shoreline shaded by whitebark and foxtail pines offers plenty of opportunities for picnics or midday naps. The little basin that cradles Robinson Lake will delight you with its view down to Onion Valley.

35. FLOWER LAKE AND KEARSARGE PASS

Distance ■	5.6 miles round trip (Flower Lake) / 11 miles round trip (Kearsarge Pass) / 13.2 miles round trip (Kearsarge Lakes)
Difficulty ■	Moderate / Strenuous / Strenuous
Starting point ■	9200 feet / 9200 feet / 9200 feet
High point ■	10,420 feet / 11,823 feet / 11,823 feet
Elevation gain ■	1220 feet / 2623 feet / 3446 feet
Trail grade ■	436 feet per mile / 477 feet per mile / 477 feet per mile
Maps ■	USGS Kearsarge Peak 7.5' and USGS Mount Clarence King 7.5', or Kings Canyon High Country Trail Map (Tom Harrison Maps)
Access road/town ■	Highway 395 to Onion Valley Road / Independence

If you must choose only one of the three routes (Hike 34, Hike 35, and Hike 36) originating from the trailheads at Onion Valley, this trek

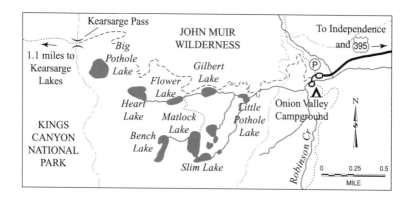

is the one to take. The trail is good, the inclines are moderate, and the vista from Kearsarge Pass is outstanding. It helps to get an early-morning start on this challenging day hike. Carry plenty of liquids for the climb and a windbreaker for the pass.

From the town of Independence (45 miles south of Bishop), turn west on Onion Valley Road and drive 13 miles to its end. Park in the lot adjacent to Onion Valley Campground. Look for a trailhead information sign denoting the Kearsarge Pass Trail.

Start with a gentle ascent beside Independence Creek and climb across a sage-covered hillside scattered with sulfur flower and scarlet penstemon. You will pass an unmarked trail descending to the right at 0.3 mile. Continue straight ahead, climbing steadily. A sign marks the boundary of the John Muir Wilderness at 0.7 mile. A peek across the canyon will yield a view into the basin that cradles Robinson Lake (see Hike 34).

A menagerie of wildflowers will greet you at 1.1 miles as you hike beside Independence Creek. Watch for swamp onion, Bigelow's sneezeweed, bistort, mountain pennyroyal, death camas, and alpine shooting star. Pass Little Pothole Lake to the left of the trail at 1.5 miles. The moderate incline continues, as do the switchbacks. Console yourself with views of the surrounding mountains, dominated by the distinguished form of 13,632-foot University Peak.

The climb eases at 2.3 miles as you arrive at Gilbert Lake. This lake provides an excellent destination or picnic spot for those in quest of an easy hiking day, as does Flower Lake 0.5 mile ahead. Ringed by willows and foxtail pines, Gilbert Lake is particularly picturesque against the backdrop of University Peak.

Zigzag up to a signed junction for Matlock Lake at 2.7 miles.

Kearsarge Lakes as viewed from nearby Kearsarge Pass. Paul Richins Jr.

Continue to Kearsarge Pass and look for Flower Lake on your left.

Another installment of switchbacks leads up through open, rocky terrain. If it's not too late in the flower season, you will see meadow penstemon, Sierra primrose, and alpine buckwheat thriving beside the trail. Heart Lake will tug at your affections as you gain a look down into its aquamarine-colored water.

More rocky switchbacks will take you within sight of your goal. Round a bend and there it is. You will see Kearsarge Pass in the distance. Except for scattered clumps of shrubby whitebark pine, the route is almost desolate. Although the grade is moderate, the climb is steady. Big Pothole Lake will soon come into view.

Reach the 11,823-foot crest of Kearsarge Pass. The vistas are splendid from this vantage point. Explore the depths of Kings Canyon National Park with wondering eyes, drinking in the sight of a host of mountains including North Guard, Mount Brewer, South Guard, and a multitude of others. In the foreground, Kearsarge Pinnacles, Bullfrog Lake, and Kearsarge Lakes lure backpackers to their shores. Find a flat boulder, sit down, rest, and enjoy the impressive view from Kearsarge Pass.

From the pass it is only 1.1 miles to Kearsarge Lakes. Make the added effort to hike down to the lakes—the setting and vistas are outstanding. To reach the lakes, hike down the west side of the pass for about 0.5 mile to the trail junction for Kearsarge Lakes. Turn left and hike 0.6 mile to the lakes. This makes a wonderful destination whether you plan a single-day excursion or you plan to stay overnight.

36. DRAGON PEAK LAKES AND GOLDEN TROUT LAKE

Distance	■	6.2 miles round trip (Dragon Peak Lakes) / 6 miles round trip (Golden Trout Lake)
Difficulty	■	Moderate / Moderate
Starting point	■	9200 feet / 9200 feet
High point	■	11,400 feet / 11,400 feet
Elevation gain	■	2200 feet / 2200 feet
Trail grade	■	710 feet per mile / 733 feet per mile
Map	■	USGS Kearsarge Peak 7.5'
Access road/town	■	Highway 395 to Onion Valley Road / Independence

This challenging hike up a seldom-maintained trail leads to a pair of unnamed lakes near the more popular Golden Trout Lake. But who wants to call a hike description "Unnamed Lakes"? And who would want to choose such a nondescript spot for a destination? So, we have dubbed these lofty alpine tarns Dragon Peak Lakes in honor of the nearby peak that dominates the view. On this hike, you have the opportunity of visiting Dragon Peak Lakes or Golden Trout Lake, or taking side excursions to both. Both lake basins make for a memorable day hike or a weekend backpack.

To reach the trailhead for the Dragon Peak lakes follow the directions for Hike 35. Park in the lot adjacent to Onion Valley Campground. Look for a trailhead information sign denoting the Kearsarge Pass Trail. This is your starting point.

Start with a gentle ascent beside Independence Creek. The trail soon switchbacks to the right, leaving the creek. Watch for the stock trail coming in on the right. Pass the stock trail and continue to the first switchback to the left. The trail to Dragon Peak Lakes/Golden Trout Lake continues straight ahead at the switchback. Leave the Kearsarge Pass Trail and head up the valley toward the lakes.

Ascend on a trail lined with sage, sulfur flower, Indian paintbrush, and angelica. Continue beside a creek with banks aflame in fireweed and cross the creek at 0.7 mile. Note and admire the lacy waterfall far above. The top of the waterfall is your immediate goal. In the valley below the waterfall, deer are often seen early in the morning or in the evening.

Ascend a rocky section where encroaching chinquapin threatens to overwhelm the trail. You will reach the end of this unfriendly introduction to the Dragon Peak Lakes Trail at 1 mile. Pause at the crest of the hill to savor a stunning view of University Peak (13,632 feet). Continue on a rough trail lined with pungent mountain penny-royal and recross the creek (above the waterfall) at 1.1 miles.

Ascend along a rocky ridge where weather-tormented foxtail pines are grotesquely beautiful against a blue sky. Push upward along the creek on your right. In spots, the trail is faint and difficult to follow. The bright blossoms of crimson columbine and alpine shooting star abound. A trail visible on the far shore will tempt you to hop across the water. However, the best route stays along the left bank.

Continue climbing along the creek. You will arrive at what appears to be an insurmountable jumble of boulders at 1.9 miles. Look for a small rock cairn beside the creek (there may be one on both banks). This marks your crossing point.

Skip across the creek and keep climbing along the rocky path. You will recross the creek at 2 miles (just as you come to a dense willow thicket). More climbing will bring you to a grassy basin at 2.1 miles. This is an enchanting spot when the wildflowers are in full bloom. Follow an indistinct trail along the left side of the meadow and work your way through an avalanche-blighted patch of trees.

At this point the trail turns away from the basin to begin its climb toward Golden Trout Lake. If you plan to hike to Golden Trout Lake, follow the trail to the left. The route is easy to follow as it ascends the northwest side of Golden Trout Lake's outlet stream. For backpackers, there are many good camping sites at Golden Trout Lake.

If you plan to head for Dragon Peak Lakes, abandon the route and keep to the right along the meadow's perimeter. Descend into the lush center of the meadow and cross the creek again. Pause for a view

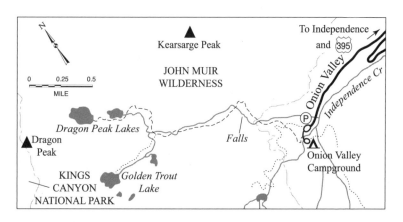

High above Golden Trout Lake on a cross-country route to Rae Lakes Basin. Paul Richins Jr.

toward the distant lowlands. It appears as though someone pushed the world off a precipice at the meadow's edge. Search for a faint path through galaxies of alpine shooting star (they're incredible in early season). Continue across the meadow and begin climbing on the rocky trail that leads out of the basin.

The two-humped crest of Dragon Peak and the Golden Trout Lake Basin comes into view. A pocket-sized meadow is soon reached and provides a brief respite.

Climb along the right side of the lower lake's outlet stream and quickly arrive at the first lake. The Lower Dragon Peak Lake is small and the water is crystal clear. Its shoreline includes a scattering of mountain heather, little elephant head, and Sierra primrose as well as a couple of tempting camping spots.

To continue on to the upper lake, traverse around the left shore of the lower lake following an indistinct trail. Ascend a small ridge to the left of the inlet stream and approach the upper lake at 3.1 miles. Another treat awaits. The Upper Dragon Peak Lake is an alpine treasure hidden in a glaciated granite cirque. Although the lake's shoreline is less inviting, its ruggedness only serves to accentuate its unspoiled beauty.

Fanciful stories often cast dragons as hoarders of precious gems. If there's any truth to these legends, then these two often-overlooked, unnamed lakes are the most prized jewels of Dragon Peak's collection.

BISHOP AREA

This region lies west of Highway 395 between Big Pine in the south and Toms Place in the north. The town of Bishop is midway along this 30-mile stretch of Highway 395. It is the largest community on the east side of the Sierra Nevada south of Carson City and Reno. There are many services, restaurants, motels, bookstores, backpacking shops, and art galleries in town: a vibrant and bustling locale.

If you need supplies for your hike, Wilson's Eastside Sports is well-stocked with outdoor equipment. It is worth the stop if only to browse the wide array of new gear they offer. Just down the street is Mountain Light, the exquisite photographic gallery of world-renowned Galen Rowell. Stop in to view (and purchase) superb photography of the Sierra Nevada and from around the world.

The Bishop area contains scores of hiking opportunities in a breathtaking setting, all within a thirty-minute drive. Rugged peaks, beautiful meadows, high mountain lakes, and numerous glaciers combine to make this area the most alpine region of the Sierra Nevada. In the Palisades region near Big Pine, Hikes 37 and 38 pass beneath the largest glaciers in the Sierra Nevada and four summits exceeding 14,000 feet—Thunderbolt Peak, North Palisade, Mount Sill, and Middle Palisade. The

An early morning view of the South Palisades group and Mount Sill along the Brainard Lake Trail (Hike 38). Paul Richins Jr.

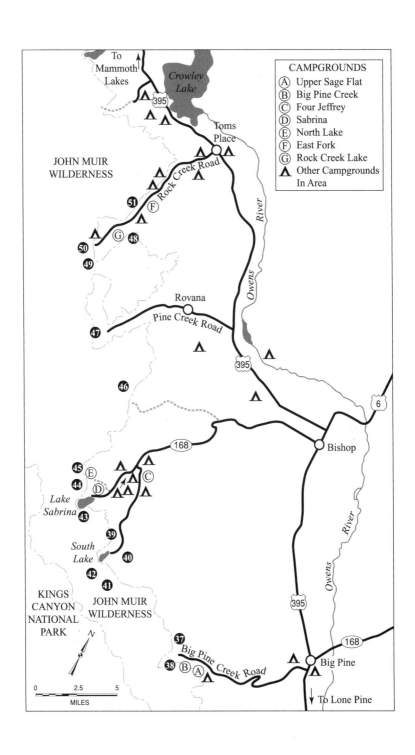

To Mammoth Lakes

Crowley Lake

395

Toms Place

JOHN MUIR WILDERNESS

Rock Creek Road

51 Ⓕ

Ⓖ **48**

50

49

Rovana

Pine Creek Road

395

47

46

6

168

Bishop

45 Ⓔ

44 Ⓓ Ⓒ

Lake Sabrina **43**

39

South Lake **40**

42

41

KINGS CANYON NATIONAL PARK

JOHN MUIR WILDERNESS

N

395

Owens River

Owens River

37

38 Ⓑ Ⓐ

Big Pine Creek Road

168

Big Pine

To Lone Pine

0   2.5   5
MILES

CAMPGROUNDS
- Ⓐ Upper Sage Flat
- Ⓑ Big Pine Creek
- Ⓒ Four Jeffrey
- Ⓓ Sabrina
- Ⓔ North Lake
- Ⓕ East Fork
- Ⓖ Rock Creek Lake
- ▲ Other Campgrounds In Area

trails west of the town of Bishop (Hikes 39–47) are equally appealing, with many beautiful lakes in a splendid alpine environment.

Little Lakes Valley, near Toms Place, provides additional opportunities to enjoy magnificent scenery over gentle terrain (Hikes 48–51). This high glacial basin is rimmed by magnificent 13,000-foot peaks: Mount Morgan, Bear Creek Spire, Mount Dade, Mount Abbott, and Mount Mills. The valley is an oasis of streams, meadows, and more than sixty lakes. This is an ideal place for a family hike in a pristine, postcardlike setting.

Many of the trailheads are above 9000 feet, providing excellent access to the backcountry for day hikers. With these high starting points, pacing yourself is important. If at all possible, allow for a day or two to acclimate by sleeping as high as you can, preferably above 8000 feet. Refer to the discussion on mountain sickness at the beginning of the book.

Trailheads in the region are often busy. As with all heavily used Sierra areas, weekday visits are much less crowded than weekends.

CAMPGROUNDS

Upper Sage Flat Campground *(Hikes 37 and 38)*. Upper Sage Flat Campground offers several pleasant sites shaded by aspens and Jeffrey pines. Drinking water is provided, as are firepits, picnic tables, and non-flush toilets. To reach the Upper Sage Flat Campground, turn west off Highway 395 in Big Pine and proceed 9 miles on the paved Big Pine Creek Road.

The campground is open May to November. Reservations accepted. Moderate fee.

Big Pine Creek Campground *(Hikes 37 and 38)*. This wonderfully situated campground is just a stroll away from the trailhead for Hikes 37 and 38. Perched near the site of the old Glacier Lodge on Big Pine Creek, the campground boasts mountain scenery and a pleasant, shaded setting. The campground has more than 30 sites for tents and RVs. Drinking water, firepits, picnic tables, and non-flush toilets are provided.

To reach Big Pine Creek Campground, turn west off Highway 395 in Big Pine and drive 10.6 miles on the paved Big Pine Creek Road to the site of the old Glacier Lodge.

Campsites may be reserved in advance. Big Pine Creek Campground is open May to November. Reservations accepted. Moderate fee.

Four Jeffrey Campground *(Hikes 39–46)*. This well-equipped campground on the South Fork of Bishop Creek is one of the few campgrounds in the area that consistently has available sites. Four Jeffrey's limited popularity is probably due in part to its distance from the trailheads and meager fishing opportunities.

The campground's more than 100 sites for tents and RVs are provided with drinking water, firepits, picnic tables, and non-flush toilets. Some sites are shaded but most are exposed to the sun. The campground's namesake four Jeffrey pines are by far the dominant trees in the vicinity.

To reach the campground from Bishop, turn west onto Highway 168 (signed for Lake Sabrina and South Lake). At the junction for South Lake (15.1 miles from Bishop), turn left and continue 1.1 miles to the entrance of the campground.

Four Jeffrey Campground is open April to November. Reservations accepted. Moderate fee.

Sabrina Campground *(Hikes 43–45)*. Convenient trailhead access and excellent fishing opportunities combine to make Sabrina an especially popular campground.

To reach the campground from Bishop, turn west onto Highway 168 (signed for Lake Sabrina and South Lake) and drive 18.5 miles toward Lake Sabrina.

Sabrina Campground's 18 sites for tents and RVs are sprinkled along the North Fork of Bishop Creek. Campsites include picnic tables, firepits, drinking water, and toilets.

Sabrina Campground is open May to September. Reservations accepted. Moderate fee.

North Lake Campground *(Hikes 43–45)*. This pleasant little campground is located near the trailheads on the North Fork of Bishop Creek. In fact, it's within walking distance of Hikes 44 and 45. Drinking water is provided at North Lake Campground, as are toilets, picnic tables, and firepits. The campground has about a dozen sites (less than half are suitable for RVs) and is on the shores of lively Lamarck Creek, not far from North Lake, a popular destination for fisherman. A few walk-in sites are available as well.

To reach North Lake Campground, follow the driving directions given for Sabrina Campground, but just before reaching Sabrina Campground turn right on the road to North Lake. Follow this intermittently paved road 2 miles to the campground.

North Lake Campground is open June to October. Reservations accepted. Moderate fee.

East Fork Campground *(Hikes 48–51)*. This large campground located along Rock Creek offers 133 sites for tents and RVs. Picnic tables, firepits, drinking water, and flush toilets are available. The grove of aspens provides shade to the well-spaced campsites.

East Fork Campground makes a great launching pad for the many hikes in Little Lakes Valley. To reach the campground, turn off Highway 395 at Toms Place (15 miles south of Mammoth Lakes Junction) and drive 6 miles on the paved Rock Creek Road.

East Fork Campground is open May to October. Reservations accepted. Moderate fee.

Rock Creek Lake Campground *(Hikes 48–51)*. This popular campground includes scenic views near the lake's shore and is an excellent home base for Hikes 48–51. The trail to Dorothy Lake leaves right from the campground, and the others aren't far away.

The campground's forty-seven sites for tents and RVs offer picnic tables, firepits, drinking water, and flush toilets. Several walk-in sites are a latecomer's best chance of claiming an open spot.

The campground is located just off Rock Creek Road about 8.7 miles south of Highway 395 and Toms Place. Once you reach the lake, drive along the lakeside road for 0.4 mile to reach the campground along the shore of the lake.

Rock Creek Lake Campground is open May to October. Reservations accepted. Moderate fee.

37. BIG PINE LAKES

Distance ■	9.8 miles (Second Lake) / 13.1 miles (Big Pine Lakes loop)
Difficulty ■	Moderate / Strenuous
Starting point ■	7800 feet / 7800 feet
High point ■	10,060 feet / 10,800 feet
Elevation gain ■	2260 feet / 3000 feet
Trail grade ■	461 feet per mile / 500 feet per mile
Maps ■	USGS Coyote Flat 7.5', USGS Mount Thompson 7.5', and USGS Split Mountain 7.5', or Kings Canyon High Country Trail Map (Tom Harrison Maps)
Access road/town ■	Highway 395 to Big Pine Creek Road / Big Pine

There are few trails in the Sierra Nevada that have more lake and mountain scenery packed into 13 miles than this Big Pine Lakes loop.

You will pass a handful of enchanting lakes and view the sheer granite face of Temple Crag rising above the turquoise waters of First and Second Lakes. Not only will you get a peek at the Palisade Glacier, the largest in the Sierra Nevada, the trail passes beneath Mount Sill, North Palisade, and Thunderbolt. These peaks tower above the magical 14,000-foot plateau.

To reach the trailhead, turn west off Highway 395 in Big Pine onto Big Pine Creek Road. Drive 10.6 miles to day-use parking area at the end of the paved road. There's additional day-use parking on the spur road to Big Pine Creek Campground, the site of the old Glacier Lodge, which burned down in the 1990s. Drinking water and restroom facilities are available at the trailhead. Backpackers must use the overnight parking lot near the pack station a short distance to the east.

Begin by walking up the Big Pine Creek Trail. The trail starts alongside Big Pine Creek and the old washed-out road. At the start, you will pass a handful of private cabins. Cross a sturdy bridge across the North Fork Big Pine Creek at 0.3 mile. Continue to a trail junction and turn right up the North Fork Trail. The trail to the left continues up the South Fork of Big Pine Creek to Brainard and Finger Lakes (Hike 38).

Ascend several switchbacks, traversing a rugged hillside dotted with sage and mountain mahogany. Fine views into the canyon of the South Fork Big Pine Creek will entertain you as you climb. This is the Middle Palisades group; its impressive glaciers and peaks also rise above 14,000 feet. The switchbacks end at 0.9 mile and level walking will take you to a reunion with the abandoned road. Turn right and follow the old road.

Recross the North Fork on another footbridge. Immediately after

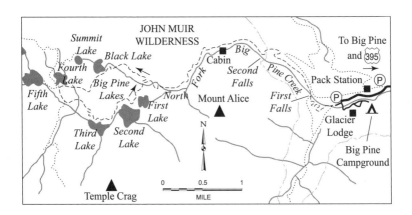

The emerald-green waters of First Lake and Second Lake contrast strikingly against the black granite of Temple Crag. Paul Richins Jr.

crossing this bridge a short trail connects the lower road with the upper trail. The upper trail starts at the pack station and the overnight parking trailhead. Take this connector trail to the upper trail or follow the road along the creek. Either option is fine, although the road is slightly longer. Second Falls comes into view at 1.2 miles. Your admiration of the lofty waterfall may dim when you realize the trail ascends to the top of it. The old road narrows to a trail in a quaking aspen grove at 1.5 miles.

Ascend the shadeless hillside in several long switchbacks and reach the upper trail, Baker Creek (straight), and Big Pine Lakes (left). Turn left toward Big Pine Lakes. A sign marks the boundary of the John Muir Wilderness at 2.2 miles. The trail soon approaches the creek near the top of the second falls.

Pass several use trails leading down to fishing holes and campsites on the creek. The climb eases at 2.6 miles as you hike through a meadow area inhabited by monkshood, ranger buttons, arrowleaf groundsel, and lupine. Watch for a rock-walled cabin set near the creek at 2.9 miles. It was built by film star Lon Chaney.

Resume climbing as the creek's downhill tumble intensifies. You will be treated to a fine view of the imposing granite face of Temple Crag as you round a bend at 3.8 miles. The peaks to the right of Temple Crag will soon come into view. Look for the 14,242-foot North Palisade (the summit with the broadband glacier near its top), Mount Sill, Thunderbolt Peak, Mount Winchell, and Mount Agassiz.

Enjoy level walking until you cross Black Lake's outlet creek at 4.2 miles and then ascend several switchbacks once again. At 4.6 miles you will reach the junction to Black Lake. This 13.1-mile loop route makes the jog to Black Lake and returns via Fourth, Third, Second, and First Lakes. If you feel your energy or time is running low you can shorten the trek to 9.8 miles (round trip) by cutting out the Black Lake loop and proceeding to the Big Pine lakes. Go as far as the scenic Second Lake and then backtrack to your starting point.

To continue along the longer loop route, head to Black Lake at the trail junction. Climb a series of switchbacks and enjoy your first peek of First Lake at 4.8 miles. Second Lake, Temple Crag, and Mount Gayley will soon come into view. The lake's unusual turquoise hue is so unlike the deep-blue color of most Sierra Nevada alpine lakes. First Lake's color is a result of extremely fine microscopic granite particles suspended in the glacial runoff.

The climb eases at 5.4 miles and a willow-filled ravine leads gently upward to the shore of Black Lake at 5.7 miles. You will know this lake isn't glacier-fed at once. Its dark water looks as though it was filmed in black and white. It is in stark contrast to the blazing Technicolor of First and Second Lakes. Even so, Black Lake is pretty, tucked into a granite slope, and edged with Labrador tea and mountain heather.

Leave the scattered campers and anglers on Black Lake's shore and climb once more. At the 6-mile point, just as the trail begins a brief descent, there is a nice view of the area's 14,000-foot peaks and the edge of the famed Palisade Glacier.

A gentle downhill stroll leads to the edge of Fourth Lake at 6.3 miles. This lovely little gem is also not in the path of descending glacial silt, so it has a more traditional color. Leave Fourth Lake to descend to a four-way junction at 6.4 miles. Turn left to begin your trek past Third, Second, and First Lakes. Alternatively, the short hike up to Fifth and Sixth Lakes should be considered if time and energy permit.

Wonderful views of the mountains, coupled with the roar of the rowdy North Fork Big Pine Creek, will accompany you as you descend. Reach a junction with the Palisade Glacier Trail at 6.7 miles and continue straight through a meadow basin awash in wildflowers.

The descent to Third Lake goes quickly. Third Lake is the milkiest of the trio of lakes you will pass because it is first in line for the glacier's handouts. Walk beside Third Lake at 7.4 miles and continue to the edge of Second Lake. Second Lake is the most beautiful lake of the group. With statuesque granite shores and flawless turquoise waters, Second Lake is framed perfectly by the surrounding peaks and the granite face of Temple Crag.

Leave Second Lake at 8.2 miles and take time to look back for one last spectacular view. First Lake is soon passed as you descend past the Black Lake junction at 8.5 miles. Keep to the right at the junction and close the loop back to your starting point. This gem is one that will be long remembered.

38. BRAINARD LAKE AND FINGER LAKE

Distance ■	11.4 miles round trip (Brainard Lake) / 12.6 miles round trip (Finger Lake)
Difficulty ■	Strenuous / Strenuous
Starting point ■	7800 feet / 7800 feet
High point ■	10,260 feet / 10,800 feet
Elevation gain ■	2660 feet / 3200 feet
Trail grade ■	450 feet per mile / 508 feet per mile
Maps ■	USGS Coyote Flat 7.5' and USGS Split Mountain 7.5', or Kings Canyon High Country Trail Map (Tom Harrison Maps)
Access road/town ■	Highway 395 to Big Pine Creek Road / Big Pine

Brainard Lake and Finger Lake are located in the glacier cirque of the Middle Palisades group. The cirque is ringed by some of the most rugged peaks in the Sierra Nevada. The Thumb, Disappointment Peak, Middle Palisade, and Norman Clyde Peak are coveted summits. This beautiful cirque is located just south of the North Palisades group. Middle Palisade and Norman Clyde Glaciers feed the streams and lakes below and provide an emerald tint to both Finger Lake and Brainard Lake.

This hike is challenging but will be enjoyed by hikers in good physical condition. The trail is a little rough in spots but can be easily followed to Brainard Lake. To reach the impressive Finger Lake, 0.6 mile of cross-country travel over a use trail is necessary. Finger Lake, as the name implies, is a long sliver of a lake about 50 feet wide and 0.75 mile long formed between the faults of two granite masses.

To begin the hike, refer to the beginning of Hike 37. Start up the Big Pine Creek Trail. From the junction just beyond the bridge across the North Fork Big Pine Creek (0.3-mile point), turn left onto the South Fork Trail. Follow a gentle uphill route along a sage-covered hillside. The trail now follows the South Fork Big Pine Creek.

Palisade Crest and Norman Clyde Peak fill the view while sulfur flower and mountain pennyroyal frolic in your footsteps. Reach an abandoned roadbed at 0.6 mile. Cross the road and continue up the trail. Hike gradually uphill on a sometimes-rocky path that winds through sage and blue elderberry.

The trail approaches the South Fork of Big Pine Creek at 1.2 miles and continues to a creek crossing at 1.8 miles. The steady but easy climb eases for a time as you savor a view of the South Fork spilling down the canyon wall. Alas, the ascent renews with a vengeance at 2 miles. Climb a series of switchbacks that ascends to a ridge crest at 3.6 miles. The

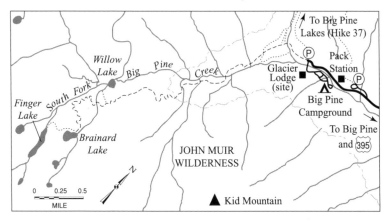

Sunrise on Middle Palisade and the South Palisades group. Paul Richins Jr.

ridge crest above Willow Lake provides a dramatic and inspiring mountain panorama. From left to right, marvel at The Thumb, Disappointment Peak, Middle Palisade Peak, Middle Palisade Glacier, Palisade Crest, Norman Clyde Glacier, Mount Jepson, and Mount Sill. There are great views along the trail for the next 0.2 mile.

If your legs have had all the uphill going they can take, consider this spot your turnaround point. Break out lunch and enjoy the scenery.

To continue to Brainard Lake and Finger Lake head down a gentle hill through willows and wildflowers. Catch sight of Willow Lake at 4 miles as you negotiate a slight descent. The cutoff trail to Willow Lake is passed at 4.2 miles. Continue to Brainard Lake wading through a stream of wildflowers.

Follow the undulating trail through whitebark and lodgepole pines and hop across Brainard Lake's outlet creek at 4.4 miles. Pass through a lush meadow and ascend a lodgepole-shaded hillside. Soon you will come alongside Finger Lake's outlet stream. Leave the creek at 5.2 miles, pass a small pothole lake, and continue upward. The trail dips into a shady, willow-filled ravine at 5.3 miles.

The climb resumes with a final steep ascent that leads to the shore of Brainard Lake at 5.7 miles. The waters of the lake are home to the much-prized golden trout, and the lakeshore is edged with mountain heather, Labrador tea, and willows. Scattered campsites tempt overnighters and possibilities for exploration abound. Best of all, Brainard Lake is secluded and is an ideal base camp for ventures to Finger Lake, Middle Palisade Glacier, and the summits of the Middle Palisades group.

To reach Finger Lake, hike along an ill-defined use trail around the west shore of Brainard Lake. Hike halfway along the right shore of the lake. Look for rock ducks or cairns marking the trail. The trail will pass a large foxtail pine before ascending a scree and talus slope. The trail gains a slight ridge above Finger Lake's outlet stream. Follow the ridge by heading southwest to the emerald-blue lake. A camera is essential, as the views of the lake are indescribable. If you plan to stay overnight, great campsites are located at the lower end of the lake.

39. TYEE LAKES

Distance ▪	7.6 miles round trip
Difficulty ▪	Moderate
Starting point ▪	9080 feet
High point ▪	11,020 feet
Elevation gain ▪	1940 feet
Trail grade ▪	511 feet per mile
Maps ▪	USGS Mount Thompson 7.5', or Mono Divide High Country Trail Map (Tom Harrison Maps)
Access road/town ▪	Highway 395 to Highway 168 / Bishop

Among the wealth of hiking opportunities on the South Fork of Bishop Creek, this offers one of the best opportunities for quiet solitude. A string of lakes along the way and a scenic lakeside destination make this an entertaining outing, full of "perks" for younger hikers although the uphill climb pushes this hike into the moderately difficult category.

To reach the trailhead, turn west off Highway 395 in Bishop onto Highway 168 (to Lake Sabrina and South Lake). Drive 15.1 miles to the South Lake junction and turn left. Continue 5 miles on this paved road. Look for a footbridge across the South Fork of Bishop Creek located just before Willow Campground. The bridge marks the start of the Tyee Lakes hike.

Cross the South Fork on the footbridge. Ascend through sage

and quaking aspens. As you gain elevation, lodgepole pine will provide some welcome shade.

The trail will begin its ascent of more than twenty switchbacks at 0.7 mile. This challenging section rises nearly 1000 feet. The views improve as you ascend the slopes of Table Mountain. Enjoy chinquapin and Labrador tea along the way. Cross over Tyee Creek at 1.9 miles and continue through a pine forest.

At 2.2 miles the trail flattens out at last as you approach the first of the Tyee lakes. This midsize lake has a wildflower-decked shoreline bright with Indian paintbrush, fireweed, larkspur, and ranger buttons. The color-burst from common monkeyflower will draw your attention as you loop around the lakeshore.

More switchbacks slice through the trees to the second lake at 2.9 miles. This lake is a smaller version of the first. Push onward and upward—the best is yet to come.

The ascent continues as more switchbacks ascend to the upper lakes. When the hillside opens up to boulders and scrubby whitebark pines, look for the cheery faces of Sierra primrose smiling among the rocks. Level ground will greet you at the 3.2-mile point and you will arrive at the third lake 0.2 mile later.

The climb now begins to seem worthwhile. This lake is an alpine beauty with a rocky shore and a deep, cold center. Rainbow and brown trout fishing opportunities abound. But don't stop. Push on to the fourth and final lake of the hike—this is the nicest of the group.

Sierra primrose, Coville's columbine, and mountain sorrel are

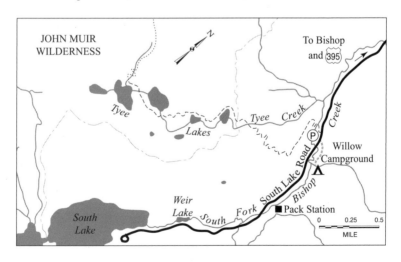

A packer follows his loaded mules into the backcountry. Paul Richins Jr.

scattered among the rocks beside the trail. The brief climb ends at 3.8 miles as you emerge on the fourth lake's beachlike shoreline.

The lake's sandy banks will tempt anglers and swimmers alike but the water is frigid. Visitors in quest of wildflowers will revel in lakeside meadows bursting with hikers gentian, primrose monkeyflower, and little elephant heads. Travelers who simply want a place to sit and rest will find this scenic perch amid the mountains to be a delicious picnic for their senses.

40. GREEN LAKE

Distance ■	5.8 miles round trip
Difficulty ■	Moderate
Starting point ■	9800 feet
High point ■	11,080 feet
Elevation gain ■	1280 feet
Trail grade ■	441 feet per mile
Map ■	USGS Mount Thompson 7.5'
Access road/town ■	Highway 395 to Highway 168 / Bishop

Like Tyee Lakes (Hike 39), the walk to Green Lake is one of the least crowded in the area and hosts some impressive mountain vistas. The hike's unique beginning—the first mile is along the route of an abandoned pipeline—may rule it out for younger hikers because the footing is frequently unsteady.

Green Lake's trailhead can be reached by turning west off Highway 395 in Bishop onto Highway 168 (to Lake Sabrina and South Lake). Drive 15.1 miles to the South Lake junction and turn left. Continue 7.2 miles on this paved road to reach South Lake. Park in the day-use parking area near the trailhead for Bishop Pass. Toilets and drinking water are available. An alternate trailhead leaves from Parcher's Rainbow Village near the pack station, 6 miles from the junction on Highway 168. This trail avoids the pipeline walk but requires an additional 500 feet of elevation gain.

From the day-use parking lot at South Lake, walk to the upper end of the overnight parking lot. Gain a gated, unpaved road that leaves from the upper parking lot. Follow this road a short distance to a small building and the start of the pipeline, which is partially hidden in the aspen and easy to miss. If you find yourself on the horse trail, you have gone too far. The horse trail is nearly level at the beginning and then trends slightly downhill to Parcher's Village and the pack station.

The beaten, old pipe that once carried creek water to South Lake is about 18 inches in diameter. The pipe is sometimes buried, sometimes raised. At times, you will be able to follow use trails beside it; at other times, encroaching ground cover will force you to tightrope-walk along

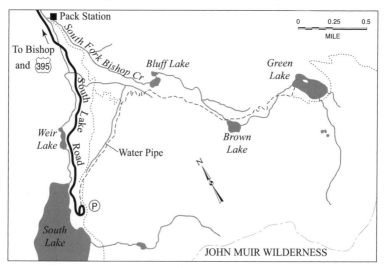

South Lake is near the Green Lake trailhead. Paul Richins Jr.

the pipe itself. It's not bad going—just be alert for spots where the metal has collapsed.

Follow the pipe's gradual uphill angle. You will hear the whisper of the water running through the metal as your footsteps echo on the rusted path. After 1 mile, the pipeline trail meets the Green Lake Trail as it ascends the hillside from the pack station at Parcher's Village.

Join the trail toward Green Lake as it continues steeply up the hill. Steep switchbacks climb beside a creek choked with willows and wildflowers. Cross the creek at 1.3 miles.

Hike upward through an avalanche-blighted ravine, marveling at the devastated landscape overrun by fireweed. The trail can be difficult to follow, as rerouting efforts are not well marked.

The grade eases at 1.5 miles. Enjoy easy walking as you approach Brown Lake. Early in the season the trail is lined with brilliantly colored shooting star, elephant heads, and primrose monkeyflower.

Cross over Brown Lake's outlet stream at 2 miles and arrive at little Brown Lake. This homely little lake is certainly no beauty queen but anglers love the fishing. Resume climbing as you leave Brown Lake, enjoying views of the South Fork of Bishop Creek across the canyon.

A gentle uphill leads to a crossing of Green Lake's outlet stream at 2.4 miles. Pause to gaze down the lake basin. Climb onward through a rocky landscape brightened by Coville's columbine and lacy white angelica.

A short, steady climb eases as you near Green Lake. The trail branches at the 2.8-mile point. Stay to the left to arrive at Green Lake at 2.9 miles. This large, attractive lake boasts a shore awash in wildflowers.

Flower lovers will find a host of blossoms early in the year. Scrubby whitebark pines offer areas of shade and the rocky slopes behind the lake heighten the beauty of the setting. Green Lake is popular with backpackers and anglers, but you shouldn't have any trouble finding a peaceful picnic spot.

41. LONG LAKE AND BISHOP PASS

Distance ■	4.6 miles round trip (Long Lake) / 12 miles round trip (Bishop Pass)
Difficulty ■	Easy / Strenuous
Starting point ■	9800 feet / 9800 feet
High point ■	10,700 feet / 11,980 feet
Elevation gain ■	900 feet / 2180 feet
Trail grade ■	360 feet per mile / 363 feet per mile
Maps ■	USGS Mount Thompson 7.5' and USGS North Palisade 7.5', or Kings Canyon High Country Trail Map and Mono Divide High Country Trail Map (Tom Harrison Maps)
Access road/town ■	Highway 395 to Highway 168 / Bishop

The hike to Long Lake and Bishop Pass, and all the other lakes along the way, is in a class by itself. Allow yourself an entire day to complete it, as it includes many beautiful lakes, tempting photo and fishing opportunities, and wonderful mountain scenery.

If you happen to get a late start or if the length of the walk to the crest of Bishop Pass is too great, get a taste of this outing by simply making the 4.6-mile round trip to beautiful Long Lake. The scenery and views are outstanding.

To reach the trailhead, turn west off Highway 395 in Bishop onto Highway 168 (to Lake Sabrina and South Lake). Drive 15.1 miles and turn left to South Lake. Continue 7.2 miles on this paved road to reach South Lake. Park in the day-use parking area near the trailhead for Bishop Pass. Toilets and drinking water are available.

Begin with a stroll along the shore of South Lake. Views of the surrounding peaks frame South Lake as you walk along an aspen-lined trail. Turn away from the lakeshore at 0.5 mile to continue ascending through a willow-filled ravine. Shooting star runs rampant early in the summer.

Continue through the trees to arrive at the Treasure Lakes (Hike 42) junction at 0.8 mile. Keep left for Bishop Pass and ascend more gently with a view of Hurd Peak. Cross a small stream at 1 mile and continue climbing, passing a cutoff trail for Marie Louise Lakes at 1.4 miles. A series of short, well-graded switchbacks provides views of Hurd Lake at 1.7 miles. Ascend to the junction for Bull and Chocolate Lakes at 1.9 miles.

Continue toward Long Lake and Bishop Pass. You will soon reach the crest of a small rise at 2.2 miles and then descend to the shore of Long Lake, a popular destination for anglers and campers. This long, narrow lake is deep, pointing like a watery arrow toward Bishop Pass. You will see Mount Agassiz to the left of the pass. The Inconsolable Range is the high ridgeline on the left.

Follow an undulating trail along a lakeshore bright with Coville's columbine and cinquefoil, and pass the cutoff trail for Ruwau and Chocolate Lakes at 2.8 miles. Stay on the main trail and leave Long Lake soon afterward. Your path will take you past little Spearhead Lake, popular

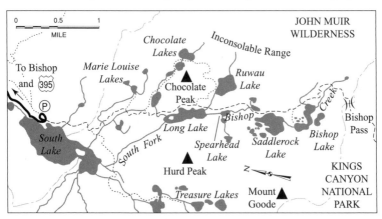

Spearhead Lake and Long Lake, viewed from the trail to Bishop Pass. Paul Richins Jr.

with campers, fishermen, and photographers. The climb intensifies along a rocky hillside scented with hearty mountain pennyroyal. Turn back for a scenic farewell to Long Lake before the trail levels off at 3.7 miles.

An easy stream crossing leads into the brief climb to Saddlerock Lake. You will find this midsize lake studded with rock islands at the 4-mile point. Mount Goode adds its dominating presence to the scene at Saddlerock Lake.

Ascend gradually from the lake and pass the unsigned spur trail to Bishop Lake at 4.5 miles. Continue along the main trail as the climb intensifies. Continue uphill on a rocky trail lined with mountain heather and shrubby whitebark pines. The small stature of the whitebark pine is a testimony to the lofty elevation.

Pick your way through several short switchbacks, looking back frequently to the sight of Bishop and Saddlerock Lakes. The ascent eases at 5.7 miles as you wind into a notch in the ridgeline. Continue up across a rock-strewn ridgeline. Not much grows on this windswept spot but tiny alpine plants and flowers, and it's not unusual to find snow late in August. Reach the crest of Bishop Pass at 6 miles. A trail sign marks the boundary of Kings Canyon National Park.

Scramble up the low ridge to the right (north) to gain a panorama view. Look out over Bishop, Saddlerock, and Long Lakes, Mount Tom, Mount Humphreys, and the Inyo Valley. This is one of the most captivating scenes in the entire Sierra Nevada.

Wander to the left (south) of the Kings Canyon sign for a peek toward Dusy Basin, Columbine Peak, and Giraud Peak. Distant mountains form a backdrop more beautiful than any artist could conceive.

42. TREASURE LAKES

Distance	■	6 miles round trip
Difficulty	■	Moderate
Starting point	■	9800 feet
High point	■	10,680 feet
Elevation gain	■	1280 feet
Trail grade	■	121 feet per mile
Maps	■	USGS Mount Thompson 7.5', or Mono Divide High Country Trail Map (Tom Harrison Maps)
Access road/town	■	Highway 395 to Highway 168 / Bishop

Those interested in a family-friendly hike will do well to investigate this hike or the one to Long Lake (Hike 41). The Treasure Lakes name is certainly appropriate—this hike is a gem! Trail grades are easy and the footing is good for walkers of all abilities. All who make the adventure will be rewarded with the lake destination and surrounding mountain scenery.

To begin the trek, refer to Hike 41. From the trail junction at 0.8 mile, turn right toward Treasure Lakes. Descend to a small stream, cross on a small bridge, and continue hiking down the hill. Look for the hulking form of 12,237-foot Hurd Peak on the left and 12,871-foot Mount Johnson on the right.

Continue your easy descent to the South Fork Bishop Creek at 1.4 miles. More downhill walking leads to the banks of the Treasure Lakes' outlet stream. Continue downstream beside the sparkling water, delighting in the mountain heather and Labrador tea. Anglers'

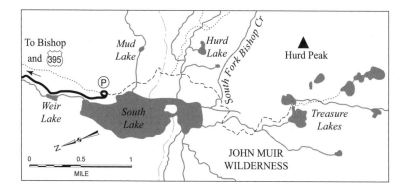

The hike to Treasure Lakes is ideal for families. Paul Richins Jr.

use trails crisscross both shores. Stick with the main trail to reach the stream crossing at 1.8 miles.

Once across the creek, leave the stream and begin the climb to Treasure Lakes. The trail winds through the woods, steadily gaining elevation. An expanding view of South Lake will greet you as you climb. The grade mellows across an open granite hillside. You will soon regain Treasure Lakes' outlet stream.

Recross the little waterway at 2.3 miles, wading through an overflow of mountain heather and leafy lupine. In all directions, there are views of nearby peaks. Continue uphill on a rocky trail, passing through small patches of shade from hearty whitebark pines. The climb intensifies by ascending a series of switchbacks and then eases at 2.8 miles.

Push on to the first of the Treasure Lakes at 2.9 miles. It's a deep blue jewel nestled into a rugged granite basin. Surrounding peaks appear to guard the lake from would-be thieves but campers, anglers, and picnickers are welcome.

Follow the path along the lakeshore. Look for an unsigned use trail departing to the left at 3 miles. The use trail leads to the second lake, just a stone's throw from the first.

This gem is tucked into the protecting shadow of Hurd Peak. It is smaller than the first lake but just as beautiful. The shoreline offers wildflowers, willows, and pines for a pleasant picnic setting.

43. BLUE LAKE AND MIDNIGHT LAKE

Distance	▪	6.4 miles round trip (Blue Lake) / 13 miles round trip (Midnight Lake)
Difficulty	▪	Moderate / Strenuous
Starting point	▪	9070 feet / 9070 feet
High point	▪	10,380 feet / 10,988 feet
Elevation gain	▪	1310 feet / 2100 feet
Trail grade	▪	409 feet per mile / 323 feet per mile
Maps	▪	USGS Mount Thompson 7.5', or Mono Divide High Country Trail Map (Tom Harrison Maps)
Access road/town	▪	Highway 395 to Highway 168 / Bishop

The hike to Blue Lake and on to Midnight Lake is one of many wonderful adventures in the Bishop Creek area. Throw in Drunken Sailor Lake and Hungry Packer Lake and this becomes one of the most rewarding and scenic hikes you will find in the Sierra Nevada. Any combination of these lakes makes an excellent day hike or overnighter. A base camp at any lake affords an opportunity to hike and explore the area with side trips to Echo Lake, Echo Col, and the towering peaks in the area.

To reach the trailhead, turn west off Highway 395 in Bishop onto Highway 168 (to Lake Sabrina and South Lake). Drive 15.1 miles to the junction for South Lake and Lake Sabrina. Continue straight ahead for another 3.7 miles to the Sabrina Basin trailhead (0.3 mile before

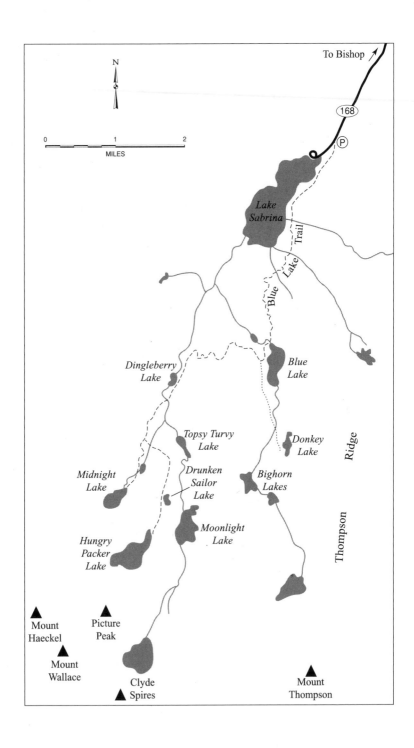

the Sabrina Lake Lodge).

The Sabrina Basin Trail begins on the left side of the road just below the Lake Sabrina dam. The trail narrows as you climb through thickets of aspen trees. The trail follows the left shore of Sabrina Lake for the first 1.3 miles. Look for Mount Wallace, Picture Peak, and Mount Haeckel. Hungry Packer, Drunken Sailor, and Midnight Lakes lie at the bases of these impressive summits.

Begin climbing away from Lake Sabrina at the 1-mile point. There is a steady climb to the trail junction at 1.3 miles. The swiftly ascending trail that exits to the left leads to George Lake and then over the ridge to the Tyee Lakes (Hike 39). Continue toward Blue Lake.

The trail toward Blue and Midnight Lakes has an awesome backdrop.
Karen & Terry Whitehill

Cross a stream and pass a second tumbling waterway at 1.6 miles. A series of short switchbacks lies ahead. Round a bend at 2.3 miles and gain a magnificent view of Mount Haeckel. A peek downhill provides an opportunity to view a ribbonlike cascade of the swiftly descending Middle Fork Bishop Creek. Angle toward the rugged Thompson Ridge as you head to Blue Lake.

This stairstepped section of the trail is the handiwork of the California Conservation Corps. Granite and gravel make for tricky footing. Start up the rocky course of a dry streambed at 2.9 miles, delighting in a flood of Coville's columbine and mountain sorrel. You will soon arrive at Blue Lake. The scene is in wonderful technicolor, filled with snow-flecked mountains and sparkling water. Gaze across Blue Lake toward the awesome backdrop formed by the 13,494-foot Mount Thompson and the Thompson Ridge.

Traverse Blue Lake's little outlet creek and follow the undulating trail along the rugged shore. You will find an ideal lunch spot at 3.2 miles. Claim a slab of granite with a view. There are many excellent campsites at Blue Lake as well as the lakes farther up the trail.

If you feel energized by the fantastic scenery, the trail continues on an easy route to Dingleberry, Midnight, Drunken Sailor, and Hungry Packer Lakes. Once you have reached Blue Lake most of the difficult climbing has been accomplished. The hike beyond Blue Lake is over an enjoyable trail with only mild elevation gains. Although easy hiking, you must pay close attention. At times, the route crosses glaciated granite slabs so it's difficult to tell its direction. In most places, an outline of small rocks marks the trail's presence and direction.

To head for these lovely lakes, hike halfway up the right side of Blue Lake to the trail junction to Donkey Lake and Hungry Packer Lake. Turn right toward Dingleberry Lake and Hungry Packer Lake. There's little elevation gain between Blue and Dingleberry Lakes.

Continue to Dingleberry Lake and follow the trail to the junction for either Midnight Lake or Drunken Sailor and Hungry Packer Lakes. These lakes are more spectacular than Blue Lake. The left fork of the trail leads to Drunken Sailor Lake and Hungry Packer Lake, two favorites. These lakes lie at the base of photogenic Picture Peak. The right fork leads to Midnight Lake. Off to the right is Mount Darwin. An overnight trip to either lake will provide added time to explore and enjoy the spectacular scenery.

44. LAMARCK LAKES

Distance ■	6.4 miles round trip
Difficulty ■	Moderate
Starting point ■	9250 feet
High point ■	10,920 feet
Elevation gain ■	1670 feet
Trail grade ■	522 feet per mile
Maps ■	USGS Mount Darwin 7.5', or Mono Divide High Country Trail Map (Tom Harrison Maps)
Access road/town ■	Highway 395 to Highway 168 / Bishop

Although the hike to Lamarck Lakes involves a challenging ascent, the distance is quite manageable. Families staying at North Lake Campground near the trailhead will find it a delightful outing. Pack a lunch and a fishing pole, and spend the day.

The Lamarck Lakes trailhead is located near North Lake. From Highway 395 in Bishop turn west onto Highway 168 (to Lake Sabrina and South Lake) and proceed 15.1 miles to a junction branching to

South Lake and Lake Sabrina/North Lake. Continue toward Lake Sabrina for another 3.1 miles and turn right to North Lake. Follow this intermittently paved road for 1.8 miles to trailhead parking.

From the parking area walk along the roadway and through the North Lake Campground to the trailhead at the far end of the camping area, 0.7 mile from the parking area (there is no trailhead parking in the North Lake Campground). Take the trail to the left crossing North Fork Bishop Creek before heading toward "Lamarck." The stream is bright with monkshood, yampah, and swamp onion. Ascend a series of switchbacks as you leave the creek among aspen and lodgepole pine.

The hillside opens up at 1.4 miles. A short incline eases slightly at 1.6 miles near the Grass Lake junction. Keep to the right angling toward Lamarck Lakes.

The ascent is continuous and you may wonder if you have somehow entered an eternal set of switchbacks. Don't despair—the crest of the climb is quickly reached at 2.5 miles. Pass a small pothole as you continue on a level trail.

Reach the short spur trail to Lower Lamarck Lake 0.1 mile later. Muriel Peak is prominent on the skyline to the west; Mount Lamarck dominates the view to the southwest. Lower Lamarck Lake is large, deep, and popular with anglers. A shoreline dotted with rocks and willows makes this the superior lunch stop of the two Lamarck lakes.

However, don't fail to take the short hike to the upper lake, as it is too beautiful to miss. To reach the upper lake, continue along the trail and cross the lower lake's outlet stream. The trail is a little rocky but

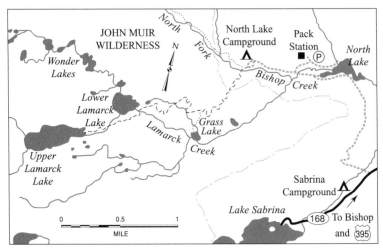

The bright colors of Piute Canyon's rock formations are attention grabbers—they include red, rust, white, black, silver, and gray. In the fall, quaking aspens add yellow and gold to the rainbow. Paul Richins Jr.

not too difficult. A handful of switchbacks leads to Upper Lamarck Lake's outlet creek.

Cross the creek and ascend its banks. Watch for ranger buttons and sassy shooting star. You will reach the upper lake at 3.2 miles. Fed by the nearby snowfields, the lake is ice cold. Its brilliant aqua hue is contrasted by the glowing granite shoreline. The lake sits in a massive glacial moraine with Mount Lamarck completing the picture-perfect scene.

45. LOCH LEVEN LAKES AND PIUTE PASS

Distance	■	6.2 miles round trip (Loch Leven Lakes) / 11 miles round trip (Piute Pass)
Difficulty	■	Moderate / Strenuous
Starting point	■	9250 feet / 9250 feet
High point	■	10,743 feet / 11,423 feet
Elevation gain	■	1493 feet / 2173 feet
Trail grade	■	482 feet per mile / 395 feet per mile
Maps	■	USGS Mount Darwin 7.5', or Mono Divide High Country Trail Map (Tom Harrison Maps)
Access road/town	■	Highway 395 to Highway 168 / Bishop

This remarkable hike passes through a canyon of red-, white-, black-, and yellow-rock formations. This outing has mile after mile of scenery as one advances past Piute Crags, Mount Emerson, Loch Leven Lakes, and Piute Lake. If the distance to Piute Pass is too much, head for Loch Leven Lakes or Piute Lake.

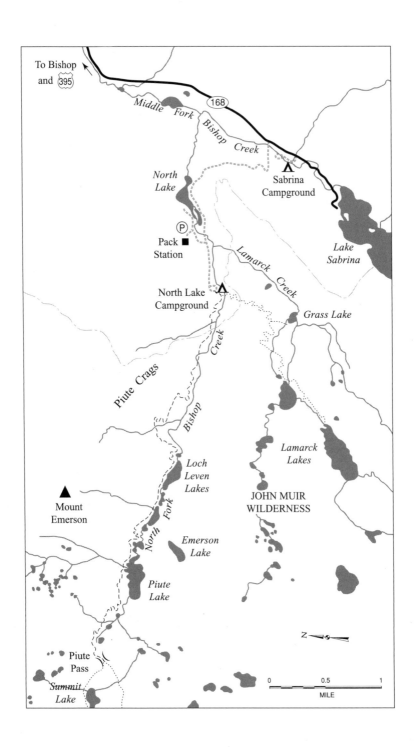

To reach the trailhead, refer to Hike 44. From the far end of North Lake Campground, turn right at the sign for Piute Pass. As you leave the campground, ascend the rocky trail through quaking aspens and lodgepole pines. Cross the North Fork Bishop Creek at 1.3 miles. You will soon traverse back to the north side of the stream. Watch for ranger buttons, Bigelow's sneezeweed, monkshood, and the elusive Sierra rein orchid. Scattered lodgepole pines offer shade as you ascend steadily. At 2 miles, pass below a rocky, red-hued slope at the base of the Piute Crags.

A series of switchbacks eases at 2.9 miles. Enjoy an easy uphill stroll to the Loch Leven Lakes at 3.1 miles. The views from this lake are dominated by the rugged peaks towering overhead. Camping and fishing spots are scattered along the shore, inviting an early stop. Gaze upward along the lake basin and you will spot Piute Pass in the distance.

Continue along the shoreline and begin climbing gently toward Piute Lake. Stubby whitebark pines, hearty mountain heather, and clumps of willows line the way as you meander through the rocky meadow sprinkled with tarns. Wildflowers are abundant early in the season.

Ascend a low ridge at 3.8 miles and then descend into a small meadow. Another gentle climb leads to Piute Lake at 4.2 miles. Piute Lake is much larger than the Loch Leven Lakes and has many fine campsites at its upper end. Above the lake are many small meadows and tarns that are enjoyable to explore.

Turn away from Piute Lake, ascending through a carpet of tiny alpine wildflowers. Climb a series of switchbacks at 4.8 miles. Pause along the way to savor satisfying vistas of Piute and Loch Leven Lakes.

The climb mellows quickly, melting into a lovely meadow walk below Piute Pass. Primrose monkeyflower, Lemmon's paintbrush, and little elephant heads thrive in lofty meadow settings above 10,000 feet.

The final ascent to Piute Pass kicks in at 5.3 miles. Ramble uphill on a rocky trail, stopping often to check the increasingly fantastic panorama. The best vista comes just before the pass, offering visual inspiration to push on to Piute Pass at 5.5 miles. Look to the west and the trail that leads toward Summit Lake. Muriel Peak, Glacier Divide, the Pinnacles, and Mount Humphreys surround the pass. Still, the best view is the one you will have when you turn homeward and gaze out over the lake basin you've just ascended.

Opposite: *Loch Leven Lakes and many small tarns along Piute Pass Trail fill Piute Canyon. Paul Richins Jr.*

46. HORTON LAKES

Distance	■	8.6 miles round trip (Horton Lake)
		11.6 miles round trip (Upper Horton Lake)
Difficulty	■	Moderate / Strenuous
Starting point	■	8000 feet / 8000 feet
High point	■	10,000 feet / 10,900 feet
Elevation gain	■	2000 feet / 2900 feet
Trail grade	■	465 feet per mile / 500 feet per mile
Maps	■	USGS Tungsten Hills 7.5' and USGS Mount Tom 7.5', or Mono Divide High Country Trail Map (Tom Harrison Maps)
Access road/town	■	Highway 395 to Highway 168 / Bishop

Horton Lake and Upper Horton Lake are beautiful, largely undiscovered destinations. Invest a day and you will reap dividends of scenic mountain vistas, abundant wildflowers, and a lovely lake. And, with any luck, you will have the whole adventure to yourself.

To reach the trailhead, turn west off Highway 395 in Bishop onto Highway 168 (to Lake Sabrina and South Lake). Drive 7.3 miles and turn right onto unpaved Buttermilk Road. The road splits after 4 miles. Keep to the right and remain on the main dirt road another 2 miles.

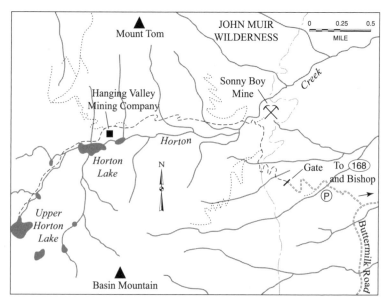

Then turn right onto an unsigned and rough spur road. Continue 0.8 mile to a split in the road. If you are driving a vehicle with good ground clearance, it is possible to keep right and drive another 0.6 mile to a gate across the road.

From the gate, hike up the abandoned mining road. The hulk of towering Mount Tom is directly ahead. Ascend a series of rugged switchbacks. Even in this dry terrain, sulfur flower, scarlet gilia, mountain pennyroyal, lupine, and mule ears brighten the harsh landscape. Reach the edge of a murmuring grove of quaking aspens at 1 mile and continue steadily uphill.

As you climb, the views expand to encompass Bishop Creek canyon, Owens Valley, and the distant White Mountains. Gain the crest of a rise at 1.6 miles and enjoy a brief descent. Pass a short spur road that heads to the abandoned Sonny Boy Mine settlement at 1.7 miles.

Quaking aspen silhouetted against the rich blue sky. In the fall, the leaves turn bright yellow and gold. Paul Richins Jr.

Cross crystal-clear Horton Creek at 1.9 miles and then enjoy level walking through a broad meadow overwhelmed with wild iris early in the season. The ascent kicks in again as you head up the canyon. Look for Basin Mountain, the Four Gables, and Mount Tom. A steady climb on a sage-lined road above Horton Creek leads to a pair of switchbacks at 2.8 miles.

Sulfur flower, red penstemon, crimson columbine, and sweet-smelling wood rose decorate the route, and a pleasing view of a small waterfall on Horton Creek will take you into another set of short switchbacks at 3.2 miles. Negotiate the subsequent straight and steady stretch of roadway, climbing another switchback at 3.8 miles.

You can avoid this switchback by watching for a faint footpath marked by a small pile of stones (it takes off from the roadway as the switchback begins). The path cuts through a stand of aspen trees and rejoins the road at 3.9 miles. A small, marshy lake, below Horton Lake, soon comes into view after the road is regained.

The rocky road branches at 4 miles. Keep left to make the short descent to Horton Lake and pass the abandoned buildings of the Hanging Valley Mining Company.

Reach the flower-covered shore of Horton Lake at 4.3 miles. No carpet could be lovelier than one made of alpine shooting star and primrose monkeyflower. The picture of Horton Lake, embraced by a close-knit brotherhood of surrounding peaks, is a nice finish to any hiking day.

For the ambitious, it is only another 1.5 miles and 900 feet elevation to Upper Horton Lake, located directly beneath the Four Gables and an impressive glacier. The trail continues up Horton Creek to the glacial cirque holding the lake. This is a worthwhile addition to your day's adventure.

47. PINE LAKE AND HONEYMOON LAKE

Distance ▪	9.4 miles round trip (Pine Lake) / 12.8 miles round trip (Honeymoon Lake)
Difficulty ▪	Strenuous / Strenuous
Starting point ▪	7400 feet / 7400 feet
High point ▪	9950 feet / 10,400 feet
Elevation gain ▪	2550 feet / 3000 feet
Trail grade ▪	543 feet per mile / 469 feet per mile
Maps ▪	USGS Mount Tom 7.5' or Mono Divide High Country Trail Map (Tom Harrison Maps)
Access road/town ▪	Highway 395 to Pine Creek Road / Rovana

This is a major route into the Mono Divide, Granite Park, and French Canyon, so it is popular with backpackers. Pine Lake is a superb hike and a worthy goal for both backpackers and day hikers.

To reach the Pine Creek trailhead, drive north of Bishop on Highway 395 and turn onto Pine Creek Road toward Rovana. Follow the paved Pine Creek Road 9.4 miles to the end of the road and a sign for the Pine Creek trailhead. There is a pack station and no drinking water so make sure you fill up before leaving town.

Begin walking up the unpaved road past the pack station. The road narrows to trail width just before a creek crossing at 0.3 mile. Ascend steadily in the shade of white firs and aspens. A stream crossing at 0.6 mile offers additional sanctuary from the sun. Soon the fir trees are supplanted by Jeffrey pines and Sierra junipers. The buildings of the sprawling Pine Creek Tungsten Mill are visible across the way at 0.9 mile. Views extend to Owens Valley and the White Mountains in the distance.

Ascend well-graded switchbacks joining an old mining road at 1.1 miles. The road snakes uphill in long switchbacks, its edges populated with mountain mahogany, sulfur flower, phlox, and unexpected explosions of giant blazing star.

There is a brief break at 1.7 miles as the road levels off to cross a creek. Climb again, enjoying the sight of stout Sierra junipers. Pass an old mine shaft and a nearby abandoned tramline at 1.9 miles.

More climbing leads to the upper reaches of Pine Creek at 2.2 miles. The water paints a lovely picture as it slides downhill through a series of granite chutes. Unfortunately, the ascent continues unabated as the trail continues upward toward the headwall of the canyon.

Leave the rock-strewn mining road at 2.8 miles and continue upward on a rocky trail. Note the appearance of whitebark pines along the hill as you gain elevation. Cross a small creek at 3.5 miles, its banks awash in Labrador tea and willow. Climb additional switchbacks to reach a sign for the John Muir Wilderness at 3.8 miles.

The climb will soon be over. Reach the crest, just past the sign, and cruise through a sparse pine forest with the rumble of Pine Creek

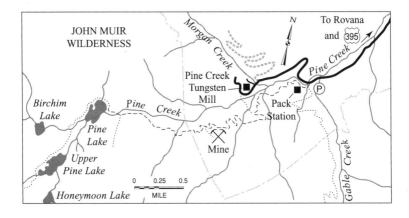

Early morning light on the colorful rocks of the canyon provides unique photo opportunities. Paul Richins Jr.

on your right. This waterway, with its scores of pools and little water-falls, is inviting.

Head toward Pine Lake, strolling through a creekside paradise. The trail crosses glowing expanses of polished granite, the handiwork of a long-departed glacier. Reach a fork in the trail at 4.5 miles. Keep to the right and look for a log to ford Pine Creek.

From the creek crossing, a gentle climb will take you to the edge of Pine Lake at 4.7 miles. An awesome mountain backdrop gives this large lake a delightful setting. And broad slopes of variegated stone add a Sierra "art deco" appearance.

The lake's deep, clear water will tempt overheated hikers. Fishing, picnicking, and camping spots abound on the spacious shoreline. An additional 1.1 miles of easy walking will take the energetic traveler to Upper Pine Lake and another 0.6 mile to Honeymoon Lake. Both are excellent reasons to continue your journey beyond Pine Lake. Honeymoon Lake sits near Granite Park, Mount Julius Caesar, Italy Pass, and Pine Creek Pass. The two upper lakes are beautiful spots and well worth the added effort.

48. DOROTHY LAKE AND TAMARACK LAKE

Distance	▪	6 miles round trip (Dorothy Lake) / 10.4 miles round trip (Tamarack Lake)
Difficulty	▪	Easy / Moderate
Starting point	▪	9700 feet / 9700 feet
High point	▪	10,560 feet / 11,600 feet
Elevation gain	▪	860 feet / 1900 feet
Trail grade	▪	287 feet per mile / 365 feet per mile
Maps	▪	USGS Mount Morgan 7.5' or Mono Divide High Country Trail Map (Tom Harrison Maps)
Access road/town	▪	Highway 395 to Rock Creek Road / Toms Place

The hike to Dorothy Lake is at its best early in the season when the flowers are in full bloom and the meadows are still green from the winter snows. A visit to the area in the autumn is also an excellent choice; during October the aspen trees display brilliant colors. The Rock Creek area is an excellent spot in which to view and photograph the changing seasons. It is a pleasant and easy hike through gorgeous terrain. When compared with the trails in Little Lakes Valley (Hikes 49 and 50), this trek is almost deserted. Yet the trail leaves from an immensely popular campground.

To reach the trailhead, turn off Highway 395 for Rock Creek Lake at Toms Place about 15 miles south of Mammoth Junction. Proceed

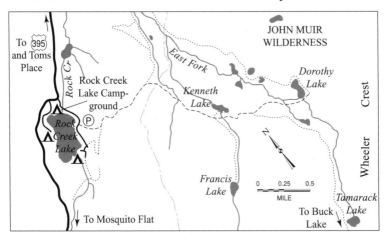

Fall colors along the trail are at their peak in October. Paul Richins Jr.

on the paved road for 8.7 miles and then turn left to Rock Creek Lake. Follow the lakeside road 0.4 mile and enter Rock Creek Lake Campground. Watch for a sign for trailhead parking.

Begin at the trailhead information board near the parking area. A steady climb through aspens leads to a junction at 0.2 mile. Continue toward Dorothy Lake while enjoying views of Rock Creek Lake as you challenge the trail's incline.

At 0.4 mile, pause for an outstanding vista of Rock Creek Canyon with the triple treat of Mount Dade, Mount Abbot, and Mount Mills. All three peaks exceed 13,000 feet. Continue uphill on a trail lined with angelica, mountain pennyroyal, and red penstemon.

The climb eases as you press onward. Scattered whitebark and lodgepole pines provide patches of cooling shade. Nearly level walking leads to a trail junction at the 1-mile point. Turn right for Kenneth Lake.

Enter a meadow and basin guarded by the rocky Wheeler Crest. Hike gently uphill on a sandy trail lined with sage and whitebark pines. The climb intensifies at 1.4 miles and then eases once again. You will find another junction at 1.8 miles. The trail to the right goes to Francis Lake while the trail to the left heads for Kenneth Lake.

Continue toward Tamarack Lake. Wander through another meadow colored by early-season wildflowers. Start a series of switchbacks at 2.1 miles. Pause at another junction 0.3 mile later. Turn left for Dorothy Lake. Continue along an undulating trail to emerge in a broad meadow after 2.6 miles. Admire the rugged shoulders of the Wheeler Crest as you walk along a grass-edged trail across the meadow.

Reach the marshy shore of Dorothy Lake at 3 miles. Although shallow, Dorothy Lake is a nice destination with a shoreline shaded by scattered pines. A lakeside meadow hides a treasure of hikers gentian, with the jewellike blossoms of alpine gentian an even rarer treat.

You will have no trouble passing an afternoon at Dorothy Lake while energetic day hikers or backpackers decide to explore the trail to Tamarack Lake. To reach Tamarack Lake, retreat toward Kenneth Lake. At the trail junction, turn left toward Tamarack and Buck Lakes. The lakes are just below the 11,600-foot level and are about 2.8 miles beyond the Kenneth Lake trail junction. The trail traverses easy terrain for the first 2 miles after which the trail gains about 800 feet in the last 0.8 mile. The lake is perched directly below Broken Finger Peak and Mount Morgan. Ascending the trail to Tamarack Lake one passes from the subalpine area of Rock Creek Lake and Dorothy

Lake (with widely spaced trees) to a more harsh alpine environment above the tree line.

49. CHICKENFOOT LAKE AND MORGAN PASS

Distance	■	5.8 miles round trip (Chickenfoot Lake) / 7.2 miles round trip (Morgan Pass)
Difficulty	■	Easy / Moderate
Starting point	■	10,300 feet / 10,300 feet
High point	■	10,800 feet / 11,100 feet
Elevation gain	■	500 feet / 800 feet
Trail grade	■	172 feet per mile / 222 feet per mile
Maps	■	USGS Mount Morgan 7.5' and USGS Mount Abbot 7.5', or High Country Trail Map (Tom Harrison Maps)
Access road/town	■	Highway 395 to Rock Creek Road / Toms Place

This delightful walk to Chickenfoot Lake is the finest treasure Little Lakes Valley has to offer. The hike begins above 10,000 feet, climbs gently, and leads to a handful of alpine lakes surrounded by 13,000-foot summits.

To reach the trailhead, turn off Highway 395 onto Rock Creek Road at Toms Place. Toms Place is about 15 miles south of Mammoth Junction. Drive up the paved Rock Creek Road 10.5 miles to the end of the road.

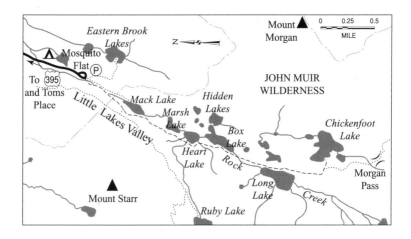

Begin walking up the gated road at the far end of the parking lot. Climb gently alongside Rock Creek with Mount Morgan, Bear Creek Spire, Mount Dade, Mount Abbot, and Mount Mills framing the setting.

Reach the boundary of the John Muir Wilderness at 0.3 mile. The trail grade increases slightly. You soon will be climbing a rocky trail lined with willows and lupine. Arrive at a trail junction at 0.5 mile, and stay left for Morgan Pass. The right fork in the trail leads to Ruby Lake and Mono Pass (Hike 50).

After a brief ascent you will be rewarded with a view of Little Lakes Valley, backed by its encircling peaks. Descend to cross a creek at 0.7 mile and gain a view of Mack Lake. Climb again, fol-

The trail toward Chickenfoot Lake winds through a beautiful high alpine valley. Karen & Terry Whitehill

lowing a wide, rocky trail. The craggy form of Bear Creek Spire is silhouetted against the sky.

You will soon spot grassy Marsh Lake at the 1-mile point. Cross a small feeder creek at 1.2 miles. Descend toward Heart Lake by tiptoeing across Ruby Lake's outlet creek. Heart Lake is surrounded by a willow-sprinkled shore.

Enjoy level terrain as you hike along the lake. Stay on the main trail, climbing gently past a flower-filled meadow. Delight in the cheery company of elephant heads and hikers gentian. The ascent mellows as you approach Box Lake at 1.7 miles. At the upper end of Box Lake, hop from rock to rock to cross the inlet stream. Continue over gentle terrain until you reach the lower end of Long Lake at 2.1 miles. Level walking leads to the far end of Long Lake.

Ascend the rocky trail to reach the trail junction for Chickenfoot Lake at 2.8 miles. The main route continues to Morgan Pass and the adjacent Pine Creek Canyon (see Hike 47). Turn left at the junction and soon arrive at Chickenfoot Lake at 2.9 miles. The alpine lake is directly below the impressive granite face of Mount Morgan. From the lake there are vistas of Mount Mills and the other peaks that rim the Little Lakes Valley.

Chickenfoot Lake is a satisfying spot to end a hiking day filled with panoramic pauses. Spread your lunch on the shoreline and soak your feet in the icy water. Energetic hikers can continue to Morgan Pass, a short hike that gains only 300 feet more.

50. RUBY LAKE AND MONO PASS

Distance	■	4.2 miles round trip (Ruby Lake) / 8 miles round trip (Mono Pass)
Difficulty	■	Easy / Moderate
Starting point	■	10,300 feet / 10,300 feet
High point	■	11,121 feet / 12,040 feet
Elevation gain	■	821 feet / 1740 feet
Trail grade	■	391 feet per mile / 435 feet per mile
Maps	■	USGS Mount Morgan 7.5' and USGS Mount Abbot 7.5', or Mono Divide High Country Trail Map (Tom Harrison Maps)
Access road/town	■	Highway 395 to Rock Creek Road / Toms Place

The hike over Mono Pass is a popular route into the Pioneer Basin and on to the Pacific Crest Trail. A healthy distance and a hefty elevation gain make Mono Pass a challenging day-hike destination, but it is worth the effort for the enchanting scenery along the way. Famed

Ruby Lake is located on the trail to Mono Pass; it makes a great day trip for the family. Paul Richins Jr.

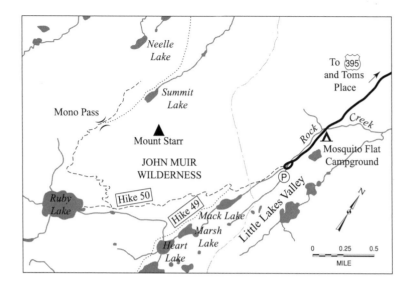

Sierra naturalist and explorer William Brewer paused at the crest of Mono Pass in 1864. The vista he saw then is the one you will see today, extending to the Mono Recess and the lake-sprinkled Pioneer Basin. This 12,040-foot pass is barren and exposed. You may need a jacket or windbreaker.

To get started on your hike to Ruby Lake and Mono Pass, refer to the beginning of Hike 49. From the junction at the 0.5-mile point, turn right toward Ruby Lake and Mono Pass. Switchbacks slice uphill through scrubby whitebark pines.

The trail straightens out before a nice viewpoint at 0.9 mile. Stop for a view of the Little Lakes Valley. You will see Mack Lake, Marsh Lake, Heart Lake, and Box Lake serenaded by a symphony of peaks.

Climb steadily with expanding views of the lake basin. Pass a small pothole lake at 1.6 miles. The grade intensifies and then eases once again. Arrive at a junction with the spur trail to Ruby Lake at 2 miles. A short stroll leads to this alpine beauty, set like a precious stone within a ring of mountains. This makes an excellent destination and turn-around point for those not planning to climb to Mono Pass.

Above Ruby Lake, the trail steepens. Views of Mount Dade and Mount Abbot are impressive. A series of short switchbacks attacks the hill. As you gain elevation, Ruby Lake will come into view at the 2.4-mile mark.

The sudden presence of lively purple rockfringe is a testimony to the increasing elevation. Round a bend at 3.1 miles and gaze up toward Mono Pass. The final climb now begins.

The setting is pure High Sierra as you push on—barren, bleak, and beautiful. You will finally see the crest ahead from the 3.4-mile mark. A sign proclaims the elevation and your victory at Mono Pass at 3.7 miles.

The view from the trail is wonderful, offering a peek downhill toward Summit Lake. For even better views, leave the trail at the sign and angle uphill to the left. A faint use trail leads to the windswept ridgeline above the pass at 4 miles. Discover a view that is magnificent. Gaze down on Pioneer Basin and its many lakes. Look out toward Mount Stanford, Mount Crocker, Red and White Mountain, and Mount Baldwin. Scramble downhill to the trail and head back to the trailhead.

51. HILTON LAKES

Distance	■	8.8 miles round trip
Difficulty	■	Moderate
Starting point	■	9840 feet
High point	■	10,370 feet
Elevation gain	■	1530 feet
Trail grade	■	205 feet per mile
Maps	■	USGS Mount Morgan 7.5' and USGS Mount Abbot 7.5', or Mono Divide High Country Trail Map (Tom Harrison Maps)
Access road/town	■	Highway 395 to Rock Creek Road / Toms Place

Hilton Lakes and Davis Lake are delightful destinations. Compared to the busy trails ascending Little Lakes Valley (Hikes 49 and 50), the trail to Hilton Lakes is nearly deserted.

To reach the trailhead, turn off Highway 395 at Toms Place (located 15 miles south of the Mammoth Lakes junction) and follow Rock Creek Road for 8.9 miles to Rock Creek Lake and the trailhead.

Begin climbing on an aspen-lined trail, enjoying views down to Rock Creek Lake and up Rock Creek Canyon to the peaks beyond. Trees obscure the vista before long.

Reach the crest of the initial ascent at 0.4 mile and ease into more level walking with some gentle ups and downs. Look for sage, lupine, nude buckwheat, sulfur flower, and scarlet gilia in the dusty ground along the way. Arrive at an entry sign for the John Muir Wilderness at 0.7 mile.

More undulating terrain follows. At the 1.3-mile point, a feeder trail joins in from the pack station. Continue toward Hilton Lakes and Davis Lake.

A long, gentle downhill levels off at 1.6 miles and then you will glide across an open hillside studded with Sierra junipers. Begin a steady climb at 2 miles. It will end atop a lodgepole-covered ridge at the 2.3-mile mark.

Stay to the right as the trail branches and continue on a wide, sandy route beneath the trees. At 2.9 miles, the gentle ascent becomes a full-fledged assault on a tree-sprinkled hillside. A half-mile of climbing leads to yet another ridge.

Continue through an avalanche-blighted area littered with uprooted trees and then start into a steep descent of switchbacks at 3.7 miles. You will groan inwardly as you start downhill on steep switchbacks, knowing that this little "detour" means more climbing on the hike out. Pause for a peek of Davis Lake through the trees.

Reach a junction at 4.1 miles and go left toward the Hilton Lakes. The trail to the right leads to Davis Lake and the second Hilton Lake.

Climb steep switchbacks, breathing threats against the person who laid out this roller-coaster ride the Forest Service calls a trail. At 4.3 miles you'll reach a viewpoint of Davis Lake and the second Hilton Lake. Beyond Davis Lake, the view extends to the Owens Valley and the distant White Mountains.

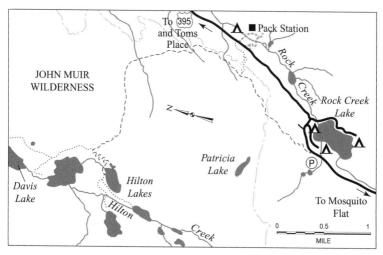

*The mountain-backed Hilton Lakes are a scenic day-hike destination. Karen &
Terry Whitehill*

Continue on a level trail to reach the shore of the third Hilton
Lake at 4.4 miles. This lovely alpine lake has a startling granite backdrop that appears to tumble into the lake's cool waters. The meadowlike
shoreline is perfect for resting and eating lunch. Find a spot beside a
mountain heather bush or find a nook filled with Labrador tea. Wiry
whitebark pines offer shade from the sun.

Anglers can explore the depths of the third Hilton Lake and its
nearby neighbors for brook trout and the much-prized golden trout.
The high elevation guarantees a chilly dip for hikers intending to take
an invigorating swim.

MAMMOTH LAKES AREA

The resort town of Mammoth Lakes is a popular year-round playground. The area's lakes are favorite fishing destinations. The nearby mountains attract rock climbers, backpackers, mountaineers, anglers, snowboarders, and skiers. There is a distinct European flair to some of the restaurants in the area, and it is not unusual to observe international travelers in the community.

One of the largest ski areas in the country is Mammoth Mountain Ski Resort, a good place to improve your backcountry skiing and snowboarding skills in the winter and spring. In the summer, Mammoth Mountain is a favorite of mountain bikers and the resort attracts many national and international mountain-bike competitions. The nearby thermal springs of Hot Creek are enjoyed by all after a hard day of playing.

Mount Ritter from Shadow Lake on Hike 61. Views like this are plentiful all the way up the trail to Shadow and Ediza Lakes. Paul Richins Jr.

The Minarets are a striking sight from Highway 395 and Minaret Summit (Highway 203). The highest and most prominent of the twenty Minaret spires is Clyde Minaret, backed by the needlelike spire of Michael Minaret. To the north, the skyline is dominated by Mount Ritter and Banner Peak. Mount Ritter was first climbed by John Muir in 1872. Shadow and Ediza Lakes (Hike 61) are located at the base of the Minarets near Mount Ritter.

If you are not familiar with the area, make the Forest Service office in the community of Mammoth Lakes your first stop. It is located on the north side of

195

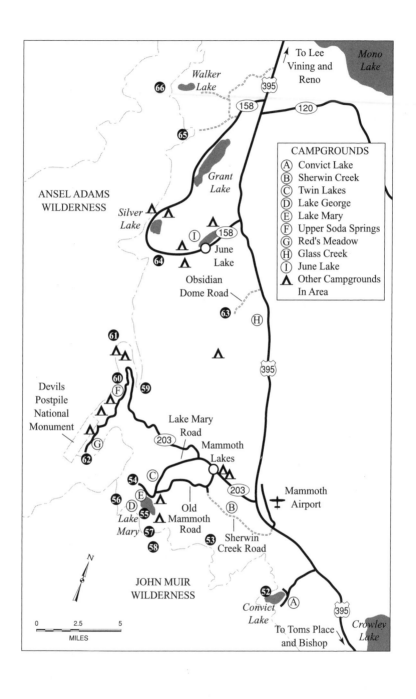

To Lee Vining and Reno

Mono Lake

Walker Lake

66

65

158

120

CAMPGROUNDS
- Ⓐ Convict Lake
- Ⓑ Sherwin Creek
- Ⓒ Twin Lakes
- Ⓓ Lake George
- Ⓔ Lake Mary
- Ⓕ Upper Soda Springs
- Ⓖ Red's Meadow
- Ⓗ Glass Creek
- Ⓘ June Lake
- ⛺ Other Campgrounds In Area

ANSEL ADAMS WILDERNESS

Silver Lake

Grant Lake

Ⓘ 158

64

June Lake

Obsidian Dome Road

63

Ⓗ

61

Devils Postpile National Monument

60

Ⓕ

59

Ⓖ

62

Lake Mary Road

203

Mammoth Lakes

395

54

Ⓒ

56

Ⓓ 55

Ⓔ

Lake Mary

57

58

Old Mammoth Road

Ⓑ

53

Sherwin Creek Road

Mammoth Airport

N

JOHN MUIR WILDERNESS

52

Ⓐ

Convict Lake

To Toms Place and Bishop

395

Crowley Lake

0   2.5   5
MILES

Highway 203 just east of the town proper. Forest Service personnel can assist with campground information, overnight wilderness permits, or entry regulations for the Devils Postpile National Monument. The visitor center includes a good selection of free literature as well as books and maps (see Appendix 1).

Those staying at one of several campgrounds in the area must pay camping fees and obtain a vehicle permit at the Devils Postpile entrance station. Entrance-station personnel keep a running total on vacancies at the campgrounds within the boundaries, and you won't be allowed to drive into the area if there aren't open sites.

If you are venturing into the Agnew Meadow–Red's Meadow area and Devils Postpile National Monument, all visitors without a campground vehicle permit must use the shuttle bus when traveling to and from area trailheads (Hikes 60–62). The shuttle runs frequently, is easy to use, and reduces traffic on the twisting, narrow Devils Postpile road. Day visitors to Devils Postpile National Monument must leave their vehicles at the Mammoth Mountain ski area and board the shuttle bus. Ask at either the Mammoth Visitor Center or at the Mammoth Mountain ski area for a bus schedule and fee information.

The hikes in the Mammoth Lakes area are accessed from three areas along Highway 395. Hike 52, Convict Lake, is reached by turning onto Convict Lake Road, located several miles south of Mammoth Lakes. Hikes 53–62 are located near Mammoth Lakes and/or the Devils Postpile National Monument off of Highway 203. Hikes 63 and 64 are in the general vicinity of June Lake and Hikes 65 and 66 are just south of Lee Vining.

CAMPGROUNDS

Convict Lake Campground *(Hike 52)*. This popular campground offers great access to Convict Lake, where boaters, swimmers, and anglers abound. Arrive early to improve your chances of claiming a site.

To reach Convict Lake Campground, turn southwest off Highway 395 at the sign for Convict Lake, 4.5 miles south of the Mammoth Lakes Junction with Highway 203. Drive the paved road 2.3 miles and then angle left for "day use parking." Continue 0.1 mile and veer left again to enter the campground.

Convict Lake Campground's 88 sites for tents and RVs include picnic tables, firepits, drinking water, and flush toilets. Shade is a scarce commodity. Some of the nicest sites are scattered along Convict Creek.

Convict Lake Campground is open April to October. No reservations. Moderate fee.

Sherwin Creek Campground (*Hike 53*). Secluded Sherwin Creek Campground is an excellent camping option. When you can't find an open campsite at other places, you might find one here. The campground is pleasant and attractive, set along Sherwin Creek and shaded by tall Jeffrey pines.

To reach Sherwin Creek Campground, turn off Highway 395 at Mammoth Lakes Junction. Follow Highway 203 to Mammoth Lakes. Turn south on Old Mammoth Road and drive 0.8 mile. Veer left onto Sherwin Creek Road. Continue to the campground entrance.

Sherwin Creek Campground's 87 sites for tents and RVs offer picnic tables, firepits, drinking water, and flush toilets. The majority of sites are first-come, first-served, but some sites can be reserved through the Forest Service (see Appendix 1).

Sherwin Creek Campground is open May to October. Reservations accepted. Moderate fee.

Twin Lakes Campground (*Hikes 54–62*). This developed campground adjacent to Twin Lakes absorbs a large portion of the camping crowd that floods the Mammoth Lakes area. With 95 sites for tents and RVs, Twin Lakes Campground includes horseback riding, boat rental, and a grocery store as well as the more mundane features of picnic tables, firepits, drinking water, flush toilets, and showers.

To reach the campground, turn off Highway 395 at Mammoth Junction, and follow Highway 203 through the town of Mammoth Lakes. Reach the Lake Mary Road after 3.7 miles. Continue straight and proceed 2.3 miles to a sign for Twin Lakes Campground. Veer right onto a paved side road and reach the campground entrance after 0.5 mile.

Despite its size and hectic atmosphere, Twin Lakes Campground is quite pleasant with many scenic, shaded sites.

Twin Lakes Campground is open June to October. No reservations. Moderate fee.

Lake George Campground (*Hikes 54–62*). The Lake George Campground is a favorite for families and anglers, and it's an ideal launching pad for day hikes in the Mammoth Lakes area. Set on the shore of Lake George, the campground's 16 sites for tents and RVs include picnic tables, firepits, drinking water, and flush toilets. An early arrival time is essential if you hope to claim a vacant site. The best sites offer a view of the lake.

To reach Lake George Campground, turn off Highway 395 at

Mammoth Junction and follow Highway 203 through the town of Mammoth Lakes for 3.7 miles. Continue through the intersection and follow Lake Mary Road for 3.9 miles before veering left onto Road 4S09 (signed for Lake Mary and Lake George Campgrounds). Follow Road 4S09 for 0.3 mile and turn right to Lake George. Arrive at the campground in 0.3 mile.

Lake George Campground is open June to October. No reservations. Moderate fee.

Lake Mary Campground (*Hikes 54–62*). Like the nearby Lake George Campground, Lake Mary Campground is a popular spot. Its 48 sites for tents and motor homes are set near the shore of Lake Mary. Some sites have a fine view of the lake and the campground offers the usual selection of picnic tables, firepits, drinking water, and flush toilets.

To reach the campground, turn off Highway 395 at Mammoth Junction and continue on Highway Road 203 through the town of Mammoth Lakes. Reach Lake Mary Road after 3.7 miles and continue through the intersection for 3.9 miles before veering left onto Road 4S09 (signed for Lake Mary and Lake George Campgrounds). A brief 0.1 mile on Road 4S09 leads to Lake Mary Campground.

Lake Mary Campground is open June to October. No reservations. Moderate fee.

Upper Soda Springs Campground (*Hikes 60–62*). Upper Soda Springs Campground is located within the Agnew Meadows–Red's Meadow area, making it subject to the special camping requirements discussed in this section's introductory paragraphs. This campground is usually a good bet for late arrivers.

The campground's 29 roomy sites for tents and RVs are set near the San Joaquin River and provide excellent access to the San Joaquin Trail. Sites offer picnic tables, firepits, drinking water, and non-flush toilets.

To reach the campground, turn off Highway 395 at Mammoth Junction and follow Highway 203 through the town of Mammoth Lakes. Reach an intersection signed for Lake Mary Road and Mammoth Mountain–Devils Postpile after 3.7 miles. Turn right for Devils Postpile and continue 5.6 miles to the Devils Postpile entrance station. You will need to pause to check on site availability and obtain your vehicle pass. While you are in the vicinity, be sure to check out the Minaret Vista (the vista is on the right just before the entrance station).

The aptly named vista parking area boasts views of Mount Ritter, Banner Peak, and the Minarets. A plaque, mounted at the 9265-foot parking spot, identifies each of the surrounding peaks. This is also the start of Hike 59, San Joaquin Ridge.

To continue your drive to Upper Soda Springs Campground, leave the entrance station and proceed 5 miles on the paved road toward Devils Postpile National Monument. Turn off the road at a sign for Upper Soda Springs Campground and gain the campground entrance 0.2 mile later.

Upper Soda Springs Campground is open June to October. No reservations. Moderate fee.

Red's Meadow Campground *(Hikes 60–62)*. This is probably the most popular campground in the Agnew Meadows–Red's Meadow area. It includes a bonus: a bathhouse with hot showers fueled by a natural hot spring! Even if you are not able to get a site at Red's Meadow Campground, you can use the showers while camping in the area. There is a small visitors' parking lot beside the bathhouse.

Additional features of Red's Meadow Campground seem anticlimactic after such a treasure. The campground's 56 sites for tents or RVs are pleasantly situated in a shady grove of Jeffrey pines. Campsites offer picnic tables, firepits, drinking water, and flush toilets.

To reach Red's Meadow Campground, turn off Highway 395 at Mammoth Junction and follow Highway 203 through the town of Mammoth Lakes. After 3.7 miles, reach the junction for Lake Mary Road and Mammoth Mountain–Devils Postpile. Turn right for Devils Postpile and drive 5.6 miles to the Devils Postpile entrance station. You will need to pause to check on site availability and obtain your vehicle pass.

From the entrance station, continue 7.7 miles on the paved road toward Devils Postpile National Monument and turn left at the sign for Red's Meadow Campground.

Red's Meadow Campground is open June to October. No reservations. Moderate fee.

Glass Creek Campground *(Hikes 63–66)*. This easy-to-miss campground just north of the Mammoth Lakes junction is probably the best accommodation bargain to be found in the entire Mammoth Lakes area. Granted, Glass Creek Campground lacks certain luxuries such as flush toilets and running water. However, the campground is free and it is so large and unstructured that one can almost always find a site.

To reach the campground, turn west off Highway 395 on Glass Creek Road. This junction is located 6 miles south of the more southerly of the two June Lake junctions. Drive a short distance to the camping area located along tiny Glass Creek.

The campground's 50 sites for tents and RVs offer picnic tables, firepits, and non-flush toilets. You will have to provide your own drinking water.

While you are at the campground be sure to check out the nearby Obsidian Dome. This impressive mound was formed by lava that escaped from a crack in the earth's surface thousands of years ago. The rugged surface of the dome is sprinkled with large chunks of obsidian and it looks more like some surreal moonscape than a typical Sierra scene. Reach Obsidian Dome via Obsidian Dome Road, 2.3 miles north of the Glass Creek Campground.

Glass Creek Campground is open May to November. No reservations. No fee.

June Lake Campground *(Hikes 63–66)*. The pleasant June Lake Campground includes 28 roomy sites for tents and RVs. Many of the sites are close to the shoreline of June Lake and all offer picnic tables, firepits, flush toilets, and drinking water.

June Lake Campground is popular on weekends. Come early or make reservations (see Appendix 1).

To reach the campground, turn off Highway 395 at the more southerly of the two June Lake junctions. Drive 2.5 miles to the sign for June Lake Campground and turn right.

June Lake Campground is open May to November. Reservations accepted. Moderate fee.

52. CONVICT LAKE

Distance ■	2.8-mile loop
Difficulty ■	Easy
Starting point ■	7640 feet
High point ■	7670 feet
Elevation gain ■	30 feet
Trail grade ■	21 feet per mile
Maps ■	USGS Convict Lake 7.5' or Mammoth High Country Trail Map (Tom Harrison)
Access road/town ■	Highway 395 to Convict Lake Road/ Mammoth Lakes

The trailhead at Convict Lake offers access to some ruggedly beautiful backcountry, including Mildred Lake and Lake Dorothy. Unfortunately, the length and difficulty of the trail rule out a day hike for all but the most able hikers. A hike to Mildred Lake would be about 10 miles round trip and involve 2300 feet of elevation gain. An easy, family-style jaunt around the shore of Convict Lake seems more in order.

This pleasant excursion along the shore of Convict Lake provides mountain vistas and many opportunities for fishing, picnicking, and exploring. The hike is especially convenient for those staying at Convict Lake Campground, because there is no need to drive to the trailhead.

To reach the Convict Lake Trail, turn southwest off Highway 395 toward Convict Lake (4.5 miles south of Mammoth Lakes Junction, Highway 203). Proceed 2.3 miles to the lakeside day-use parking lot. Toilets are available near the parking area. The circumnavigation of the lake can be done in either direction. The following description begins on the right side of the lake near the small marina and continues in a counterclockwise direction.

Leave the day-use parking area and descend to the paved lakeside path. Convict Lake is a beautiful lake in an impressive setting—the color of the water is deep blue and the sheer north face of Mount Morrison rises in the background. Linger long enough to read the information plaques along the lakeshore. They detail the history, geology, and botany of the area.

Convict Lake was named for a group of prison escapees who fled to the spot in 1871. They headed up Convict Canyon (at the upper end of the lake), with a pursuing posse hot behind them. The resulting gun battle left the posse leader dead (Mount Morrison is named for him). Several of the convicts were killed or captured.

Mount Morrison towers over the scene on your left. At 0.2 and 0.3 mile the trail from the backpackers' trailhead joins from the right.

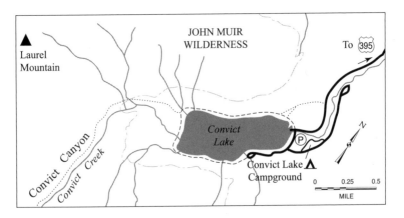

Anglers along the shore and in their boats are common.

Pass a lone Jeffrey pine at 0.8 mile, its butterscotch-scented bark clinging like a rough hide to the stout trunk. Reach the upper end of Convict Lake and a fork in the trail at the 1.2-mile mark. The route to the right leads up into Convict Canyon and Mildred and Dorothy Lakes.

If you have the time and don't mind lengthening your day a bit, it is well worth the effort to explore an additional 0.9 mile beyond the

The hike to Convict Lake is short and enjoyable, providing many fishing opportunities. Paul Richins Jr.

junction. Climb steadily along the trail heading toward Mildred Lake and earn a view into the legendary Convict Canyon. Red Slate Mountain sits at the head of the canyon.

To continue your lakeshore loop, angle left from the junction and hike in the company of Sierra junipers, mountain mahogany, Fremont cottonwoods, and quaking aspens. Reach the banks of Convict Creek at 1.4 miles. The water trickles into Convict Lake in a host of rivulets with a grove of quaking aspens nearby.

Continue around the southeast side of Convict Lake and close the loop. The last part will be a short walk along the lakeside road back to your car.

53. SHERWIN LAKES AND VALENTINE LAKE

Distance ■	5.8 miles round trip (Sherwin Lakes) / 12 miles round trip (Valentine Lake)
Difficulty ■	Easy / Moderate
Starting point ■	7800 feet / 7800 feet
High point ■	8640 feet / 9710 feet
Elevation gain ■	840 feet / 1910 feet
Trail grade ■	290 feet per mile / 318 feet per mile
Maps ■	USGS Bloody Mountain 7.5' or Mammoth High Country Trail Map (Tom Harrison)
Access road/town ■	Highway 395 to Highway 203 to Sherwin Creek Road / Mammoth Lakes

Although the 12-mile round-trip distance for this trek may seem a bit long, Valentine Lake isn't an unreasonable day-hike destination, even for hikers of moderate ability. The trail is well graded and pleasant surroundings make the miles pass easily. An alternative destination less than 3 miles from the trailhead is Sherwin Lakes.

To reach the trailhead, turn off Highway 395 at Mammoth Lakes Junction. Follow Highway 203 to the town of Mammoth Lakes and turn south on Old Mammoth Road. Drive 0.8 mile and veer left onto Sherwin Creek Road. Continue 1.3 miles and turn right at the sign for the Sherwin Lakes trailhead. You will arrive at the trailhead parking area in 0.4 mile. A boys' camp is located near the trailhead and the jubilant voices of young campers may drift your way at the start.

Begin the hike at the sign for Sherwin Lakes among scattered white firs and Jeffrey pines. Descend and cross over Sherwin Creek at 0.2 mile and then climb gently, easing into a series of long switchbacks. The mellow grade intensifies at 0.9 mile and you will pick up views of Mammoth Lakes.

Reach the crest of the switchback-scribbled hill at 2.1 miles and relax on a stretch of downhill and level walking. A good view of 11,053-foot Mammoth Mountain is on the right. At 2.5 miles, a trail to the right leads to the first of the Sherwin lakes. Small and rocky, the lake

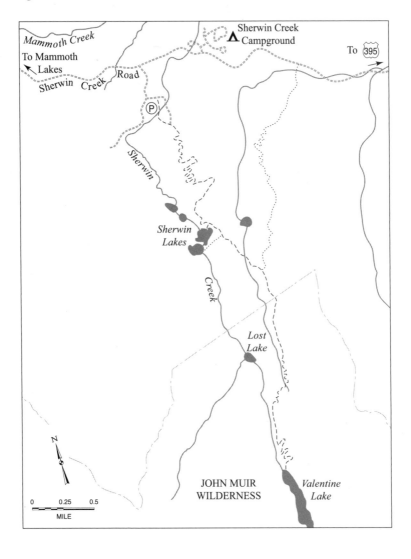

The boulder-strewn shores of Valentine Lake lend themselves to relaxing. Karen & Terry Whitehill

is certainly not spectacular, but it's nice enough to invite a rest break. Continue along the main trail and wind through the trees. Arrive at a junction at 2.7 miles. A spur trail to the right leads a short distance to the largest of the Sherwin lakes. For those planning a hike to Sherwin Lakes turn off the main trail and continue to the water's edge.

For those headed to Valentine Lake, stay on the main trail continuing on an undulating path through a dry landscape dotted with ancient-looking Sierra junipers. Cross a small creek at 3.1 miles and climb steadily for a few minutes. The route levels off before another trail junction at the 3.3-mile point. Pass a side trail joining in from the left (this comes from a secondary trailhead) and continue toward Valentine Lake. Enjoy a short stretch of easy walking through junipers and pines, and then resume climbing to reach an entry sign for the John Muir Wilderness.

A gentle climb beside an aspen-lined creek leads to a marshy wildflower wonderland at 4.2 miles. Look for ranger buttons, pink monkeyflower, angelica, and Sierra rein orchid. Cross a small creek at 4.6 miles and continue your ascent with a view down to Lost Lake. Droopy mountain hemlocks edge the trail. The vegetation becomes less dense allowing good views of the surrounding peaks and rugged canyon.

Pass a small, grass-lined pond at 5.1 miles. The trail soon approaches Sherwin Creek. Many ferns and wildflowers grow along its banks. The trail zigzags steadily uphill while Sherwin Creek tumbles downward through a boulder-strewn ravine.

The switchbacks cease at 6 miles and you will emerge on the lower lip of long and lovely Valentine Lake. Surrounding mountains wrap around the lake's blue water, encircling it like a beau's strong arms. And Valentine Lake snuggles happily into its boulder-strewn shores, clinging to the peaks even as its outlet stream tumbles headlong toward the distant valley floor.

Pick a spot along the lakeshore and settle in for lunch, some afternoon fishing, or a short nap. Not to be missed is a scramble up the small bluff on the north side of the lake's outlet stream. The short climb yields a vista of the valley below.

54. McLEOD LAKE

Distance	■	1.2 miles round trip
Difficulty	■	Easy
Starting point	■	8990 feet
High point	■	9320 feet
Elevation gain	■	330 feet
Trail grade	■	550 feet per mile
Maps	■	USGS Crystal Crag 7.5' or Mammoth High Country Trail Map (Tom Harrison)
Access road/town	■	Highway 395 to Highway 203/Mammoth Lakes

This short walk to McLeod Lake makes a super family outing, especially for those with junior hikers in their ranks. Although the climb to the lake is steep, it is short and youngsters can be lured along with promises of picnic treats.

To find the trailhead, turn off Highway 395 at Mammoth Lakes Junction and proceed on Highway 203 through the town of Mammoth Lakes. Reach Lake Mary Road after 3.7 miles. Continue straight through the intersection and proceed 5 miles to the road's end and a large parking area beside Horseshoe Lake.

Begin walking at a sign for the Mammoth Pass Trail. Climb through a forest of lodgepole pines and scattered mountain hemlocks. Continue along the main trail to reach a junction at 0.1 mile and keep to the left for McLeod Lake.

The grade eases slightly as you press on through a sampling of western white and whitebark pines and red firs. Savor views of the Mammoth Crest to the left as you continue up the hill and watch for Mammoth Mountain on the right. Pass a second trail junction at 0.6 mile.

The trail to the right leads on to Mammoth Pass and the Devils Postpile area. The largely vista-less Mammoth Pass is the lowest gap between east and west in the entire central portion of the Sierra Nevada. Rainfall on the west side of the pass flows into San Francisco Bay while rain and snow that fall on the east side flow toward the Owens River Valley and the Los Angeles Aqueduct.

Take the trail angling left from the junction and you will soon reach the shore of McLeod Lake. The lake boasts a sandy shoreline

McLeod Lake waits at the end of a brief walk. Karen & Terry Whitehill

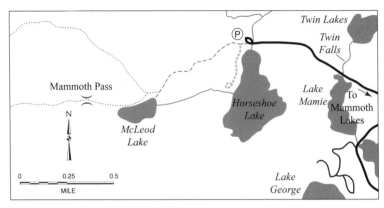

and a lakeside path sure to tempt children with excess energy. Picnic spots abound, and fishing is permissible on a catch-and-release basis. The impressive form of Mammoth Crest rises above the lake's far shore.

55. TJ LAKE AND LAKE BARRETT

Distance	▪	1.7-mile loop
Difficulty	▪	Easy
Starting point	▪	9020 feet
High point	▪	9350 feet
Elevation gain	▪	330 feet
Trail grade	▪	330 feet per mile
Maps	▪	USGS Crystal Crag 7.5' or Mammoth High Country Trail Map (Tom Harrison)
Access road/town	▪	Highway 395 to Highway 203 / Mammoth Lakes

Like the preceding hike to McLeod Lake (Hike 54), this short walk to TJ Lake and Lake Barrett is an ideal family outing. Those staying at the Lake George Campground will find it especially handy—there's no need to drive to the trailhead.

To reach the trailhead, refer to the driving directions for Lake George Campground at the beginning of this section. Park your vehicle in the day-use parking area beside the campground and begin at the sign for TJ–Barrett Lakes.

Set out on a wide trail along the shore of Lake George, admiring the picturesque Crystal Crag. This pinnacle dominates the views in the area along with Mammoth Crest in the background.

The wide path narrows to a trail at the 0.2-mile point. Cross Lake George's outlet stream on a footbridge amid a leafy hedge of willows and alders. Leave the lakeside trail at 0.3 mile, turning left for Lake Barrett.

Climb steeply on a rocky trail, ascending alongside Lake George's inlet stream. The hillside is laced with fireweed and angelica, and stout western white pines compete with bushy whitebark pines for footholds in the rocky soil. The incline eases slightly at 0.4 mile.

Climb steeply once more in the welcome shade of shaggy mountain hemlocks. At 0.6 mile, the trail branches and flattens out. Keep to the right and you will soon arrive at Lake Barrett. If you are hiking with children they will surely want to stop and explore this little lake, but it's really not as scenic as TJ Lake. Take a brief breather and push on to TJ Lake.

Follow the gently climbing trail along the right shore of Lake Barrett. A confusing mix of use trails mars the landscape. Leave Lake Barrett and ascend a short distance to gain sight of TJ Lake ahead. A quick descent leads to the lakeshore at 0.8 mile.

TJ Lake is a beautiful little gem with enchanting Crystal Crag dominating the viewscape and a shoreline lush with Labrador tea and mountain heather. This is a great spot for a picnic or wading.

To continue your loop, take the unmarked trail that leads downhill beside TJ Lake's outlet stream. Stay close to the creek when the trail branches. You will gain a view of Lake George and out toward Mammoth Mountain at the 1-mile point.

The descent picks up momentum quickly as you continue down

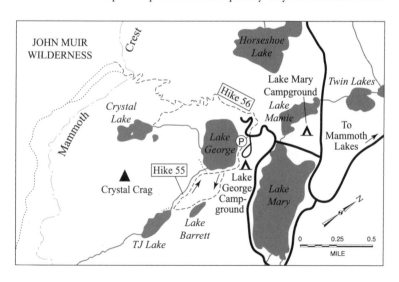

Crystal Crag rules the placid waters of TJ Lake. Karen & Terry Whitehill

along the creek. The footing is tricky at times so young children may need assistance.

Reach the shore of Lake George at 1.2 miles and go right on the lakeside trail. You will reach the junction for Lake Barrett after 0.2 mile. Continue along the shore of Lake George, retracing your steps to regain your starting point after 1.7 miles.

56. CRYSTAL LAKE AND MAMMOTH CREST

Distance	■	2.6 miles round trip (Crystal Lake) / 5.6 miles round trip (Mammoth Crest)
Difficulty	■	Easy / Moderate
Starting point	■	9020 feet / 9020 feet
High point	■	9640 feet / 10,560 feet
Elevation gain	■	620 feet / 1540 feet
Trail grade	■	477 feet per mile / 616 feet per mile
Maps	■	USGS Crystal Crag 7.5' or Mammoth High Country Trail Map (Tom Harrison)
Access road/town	■	Highway 395 to Highway 203 / Mammoth Lakes *See map page 210*

This hike shares its starting point at Lake George Campground with the preceding hike, TJ Lake and Lake Barrett, but proceeds around the

north and west sides of the lake rather than the east side. Crystal Lake is a real gem and the views are expansive from the Mammoth Crest. Carry a light windbreaker, as the crest can be breezy any time of the year.

To reach the trailhead for Crystal Lake and Mammoth Crest, refer to the driving directions for Lake George Campground at the beginning of this section. Park your vehicle in the day-use parking area beside the campground and look for the trailhead directly opposite the parking-area entrance.

Start out beside a sign for Crystal Lake–Mammoth Crest and climb on a sandy trail shaded by an assortment of pines, firs, and hemlocks. You will soon gain views toward Duck Pass, Mammoth Crest, and Crystal Crag.

A challenging ascent eases briefly at 0.4 mile. Continue onward through the trees and climb steadily to reach a superb viewpoint above Lake George at the 0.7-mile point. Continue uphill in shaded switchbacks, arriving at a trail junction at 1 mile.

Turn left to make the short side trip to Crystal Lake. Crystal Lake is nestled into an amphitheater created by the steep sides of the Mammoth Crest. Crystal Crag dominates the scene, guaranteeing panoramic views.

Retrace your steps to the junction. Press on toward the Mammoth Crest. The well-graded trail climbs steadily. Stubby whitebark pines and mountain hemlocks dot the hillside.

A particularly steep section must be climbed near the 2-mile mark. As you ascend, the views of Mammoth Lakes and Mammoth Mountain improve. Horseshoe Lake, Twin Lakes, and Lakes Mamie, Mary, and George can be seen sparkling in the basin below.

Just off the trail, there is a vista of the Minarets, Mount Ritter, and Banner Peak to the northwest. Continue ascending steadily. Crystal Lake comes into view at 2.4 miles and a handful of switchbacks leads to an entry sign into the John Muir Wilderness.

Continue up across a barren landscape of reddish volcanic stone. You will top a rise at 2.6 miles and start downhill along the main crest. Watch for a use trail exiting to the right just after the descent begins and take this footpath to angle uphill toward the summit of the red-hued knoll ahead.

Opposite: *The trailhead for Crystal Lake and the Mammoth Crest starts at Lake George. Crystal Crag is a distinctive feature in the Mammoth Lakes region. Paul Richins Jr.*

A steep scramble ends atop a volcanic mound at 2.8 miles. You have ascended the Mammoth Crest and can enjoy its magnificent 360-degree vistas. The views, on a clear day, are extensive. Look for the Minarets, Mount Ritter, and Banner Peak to the northwest. The ragged line of Mammoth Crest runs to the southeast. To the east, the White Mountains and Nevada fade into the blue-gray distance, and an eagle's vista of the Mammoth Lakes basin completes the scene.

57. EMERALD LAKE AND SKY MEADOWS

Distance	▪	1.8 miles round trip (Emerald Lake) / 4 miles round trip (Sky Meadows)
Difficulty	▪	Easy / Easy
Starting point	▪	9080 feet / 9080 feet
High point	▪	9440 feet / 10,050 feet
Elevation gain	▪	360 feet / 970 feet
Trail grade	▪	400 feet per mile / 485 feet per mile
Maps	▪	USGS Bloody Mountain 7.5' or Mammoth High Country Trail Map (Tom Harrison)
Access road/town	▪	Highway 395 to Highway 203/Mammoth Lakes

Although it involves a moderate climb, the hike to Emerald Lake and Sky Meadows is quite pleasant. Time your outing for the height of the wildflower season (July and August), and you will find a blossoming bonanza in Sky Meadows. The trail beyond Emerald Lake may not be of much interest to youngsters. However, most children will be happy with a stop at Emerald Lake. Leave the kids with an adult at the lake, while the rest of the party presses on to Sky Meadows.

To find the trailhead, turn off Highway 395 at Mammoth Lakes Junction and drive through the town of Mammoth Lakes on Highway 203. Reach the Lake Mary Road after 3.7 miles. Continue through the intersection and proceed 3.9 miles before turning left onto Road 4S09 to Lake Mary and Lake George Campgrounds. Drive 3.6 miles and turn left toward Coldwater Campground. Keep to the right as you pass the large campground along Coldwater Creek. You will see a sign for Emerald Lake parking after 0.7 mile. Toilets and drinking water are available.

Begin at the trailhead for Emerald Lake–Sky Meadows. This parking area serves the Duck Pass trailhead (Hike 58) as well. Be sure to

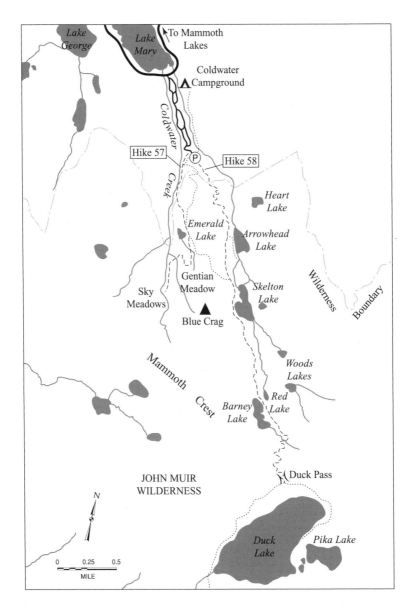

head up the correct trail. A gently ascending path leads through a lodgepole pine forest alongside Coldwater Creek.

Reach a junction with a horse trail at 0.1 mile. Keep to the right and climb steadily, savoring the enchanting selection of wildflowers. Look for arrowleaf groundsel, ranger buttons, common monkeyflower,

Monkeyflowers are just one variety of blooms lining the trail to Sky Meadows. Karen & Terry Whitehill

fireweed, and purple-blossomed lupine.

Angle left at 0.6 mile, arriving at a trail sign for Emerald Lake. Leave the creek to climb once more. You will merge with the horse trail at 0.7 mile and then enjoy a gentle uphill route across a lodgepole-sprinkled hillside. Views to the right reveal the impressive Mammoth Crest.

Gain the shore of tiny Emerald Lake at 0.9 mile. Blue Crag looms above the lake, making this a particularly scenic stopping point for those desiring an easy hiking day. Picnicking and fishing opportunities are plentiful.

To continue toward Sky Meadows, angle to the left around the lake. You will have to sift through a confusing profusion of use trails as you climb to a trail junction just above Emerald Lake. Go right for Gentian Meadow–Sky Meadows.

Ascend the trail beside Emerald Lake's tumbling inlet stream. Swamp onion paints the air with its pungent purple flowers and monkeyflowers frolic on the banks of the creek. Cross the waterway at 1.1 miles.

The grade intensifies again as you approach Gentian Meadow (with its nice view of Blue Crag) at 1.2 miles. Descend briefly to cross over Coldwater Creek at 1.5 miles. More climbing follows. Link up with another arm of Coldwater Creek at 1.7 miles. Follow the trail along the creek. You will soon arrive at a waterfall.

Leave the waterfall for the final ascent. You will reach the edge of Sky Meadows at 2 miles. The flowers are magnificent—Lemmon's paintbrush, little elephant heads, yampah, California corn lily, and willows. Please be careful as you explore the area. The popularity of this trail has taken its toll on the delicate alpine terrain. Stay on established trails, don't discard your trash, and don't pick the flowers.

58. SKELTON LAKE AND DUCK PASS

Distance ■	3.6 miles round trip (Skelton Lake)
	8.2 miles round trip (Duck Pass)
Difficulty ■	Easy / Moderate
Starting point ■	9080 feet / 9080 feet
High point ■	9900 feet / 10,800 feet
Elevation gain ■	820 feet / 1720 feet
Trail grade ■	456 feet per mile / 420 feet per mile
Maps ■	USGS Bloody Mountain 7.5' or Mammoth High Country Trail Map (Tom Harrison)
Access road/town ■	Highway 395 to Highway 203/Mammoth Lakes
	See map page 215

The ascent to Duck Pass is a rewarding and worthwhile adventure. The views of Mount Ritter, Banner Peak, and the Minarets are exhilarating. If the pass is farther than you wish to hike, Skelton or Barney Lakes are excellent destinations.

Barney Lake as viewed from below Duck Pass. Paul Richins Jr.

To reach the trailhead, refer to the driving directions for the preceding hike, Emerald Lake and Sky Meadows. Proceed to the far end of the trailhead parking lot near Coldwater Campground and begin walking at the sign for the Duck Pass Trail, not Emerald Lake.

The trail climbs gently to the John Muir Wilderness boundary at 0.1 mile. Merge with the horse trail arriving from the pack station. Ascend steadily through a varied forest of lodgepole pines, western white pines, and mountain hemlocks. Pick up Mammoth Creek at 0.9 mile and enjoy easier walking as you press on to the trail junction to Arrowhead Lake.

Stay on the main trail and gain glimpses of Arrowhead Lake on your left. A moderate grade will take you to a rocky ridge at 1.3 miles. The trail degenerates a bit in this area. Enjoy easier walking through a meadowlike basin fed by Mammoth Creek.

Pass the first of a handful of unmarked cutoff trails heading to Skelton Lake. Continue on the main trail and you will soon reach the shore of the lake at 1.8 miles. This charming lake is a fine destination for those desiring a shorter hiking day. The nearby shoreline is gentle with an occasional rock outcropping, whereas the far shoreline is guarded by a continuous cliff.

Resume climbing as you leave Skelton Lake. The steady grade eases after 0.3 mile. Head into a grassy basin brightened with a wealth of wildflowers—hikers gentian, yampah, ranger buttons, and little elephant heads line the way.

The ascent continues as you leave the meadow. There are good views of Mammoth Mountain across the way. Begin the short descent to Barney Lake at 2.6 miles. There are many downed and broken trees scattered around Barney Lake. This is the result of a powerful avalanche that swept down from the steep mountain slopes above the lake.

You will be reminded of the increasing elevation as you gaze at Barney Lake. This lake is more barren than its lower neighbors as is apparent from its rocky shoreline of willows, mountain hemlocks, and whitebark pines. Many backpackers choose Barney Lake as their first-day destination, and the lakeshore is sprinkled with campsites.

Continue along the trail and cross over Barney Lake's outlet stream. Duck Pass, the notch in the ridgeline, lies ahead. The ascent to the pass reaches full stride at 3 miles. Ascend through a landscape of talus and scrubby whitebark pines. You will spot a new breed of flowers hiding among the rocks at this high elevation. Coville's columbine, mountain sorrel, alpine gentian, and brightly colored rockfringe thrive above 10,000 feet.

Ascend a series of well-graded switchbacks. The views continue to unfold as you gain elevation. Barney and Red Lakes are just below, and Skelton Lake nestles among green pines. Look for Mammoth Mountain towering above. Mount Ritter and Banner Peak come into view as you approach the crest.

Finally reach Duck Pass at 4 miles with its delightful views of jagged peaks. Duck Lake, just below the pass, is a deep-blue alpine lake. Lovely Pika Lake beckons backpackers to its secluded shores.

Press on 0.1 mile beyond the pass to gain the best view of Duck Lake. To the southwest, the peaks of the rugged Silver Divide glitter in the thin atmosphere. Choose your favorite vista and take in the view before beginning the downhill hike back to your starting point.

An experienced hiker equipped with map, compass, and cross-country skills can turn the hike into a loop by continuing cross-country along the Mammoth Crest to Deer Lake where the trail continues along the crest and descends via the Crystal Lake Trail to Lake George Campground (see Hike 56). However, this requires routefinding and scrambling skills. You will also need an auto shuttle back to Coldwater Campground.

59. SAN JOAQUIN RIDGE

Distance ▪	4.8 miles round trip
Difficulty ▪	Easy
Starting point ▪	9265 feet
High point ▪	10,255 feet
Elevation gain ▪	990 feet
Trail grade ▪	413 feet per mile
Maps ▪	USGS Mammoth Mountain 7.5' or Mammoth High Country Trail Map (Tom Harrison)
Access road/town ▪	Highway 395 to Highway 203/Mammoth Lakes

Nearly every step of this hike is steeped in spectacular mountain scenery. You certainly will want to bring your camera and extra film. This day hike begins at the 9265-foot Minaret Vista with its superb views of the Minarets, Mount Ritter, and Banner Peak. The vistas improve as you hike along the ridge toward Deadman Pass.

To find the trailhead, turn off Highway 395 at Mammoth Lakes

Junction and drive through the town of Mammoth Lakes on Highway 203. After 3.7 miles, turn right at the junction toward Mammoth Mountain–Devils Postpile.

Drive past the Mammoth Mountain Resort and Lodge to the Minaret Vista. The vista's entry road exits to the right, just before the Devils Postpile entrance station. Drive to the vista's parking area in 0.3 mile.

The vista's information plaque has information to help familiarize you with Mount Ritter, Banner Peak, the Minarets, and the other mountains that will be your hiking partners for the day. Leave from the far end of the parking area, passing a small toilet building, and quickly descend to a four-wheel-drive road.

Turn left up the road as it heads to the north. (It is easy to miss the vista parking lot on your return, so make a special note of the point

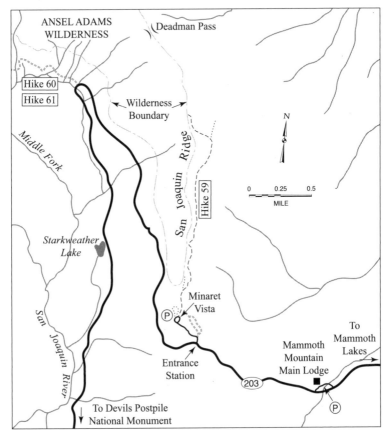

Sunrise views of Mount Ritter and Banner Peak along the San Joaquin Ridge. Paul Richins Jr.

where you join the road.) The road does have infrequent four-wheel-drive traffic, but with luck you may not encounter any vehicles. The roadway is lined with scattered whitebark and lodgepole pines, mountain hemlocks, and red firs. Ascend to a fork at 0.3 mile. Keep to the right and continue along the ridgeline.

You will be walking on the Sierra Nevada Divide throughout this hike. This ridge is the watershed between east and west. Tiny alpine flowers are nestled among the rocks. Look for miniature lupine, sulfur flower, and penstemon. The much larger mule ears thrive in this dry climate as well.

Awesome views of the peaks to the north and northwest unfold as you hike along the ridge: Mammoth Mountain fills the skyline at your back. A challenging ascent eases briefly at 0.5 mile but the climb resumes less than 0.5 mile later. Another somewhat level stretch will offer a breather at the 1.1-mile point. The view to the south and east encompasses Lake Crowley and the White Mountains. Start up another hump in the ridge. Continue past clumps of weather-twisted whitebark pines and colorful patches of mat lupine. Keep to the left when the road branches at 1.6 miles. Up ahead the trail ascends steeply.

Start into the steepest section of the hike at 1.7 miles. Fortunately, this continues for only 0.2 mile, followed by easier walking with an expanding view to the north. On a clear day the vista extends to Yosemite National Park's highest peak, Mount Lyell.

There is one more climb. Start into the final incline at 2.1 miles and stand atop a 10,255-foot knob in the San Joaquin Ridge at 2.4

miles. From here, a footpath descends to Deadman Pass, a sandy saddle in the ridgeline. But why go on? The view doesn't get any better than this 360-degree panorama.

60. SAN JOAQUIN TRAIL TO DEVILS POSTPILE NATIONAL MONUMENT

Distance	▪	7.4 miles one way
Difficulty	▪	Moderate
Starting point	▪	8330 feet
High point	▪	8330 feet
Elevation gain	▪	-700 feet
Trail grade	▪	-85 feet per mile
Maps	▪	USGS Mammoth Mountain 7.5' and USGS Crystal Crag 7.5', or Mammoth High Country Trail Map (Tom Harrison)
Access road/town	▪	Highway 395 to Highway 203/Mammoth Lakes

The San Joaquin Trail offers an ideal family outing for those camping in or visiting the Devils Postpile area. The shuttle makes one-way hiking easy and convenient and you can tailor your walk's length to the abilities and energies of your party.

This trek along a portion of the Pacific Crest Trail follows the San Joaquin River gently downhill for 6 miles to enter the Devils Postpile National Monument. It then passes the impressive landmark for which the monument is named and returns to the main road at the Red's Meadow Campground shuttle stop. Pack a lunch, a camera, and a swimming suit.

To find the trailhead, turn off Highway 395 at Mammoth Junction and follow Highway 203 through the town of Mammoth Lakes. Reach the junction of Lake Mary Road and Mammoth Mountain–Devils Postpile after 3.7 miles. Turn right toward Devils Postpile and continue 5.6 miles to the Devils Postpile entrance station. From the entrance station, drive 2.7 miles on the paved road toward the Devils Postpile National Monument. Then turn off the pavement at the sign for Agnew Meadows Campground. You will find a trailhead parking lot beside the campground entry road after 0.3 mile. Drinking water and toilets are available at the lot. (If you are not camping in the Devils Postpile area, leave your vehicle at the Mammoth Mountain ski resort and take the

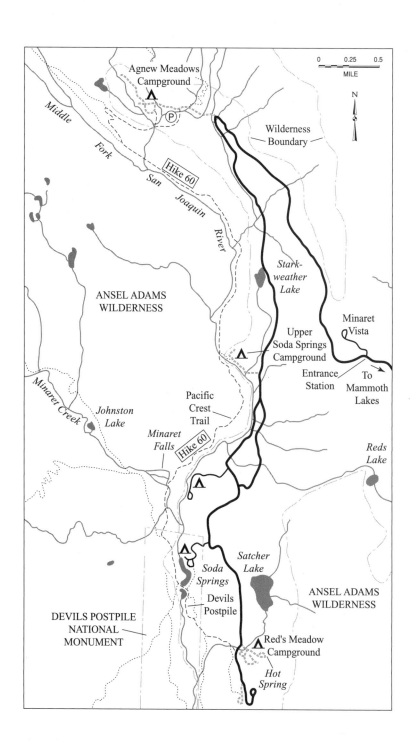

Agnew Meadows
Campground

Wilderness
Boundary

0   0.25   0.5
MILE

N

Middle

Fork

San

Joaquin

River

Hike 60

Stark-
weather
Lake

ANSEL ADAMS
WILDERNESS

Upper
Soda Springs
Campground

Minaret
Vista

Entrance
Station

To
Mammoth
Lakes

Minaret Creek

Johnston
Lake

Pacific
Crest
Trail

Minaret
Falls   Hike 60

Reds
Lake

Satcher
Lake

Soda
Springs

ANSEL ADAMS
WILDERNESS

Devils
Postpile

DEVILS POSTPILE
NATIONAL
MONUMENT

Red's Meadow
Campground

Hot
Spring

shuttle to the stop at Agnew Meadows Campground. Refer to this section's introduction for additional information on the shuttle.)

From the parking area, take the trail to Shadow Lake and proceed 0.1 mile to a second parking lot beside the fenced Agnew Meadows. (This hike's mileage count starts here so add 0.4 mile to your total if you begin walking at the shuttle stop.) Find another trailhead sign at the second lot. Cross a small creek and angle right along the path beside the heavily grazed Agnew Meadows. Look for an interesting assortment of mountain hemlocks, lodgepole pines, red firs, Jeffrey pines, and scattered Sierra junipers along the way.

Recross the creek at 0.3 mile and continue on a shaded path. Reach a trail junction after 0.8 mile. Turn left for Red's Meadow and begin a gentle descent toward the San Joaquin River. Travel downhill over several well-graded switchbacks, crossing an open hillside sprinkled with sage and manzanita.

Look for vistas of 11,053-foot Mammoth Mountain to the southeast as you descend. Arrive at a second junction at the 1.5-mile point. Continue toward Red's Meadow. Cross an aspen- and alder-choked creek

Devils Postpile National Monument attracts a steady stream of visitors. Karen & Terry Whitehill

and enjoy more level walking with a view of Mammoth Mountain.

Follow an undulating trail on the hillside above the San Joaquin River. Reach the river level at 2.6 miles and continue along beneath red firs and lodgepole pines.

A wildflower-edged inlet stream may require some rock hopping to cross at 3 miles. You will be treated to glimpses of the San Joaquin River's many tempting sparkling pools and rivulets as you hike. This is one of the nicest sections of the river this outing has to offer.

Savor easy downhill walking to a sturdy bridge across the river at 4 miles. (A use trail continues toward Upper Soda Springs Campground and a shuttle stop.) Cross the San Joaquin and continue on through trees, climbing gently for a time. Views to the left encompass the San Joaquin Ridge and Deadman Pass (see Hike 59).

The descent resumes through a red fir forest. Note the glowing white of Pumice Flat to the left of the trail at 4.8 miles. This outburst of volcanic rock is a reminder of the explosive history of the area.

Rejoin the San Joaquin and continue on an undulating trail to reach Minaret Falls at 5.5 miles. Cross the stream below the falls and take the short spur trail to its base. If you're looking for a picnic spot, you might pause to enjoy the view of the falls: icy water tumbling down a rocky ladder, with bright yellow patches of Sierra arnica clinging to every dripping foothold.

Return to the main trail and hike uphill through lodgepole pines. A sign at 6 miles announces the boundary of the Devils Postpile National Monument. Arrive at a trail junction soon after. The Pacific Crest Trail continues ahead but abandon that route and turn left to descend toward the river.

Reach another junction at 6.4 miles and continue toward Devils Postpile. Look for a reddish splash of soil on the San Joaquin shoreline, just to the left of the trail. This signals the presence of Soda Springs. Keep to the right and cross the river on a footbridge.

A brief climb leads to another junction. Turn right toward Devils Postpile. An informative display board explains the geologic phenomenon of the area. Devils Postpile is symmetry in stone, softened by the touch of bright green lichen. Broken columns are crumpled at the bases of their upright companions, looking like the pieces of a Roman ruin. Yet Rome was vibrant only yesterday when compared with the timelessness of these ancient stones.

When you are ready to move on, stay on the main trail and climb away from Devils Postpile and the river. Sneak a view of the "back side" of Devils Postpile as the ascent eases at 6.8 miles. A brief descent leads past fragrant Jeffrey pines. Leave the boundary of the national monument as the trail levels out.

Reach a junction at 7 miles and turn left toward Red's Meadow. Cross a small stream and arrive at another junction. Stay to the left for Red's Meadow and the campground and reach the main road at 7.3 miles. Follow the main road to the left to arrive at the shuttle stop beside Red's Meadow Campground.

You can use the shuttle to close your loop to Agnew Meadows Campground, the Mammoth Mountain ski area, or wherever you began your hiking day.

61. SHADOW LAKE AND EDIZA LAKE

Distance ■	7.2 miles round trip (Shadow Lake) / 14.8 miles round trip (Ediza Lake)
Difficulty ■	Moderate / Strenuous
Starting point ■	8330 feet / 8330 feet
High point ■	8750 feet / 9265 feet
Elevation gain ■	1020 feet / 1660 feet
Trail grade ■	283 feet per mile / 224 feet per mile
Maps ■	USGS Mammoth Mountain 7.5' and USGS Mount Ritter 7.5', or Mammoth High Country Trail Map (Tom Harrison)
Access road/town ■	Highway 395 to Highway 203/Mammoth Lakes

Shadow Lake and Ediza Lake lie at the base of a distinctive cluster of peaks in the Sierra Nevada. Mount Ritter, Banner Peak, and the Minarets, along with the enchanting meadows and lakes in the area, make this hike one of the best single-day or overnight trips in the entire Sierra Nevada. The hike to Ediza Lake is a bit farther than Shadow Lake but is worth undertaking. I have made the pilgrimage many times in winter and spring on skis and in summer and fall on foot and highly recommend it.

Although the trip to Shadow Lake involves a bit of elevation gain, the trail is suitable for hikers with a wide range of abilities. You can spend an entire afternoon in Shadow Lake's spectacular surroundings; however, the scenery improves dramatically as you close in on Ediza Lake.

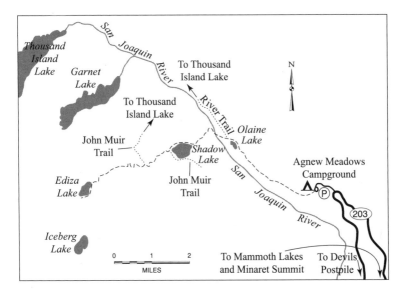

Refer to Hike 60 for driving and hiking directions. From the junction at the 0.8-mile point, stay to the right for Shadow Lake and continue a gentle descent to the San Joaquin River.

Traverse an open hillside sporting manzanita, canyon live oaks, sage, and brilliant California fuchsia. The descent becomes an easy uphill at 1.4 miles. Continue along the San Joaquin River on a sandy trail lined with Sierra junipers and lodgepole pines. Angle away from the river and climb to the shore of Olaine Lake at 2 miles. Olaine Lake is hemmed in by a forested shoreline and marshy shallows and does not offer much of a stopping point.

Continue through cool lodgepole shade, ascending gently to a trail junction at 2.3 miles. The riverside trail continues to the right. Turn left toward Shadow Lake. Cross the San Joaquin River on a footbridge at 2.5 miles where the climb to Shadow Lake begins in earnest.

The trail ascends a series of switchbacks. Enjoy the fine views of distant Mammoth Mountain as you climb higher. Look for chinquapin and manzanita beside the trail. Twisted old Sierra junipers contribute to the harsh and beautiful landscape.

Vistas improve as you gain elevation. You will spot the aptly named Two Tits atop the barren ridgeline just across the San Joaquin River. Gain your first look at the lovely waterfall tumbling out of Shadow Lake's basin at 3.3 miles.

Push on toward the falls on a steadily climbing trail. Shadow Lake is just around the corner. The ascent eases at 3.5 miles. Hike along Shadow Lake's rushing outlet stream while enjoying a host of creekside wildflowers.

Arrive at Shadow Lake. Not only is this large lake a treasure, its appeal is magnified by the beauty of the surrounding peaks (Mount Ritter, Banner Peak, and the Minarets). These spires tower above the lake reaching more than 13,000 feet. Claim a seat on the shoreline softened by Labrador tea and mountain heather and settle in to savor this lofty setting.

It may be a bit of a challenge but if you made an early start, the 3-mile hike on to Ediza Lake is manageable and should be considered. The trail makes its way up the stream and through meadows. Approaching Ediza Lake, one is left with the sense that the jagged Minarets are so close that all it would take to touch these serrated summits would be simply extending an arm. The meadows, flowers, granite cirques, glaciers, and majestic mountain backdrop all add to the luster of the setting.

Camp near Ediza Lake with the spectacular backdrop of the Minarets at your tent flap. Paul Richins Jr.

62. RAINBOW FALLS

Distance	■	2.6 miles round trip
Difficulty	■	Easy
Starting point	■	7660 feet
High point	■	7660 feet
Elevation gain	■	300 feet
Trail grade	■	231 feet per mile
Maps	■	USGS Crystal Crag 7.5', or Mammoth High Country Trail Map (Tom Harrison)
Access road/town	■	Highway 395 to Highway 203/Mammoth Lakes

Although there isn't a pot of gold at the end of the trail, this easy hike leads to a beautiful natural wonder—Rainbow Falls. The Middle Fork San Joaquin River plummets 101 feet over a lava shelf in a frenzy of froth and mist. This is a great family outing.

To reach the trailhead, refer to the driving directions for Hike 60. From the Devils Postpile entrance station, continue 8 miles on the winding, paved road. Veer right at the sign for Rainbow Falls. A short spur road leads to the trailhead parking area.

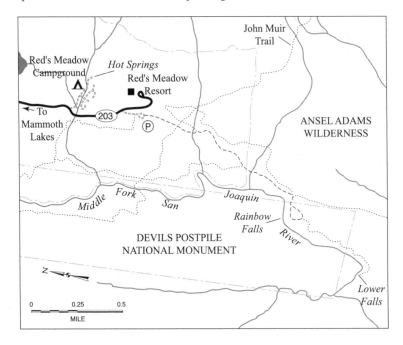

Begin hiking on the wide, sandy trail. It is a short descent of about 300 feet over 1.3 miles to the waterfall. This trek is unique by Sierra standards, as you will hike downhill, not uphill, to reach your destination.

At 0.1 mile, reach a junction with the John Muir Trail and continue toward Rainbow Falls. You will be joined by a trail from the Red's Meadow Resort at 0.4 mile. Another feeder trail joins from the right at the 0.7-mile point. This is the Devils Postpile National Monument Trail (Hike 60).

The descent finally eases at 0.8 mile. Continue walking to another trail junction at 1 mile. Turn right toward Rainbow Falls and gain the first view of the majestic waterfall. The beauty of the falls is impressive and much photographed. Watch with amazement as the Middle Fork San Joaquin River leaps over the lava shelf, throwing its watery arms out wide to catch the sun. The resulting spray transforms the sunlight into a thousand rainbow-colored parachutes that drop back into the river 101 feet below.

Walk to a second viewpoint at 1.2 miles. A long stairway leads down to the river level at 1.3 miles. Children will love it and the break will provide a welcome rest before the climb back to the trailhead.

63. GLASS CREEK MEADOW

Distance ▪	4 miles round trip
Difficulty ▪	Easy
Starting point ▪	8170 feet
High point ▪	8850 feet
Elevation gain ▪	680 feet
Trail grade ▪	340 feet per mile
Maps ▪	USGS Mammoth Mountain 7.5' or Mammoth High Country Trail Map (Tom Harrison)
Access road/town ▪	Highway 395 to Obsidian Dome Road/ June Lake

The walk to Glass Creek Meadow passes through a wonderland of meadows and wildflowers. The best time for this hike is in June and July, when the flowers are at their finest. The trail includes some steep

Opposite: *Popular Rainbow Falls is located near Devils Postpile. Karen & Terry Whitehill*

sections but much of the hike is over easy terrain. High-topped shoes are particularly appropriate, as sections of the trail are covered with deep, loose sand. Bring your sunglasses: the glare reflected by the harsh volcanic landscape can be hard on your eyes.

To reach the trailhead, turn off Highway 395 onto Obsidian Dome Road. The road is located just north of Deadman Summit opposite Bald Mountain Lookout Road, and 3.7 miles south of the more southerly June Lake junction.

From Highway 395, drive 1 mile and keep to your left at the first junction (signed for Obsidian Dome). As you near the trailhead, the road branches into three separate routes. Stay to the right (don't cross the creek) and you will soon reach a small parking area. From Highway 395, it is a total of 2.7 miles to the trailhead.

The trail to Glass Creek Meadow begins beside glittering Glass Creek. Climb gently at the start in loose sand studded with chunks of pumice and obsidian. Nude buckwheat, scraggly broadleaf lupine, lodgepole, and whitebark pines grow beside the trail.

Ascend through a narrow canyon alongside cascading Glass Creek as it falls precipitously through the gorge. The trail is sandy and steep and the difficult footing may be frustrating. It is surprising that the monkeyflower and larkspur survive in such a harsh environment.

After about 0.25 mile the grade mellows noticeably. Follow an easier trail through sage-dotted terrain as alpine buckwheat, sulfur

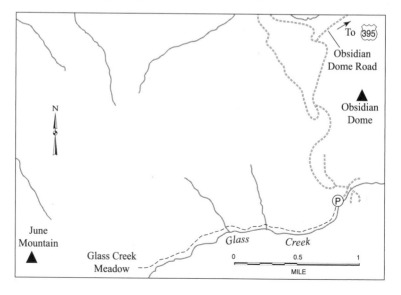

Glass Creek Meadow is abundant with wildflowers in July. Karen & Terry Whitehill

flower, and ranger buttons line the way. You may have difficulty following this section of the trail because the path is often indistinct in the rocky soil. For the easiest walking, keep Glass Creek on your left and hike along the hillside a short distance above the stream. There are numerous faint footpaths through the pumice-studded sand. As a general guideline simply follow the creek to Glass Creek Meadow.

Pause for views of Obsidian Dome behind you as you ascend through a desolate wasteland of glaring sand. Reach the crest of a low ridge at 1.6 miles. There is a nice vista of surprisingly green Glass Creek Meadow from the crest. Behind the meadow, lofty San Joaquin Mountain (11,600 feet) dominates the skyline.

Continue past patches of brilliant-hued Layne's monkeyflower as you walk through salt-and-pepper expanses of pumice and obsidian. Arrive at Glass Creek Meadow at 2 miles. This lovely mountain garden spot owes its existence to the scores of small streams that filter in from higher ground, making the soil a marshy haven for a host of wildflowers.

Those with sharp eyes and a bit of flower familiarity or a good Sierra wildflower guide will find yarrow, yampah, common monkeyflower, hikers gentian, meadow penstemon, and Brewer's lupine. Besides the lure of the meadow flowers, the backdrop of the distant mountains completes the setting of Glass Creek Meadow.

64. FERN LAKE

Distance	■	3.4 miles round trip
Difficulty	■	Moderate
Starting point	■	7330 feet
High point	■	9030 feet
Elevation gain	■	1700 feet
Trail grade	■	1000 feet per mile
Maps	■	USGS June Lake 7.5' and USGS Mammoth Mountain 7.5', or Mammoth High Country Trail Map (Tom Harrison)
Access road/town	■	Highway 395 to Highway 158/June Lake

At 1.7 miles, the hike to Fern Lake isn't long, but it makes up for its brevity with a steep climb. Even so, it is a pleasant walk, rich in wildflowers and vistas. Fern Lake is a treat for swimmers, picnickers, and anglers alike.

To reach the trailhead, take the more southerly of the two June Lake road junctions. The southerly Highway 158 turnoff to June Lake is located about 11 miles south of Lee Vining on Highway 395. Drive west on Highway 158 for 5.3 miles, passing through the small town of June Lake and the June Mountain ski resort. Leave Highway 158 at a sign for the Yost Creek Trail and drive the short distance to the trailhead. A sign for Fern and Yost Lakes marks the trail's beginning.

Start climbing immediately along a path lined with quaking aspens.

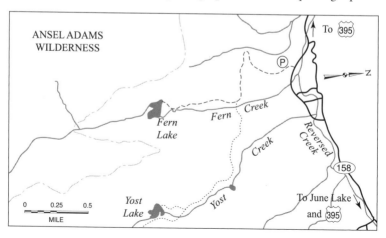

Mono Craters can be viewed to the east of Highway 395 between Mono Lake and June Lake. The trailhead to Fern Lake is near June Lake. Paul Richins Jr.

Broadleaf lupine, scarlet gilia, and mountain pennyroyal add color to the arid soil. The grade quickly increases and the aspens soon give way to white firs.

The boat-dotted Silver Lake will come into view as you gain elevation. The white firs are joined by Sierra junipers and Jeffrey pines. Traverse left across the hillside to begin a long, steep switchback. The views improve as you ascend the mountainside.

Continue upward and watch for Sierra junipers, Indian paintbrush, and yellow-blossomed mule ears. Look for views of distant June Lake and Gull Lake as you climb. You will begin to hear Fern Creek's waterfall just before you spot it through the trees.

Reach a junction at 1 mile and turn right toward Fern Lake. The other trail that continues to Yost Lake is much easier but Yost Lake isn't nearly as inviting as Fern Lake. "Steep" will gain new meaning as you scramble straight uphill toward Fern Lake for the next 0.25 mile.

Ascend steadily past thick-trunked junipers and mountain hemlocks scattered across the slope. Arrive at a meadow: there is just one final short uphill push to gain the shores of Fern Lake.

Reach your goal at 1.7 miles. Fern Lake is a gem. Rocky slopes surround the water, cradling the lake in a lofty bed of granite. Despite the steep trail and elevation gain, Fern Lake is worth the effort. Peel off your shoes, pull out your picnic, and enjoy.

65. PARKER LAKE

Distance	▪	3.8 miles round trip
Difficulty	▪	Easy
Starting point	▪	7770 feet
High point	▪	8350 feet
Elevation gain	▪	580 feet
Trail grade	▪	341 feet per mile
Maps	▪	USGS Koip Peak 7.5' or Mammoth High Country Trail Map (Tom Harrison)
Access road/town	▪	Highway 395 to Highway 158/Lee Vining

The hike to Parker Lake offers fine views of Mono Lake and plenty of easy creekside walking laced with wildflowers and quaking aspen. This is an excellent family excursion. Bring towels, fishing poles, and a lunch, and plan to spend an enjoyable afternoon.

To reach the trailhead, turn onto the more northerly of the two June Lake highway junctions. The northerly Highway 158 turnoff to June Lake is located about 4.5 miles south of Lee Vining on Highway 395. Drive along Highway 158 for 1.5 miles to a junction signed for Parker Lake. Turn onto the road for Parker Lake. Continue along the dirt road, following signs for Parker Lake at the subsequent junctions. Arrive at the small trailhead parking area after driving 2.3 miles from Highway 158.

Set out on a sandy trail, climbing steadily past aromatic sage, dusty mule ears, and yellow sulfur flower. The trail ascends a lateral moraine (rocks and sand), deposited by an ancient glacier. A similar lateral moraine on the other side of the creek forms the small gorge occupied by Parker Creek. At the entry sign for the Ansel Adams

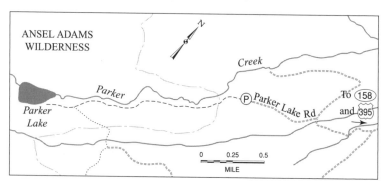

Parker Lake is a beautiful destination with many aspen trees and a colorful rock canyon. Paul Richins Jr.

Wilderness, pause for a look back toward shimmering Mono Lake.

The grade of the trail increases as you ascend past Jeffrey pines and mountain mahogany. The views back to Mono Lake improve with the increasing elevation. At this point, Parker Creek is far below in a mini-canyon formed by the lateral glacier moraines on each side of the creek.

The steady climb eases at 0.4 mile. The level walking is briefly interrupted by short spurts of uphill climbing. White-barked quaking aspen trees, lodgepole pines, and Jeffrey pines are plentiful along the trail and mountainside.

Reach a junction and a sign for Silver Lake. Continue alongside Parker Creek, savoring the bright blossoms of tower larkspur, California corn lily, and yarrow. Moisture-loving quaking aspens cluster along the creek. Over the years, some of the soft trunks of these trees have been initialed by countless pocketknife-wielding hikers. Please do not add yours.

Arrive at Parker Lake after hiking 1.9 miles. Set into an amphitheater formed by an ancient glacier, this midsize lake is framed by the rugged cliffs at its upper end. The lake is a favorite for fishing and a perfect spot to enjoy lunch and the scenery, and to explore the meadows above the lake. High above the lake are Parker Peak, Kuna Peak, and Koip Peak. These peaks form a larger granite cirque and protect a small glacier from the hot summer sun.

66. SARDINE LAKES

Distance ▪	7 miles round trip (Lower Sardine Lake) / 8.4 miles round trip (Upper Sardine Lake)
Difficulty ▪	Strenuous / Strenuous
Starting point ▪	8200 feet / 8200 feet
High point ▪	9890 feet / 10,400 feet
Elevation gain ▪	2400 feet / 2900 feet
Trail grade ▪	686 feet per mile / 690 feet per mile
Maps ▪	USGS Koip Peak 7.5' or Mammoth High Country Trail Map (Tom Harrison)
Access road/town ▪	Highway 395 to Highway 158/Lee Vining

This is a challenging hike with steep inclines, but the colorful rock formations above the rugged Bloody Canyon, the two beautiful lakes, and the views of Mono Lake make this destination well worth the effort. Lower Sardine Lake is nestled into a rugged granite basin. Upper Sardine Lake is 0.7 mile farther up the trail and is the more scenic of the two lakes. It is located below Mono Pass on gentle terrain. Backpackers will find good campsites at the upper lake.

To reach the trailhead, turn onto the more northerly of the two June Lake junctions. The northerly Highway 158 turnoff to June Lake is located about 4.5 miles south of Lee Vining on Highway 395. Follow Highway 158 for 1.5 miles to a junction signed for Parker Lake. Turn onto the unpaved road and drive 0.4 mile. Turn right toward Walker

Lake. Continue along the dirt road, following signs for Walker Lake trailhead. It is a total of 4.9 miles from Highway 395. There is a small parking area with restrooms and four campsites (no water and no fee required) spaced among the stately Jeffrey pines. Bring bug repellent, as the trail is tormented by swarms of mosquitoes in June and July.

Begin at a sign for Walker Lake–Sardine Lakes–Mono Pass. Walker Lake is popular with anglers so many along the first part of the trail will be heading to Walker Lake.

The trail begins with a short climb of the lateral moraine that divides the trailhead from Walker Lake. (A glacial moraine is a pile of rubble, rocks, and sand left behind by an ancient glacier.) After 0.1 mile of hiking gain the crest of the moraine and view Walker Lake 300 feet below. Unfortunately, the trail descends the glacial moraine to the shore of Walker Lake. Heave a sigh and start downhill, knowing that this will require an uphill climb at the end of the day.

Reach a trail junction at 0.5 mile. Although the trail sign claims that Sardine Lake is 3.5 miles ahead, it is really only 3 more miles. Turn left for Sardine Lake and angle along the hillside, descending gradually in the shade of tall white firs.

Walker Lake's shoreline and Bloody Canyon are filled with quaking aspens. This is an ideal trip to take in the fall, early- to mid-October, when the aspens are turning all shades of red, gold, and bright yellow. Cross over Walker Creek and continue through a colorful meadow of broadleaf lupine, Indian paintbrush, and tower larkspur. At the next junction, turn left.

Reach the entry sign for the Ansel Adams Wilderness at 1.2 miles. Climb a series of switchbacks as the trail ascends along Walker Creek. Turn back for a fine view of Walker Lake and Mono Lake.

Scarlet gilia, nude buckwheat, ranger buttons, crimson columbine,

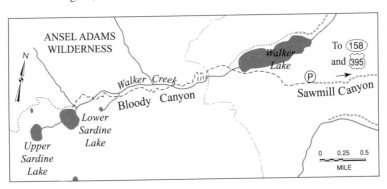

Sardine Lakes are located in an impressive basin below Mount Gibbs and Mono Pass. Paul Richins Jr.

and pink monkeyflower are well represented along this portion of the creek and trail. Recross Walker Creek and ascend a rocky slope. The grade increases as the trail switchbacks up toward Lower Sardine Lake. Enjoy a brief respite as you enter a high box canyon. The break is short but sweet.

Climb a series of switchbacks to the crest of a small ridge dotted with mountain mahogany. Enjoy easier walking for a short distance before crossing the creek again. Look for a lovely alpine waterfall framed by massive slabs of rock. Lower Sardine Lake is just above the falls.

A final brief ascent leads to the edge of 9890-foot Lower Sardine Lake. The lake is nestled into a fissure guarded by barren cliffs. Lower Sardine Lake's shoreline and its outlet creek are awash in brilliant wildflowers. The view from the lake toward Mono Lake is a special treat.

From Lower Sardine Lake, it is a short 0.7-mile jaunt with a 500-foot climb to Upper Sardine Lake. Hike around the right shore of Lower Sardine Lake to a steep gully. The trail easily ascends the gully and then traverses gentle terrain to Upper Sardine Lake and Mono Pass. Upper Sardine Lake is located in a scenic meadowlike basin with views of Mount Gibbs. It is a short, gentle hike to Mono Pass and views into Yosemite National Park and Tuolumne Meadow. Proceed around the shore of the lake to its outlet stream. This vantage point provides exquisite views of Lower Sardine Lake, Walker Lake, and Mono Lake.

APPENDIX 1
CAMPGROUND AND WILDERNESS PERMIT INFORMATION

SEQUOIA AND KINGS CANYON NATIONAL PARKS

HIKES 9, 11, 12, 15–26

Most Sequoia and Kings Canyon National Park Campgrounds are first come, first served, but some can be reserved.

http://reservations.nps.gov
800-365-2267
888-530-9796 (TDD)
301-722-1257 (international calls)

MISTIX
P.O. Box 85705
San Diego, CA 92186
800-365-2267

A wilderness permit is not required for a day hike; however, all overnight backpack trips require a wilderness permit. A wilderness permit quota system is in place on many of the popular trails during the peak summer season (May 21–September 21). Advance reservations for wilderness permits are recommended. For information on wilderness permits; campgrounds; lodging; trail, road and weather conditions; maps; books; the free park newspaper; and other information, see below.

For general information, contact:
Sequoia and Kings Canyon National Parks
47050 Generals Highway
HCR 89 Box 60
Three Rivers, CA 93271
559-565-3341 and 559-565-3134
www.nps.gov/seki

Foothills Visitor Center, 1 mile east of the park entrance on Highway 198 (559-565-3135), offers exhibits, shops, books, maps, restrooms, pay phones, and Crystal Cave tours.

Lodgepole Visitor Center, 21 miles from the Sequoia National Park entrance on Highway 198 (559-565-3782), offers the Giant Forest Museum, nature center, exhibits, food, shops, a market, a deli, a gift shop, a snack bar, horseback riding, showers, laundry, lodging, bear-proof canisters, books, and maps. Nearby are picnic areas and campgrounds—Lodgepole (258 sites) and Dorst (204 sites). Lodging 888-252-5757.

Mineral King Ranger Station, 25 miles from Highway 198 and Three Rivers on the Mineral King Road (559-565-3768), offers maps, books, and campground information. Atwell Mill (23 campground sites) and Cold Springs (37 campground sites). Silver City Resort (privately owned), located about 7 miles from the trailhead, includes a store, restaurant and lodging (559-561-3223).

Cedar Grove Visitor Center and Ranger Station, 6 miles west of Roads End on Highway 180 in Kings Canyon National Park (559-565-3793), includes a general store, a market, a restaurant, a gift shop, books, maps, campground information, and bear-proof canisters. There are four campgrounds in the Roads End and Cedar Grove area—Sentinel (82 sites), Sheep Creek (111 sites), Canyon View (37 sites) and Moraine (120 sites).

U.S. FOREST SERVICE

HIKES 1–8, 10, 13, 14, 27–66

Many Forest Service campgrounds are first come, first served, but some can be reserved in advance.

www.reserveusa.com
800-280-2267 (CAMP) or 877-444-6777
518-885-3639 (international calls)

A wilderness permit is not required for a day hike, except for the Mount Whitney Trail (Hike 32) beyond Lone Pine Lake. All overnight trips require a wilderness permit any time of the year. Depending on the wilderness, the permit quota season varies. For some trails the quotas run from the last Friday in June to September 15.

For other trails, the quotas stretch from May 1 to November 1.

Wilderness permit reservations are recommended for all trails covered by a quota system. Advance reservations can be made 6 months in advance of your departure date. Check with the appropriate Forest Service Ranger District office for their particular requirements. Wilderness permits, maps, books, trail and campground conditions, and other information can be obtained from the various Forest Service offices listed below.

For the Mount Whitney Trail (Hikes 32 and 33), the quota system is in place from May 1 through November 1. The Mount Whitney Trail is so popular that the Forest Service has implemented a lottery system to issue wilderness permits. Permit applications for the lottery must be postmarked in February for the upcoming hiking season.

Sierra National Forest
Hikes 1–8
Kings River Ranger District
34849 Maxon Road
Sanger, CA 93657
559-855-8321
www.r5.fs.fed.us/sierra

Sierra National Forest
1600 Tollhouse Road
Clovis, CA 93612
559-297-0706 or 559-487-5155
www.r5.fs.fed.us/sierra

Sierra National Forest
Pineridge Kings River Ranger District
P.O. 559
29688 Auberry Road
Prather, CA 93651
559-855-5360
www.r5.fs.fed.us/sierra

The Huntington Lake area has a number of seasonal Forest Service offices that are open from Memorial Day to Labor Day: Eastwood Visitor Center at the junction with Highway 168 and Kaiser Pass Road on the east end of Huntington Lake, 559-893-6611; High Sierra Station, on Kaiser Pass Road east of Kaiser Pass, 559-877-7173; Pineridge District Office, P.O. Box 300, Shaver Lake, CA 93664.

Sequoia National Forest
Hikes 10, 13, and 14
900 West Grand Avenue
Porterville, CA 93257
559-784-1500
www.r5.fs.fed.us/sequoia

Sequoia National Forest
Hume Lake Ranger District
35860 East Kings Canyon Road
Dunlap, CA 93621
559-338-2251
www.r5.fs.fed.us/sequoia

Inyo National Forest
Hikes 27–66
873 North Main Street
Bishop, CA 93514
Wilderness Permit Reservations: 760-873-2483
Fax: 760-873-2484
Wilderness Information Line: 760-873-2408 or 760-873-2485
www.r5.fs.fed.us/inyo

Mount Whitney Ranger Station
P.O. Box 8
640 South Main Street
Lone Pine, CA 93545
760-876-6200
www.r5.fs.fed.us/inyo

INYO NATIONAL FOREST

HIKES 37–51

White Mountain Ranger District
798 North Main Street (Highway 395)
Bishop, CA 93514
760-873-2500
www.r5.fs.fed.us/inyo

INYO NATIONAL FOREST

HIKES 52–66

Mammoth Ranger District
P.O. Box 148 (Highway 203)
Mammoth Lakes, CA 93546
760-924-5500
www.r5.fs.fed.us/inyo

Inyo National Forest
Mono Lake Ranger District
P.O. Box 429 (Highway 395, 0.5 mile north of Lee Vining)
Lee Vining, CA 93541
760-647-3044
www.r5.fs.fed.us/inyo

APPENDIX 2
USEFUL CONTACTS AND RESOURCES

GENERAL INFORMATION
Backcountry Resource Center
Valuable information for hikers, climbers, and backcountry skiers/snowboarders wishing to explore the mountains of California and beyond.

http://pweb.jps.net/~prichins/backcountry_resource_center.htm
E-mail: *prichins@jps.net*

Eastern Sierra Interpretive Association
Maps, trail guides, books, gifts, children's items, history, geology.
www.r5.fs.fed.us/inyo/esia/

MT Recreational Services
P.O. Box 430 (126 South Main)
Big Pine, CA 93513
An information source for the Sierra Nevada backcountry put together by backcountry users.
www.sierrawilderness.com

Sequoia and Kings Canyon National Parks
Park information, weather, roads, campgrounds, etc. provided by the National Park Service.
559-565-3341 and 559-565-3134
www.nps.gov/seki

Sequoia and Kings Canyon Lodging and Reservations
Official website for the Sequoia–Kings Canyon Park Services Company.
559-452-1081 or toll-free 1-866-KCANYON
www.sequoia-kingscanyon.com

Sequoia Natural History Association

HCR 89 Box 10
Three Rivers, CA 93271
Natural history, maps, books, and gifts. *The Sequoia Bark,* a free park newspaper, contains current park information, lists of facilities, and schedules of naturalist programs.
559-565-3759
www.sequoiahistory.org

SOURCES FOR MAPS

Maps can be purchased at the National Forest and the Sequoia and Kings Canyon National Parks visitor centers noted in Appendix 1, as well at backpacking and outdoor stores. Additional sources are noted below.

DeLorme Publishing Company

P.O. Box 298
Freeport, ME 04032
Topographical maps and guides to outdoor recreation, including the atlas & gazetteer.
207-846-7000 and 800-561-5104
www.delorme.com
E-mail: *info@delorme.com*

Tom Harrison Maps

2 Falmouth Cove
San Rafael, CA 94901
415-456-7940 or 800-265-9090
www.tomharrisonmaps.com

U.S. Geological Survey Maps

USGS Information Services
Box 25286
Denver, CO 80225
800-HELP-MAP
www-nmd.usgs.gov/

Wilderness Press
2440 Bancroft Way
Berkeley, CA 94704
510-843-8080 or 800-443-7227
www.wildernesspress.com

Wildflower Productions
375 Alabama Street, Suite 230
San Francisco, CA 94110
TOPO! Interactive Maps on CD-ROM
415-558-8700
www.topo.com
E-mail: *info@topo.com*

TRAILHEAD SHUTTLE SERVICES

Kountry Korners
771 North Main Street #59
Bishop, CA 93514
They will meet you at your exit point and drive you to the trailhead
to start your hike.
877-656-0756 (toll free) or 760-872-3951 (local)

Walt's Inyo Trailhead Transportation
P. O. Box 539
Lone Pine, CA 93545
760-876-0035 or 760-876-5518

Wilder House Bed and Breakfast
Shuttle Service
HCR 67 Box 275
325 Dust Lane
Fort Independence, CA 93526
760-878-2119 or 888-313-0151 (toll free)
www.wilderhouse.com
E-mail: *wilder@wilderhouse.com*

APPENDIX 3
SUMMARY OF HIKES

* Mileage is for round trip, complete length of the hike.

** Difficulty ratings: Easy—hikes 6 miles or less in length gaining less than 1000 feet. Moderate—hikes 6–12 miles gaining less than 2000 feet. Strenuous—hikes over 12 miles gaining more than 2000 feet. A hike that is within the mileage range but gains considerably more elevation than the guidelines is placed in the next higher level of difficulty. As an example, a 5-mile hike gaining 2000 feet would be rated moderate rather than easy due to the considerable elevation gain.

WESTSIDE TRAILHEADS IN ORDER OF THEIR APPEARANCE IN THE BOOK

Hike # and Name	Distance*	Elevation Gain	Difficulty**	Nearest Town
1. Bald Mountain	3.5 miles	1293 feet	Moderate	Shaver Lake
2. Mystery Lake	3.8 miles	370 feet	Easy	Shaver Lake
2. Dinkey Lakes	7 miles	790 feet	Moderate	Shaver Lake
3. Indian Pools	1.4 miles	70 feet	Easy	Huntington Lake
4. Rancheria Falls	1.6 miles	200 feet	Easy	Huntington Lake
5. Kaiser Peak	10.6 miles	3170 feet	Strenuous	Huntington Lake
6. Twin Lakes	7.2 miles	1100 feet	Moderate	Huntington Lake
6. George Lake	9.4 miles	1600 feet	Moderate	Huntington Lake
6. Twin Lakes (alternate trailhead)	5 miles	800 feet	Easy	Huntington Lake
6. George Lake (alternate trailhead)	7.2 miles	1300 feet	Moderate	Huntington Lake

Hike # and Name	Distance*	Elevation Gain	Difficulty**	Nearest Town
7. Doris Lake	1.8 miles	370 feet	Easy	Huntington Lake
7. Tule Lake	4 miles	370 feet	Easy	Huntington Lake
8. Crater Lake	8 miles	2030 feet	Moderate	Huntington Lake
9. North Grove Loop	1.8 miles	400 feet	Easy	Grant Grove Visitor Center
10. Boole Tree	2 miles	490 feet	Easy	Grant Grove Visitor Center
11. Cedar Grove Overlook	5 miles	1600 feet	Moderate	Cedar Grove Visitor Center
11. Lewis Creek Loop	8 miles	1800 feet	Moderate	Cedar Grove Visitor Center
12. Mist Falls	8.6 miles	650 feet	Moderate	Cedar Grove Visitor Center
13. Weaver Lake (Fox Meadow trailhead)	4.2 miles	810 feet	Easy	Grant Grove Visitor Center
13. Weaver Lake (Big Meadows trailhead)	7.2 miles	1110 feet	Moderate	Grant Grove Visitor Center
14. Jennie Lake (Fox Meadow trailhead)	10.4 miles	1400 feet	Moderate	Grant Grove Visitor Center
14. Jennie Lake (Big Meadows trailhead)	13.4 miles	1700 feet	Strenuous	Grant Grove Visitor Center
15. Muir Grove	5 miles	450 feet	Easy	Lodgepole Visitor Center
16. Little Baldy	3.4 miles	700 feet	Easy	Lodgepole Visitor Center
17. Tokopah Falls	3.8 miles	630 feet	Easy	Lodgepole Visitor Center
18. Heather Lake	8.2 miles	2120 feet	Moderate	Lodgepole Visitor Center
18. Pear Lake	12.4 miles	2630 feet	Strenuous	Lodgepole Visitor Center
19. Big Trees	4.3 miles	300 feet	Easy	Lodgepole Visitor Center
20. Crescent Meadow	2.3 miles	180 feet	Easy	Lodgepole Visitor Center

Hike # and Name	Distance*	Elevation Gain	Difficulty**	Nearest Town
21. Atwell Grove	3.8 miles	980 feet	Easy	Silver City Resort
21. Paradise Peak	11 miles	2842 feet	Strenuous	Silver City Resort
22. Monarch Lakes	9.4 miles	2580 feet	Strenuous	Silver City Resort
22. Sawtooth Pass	12.2 miles	3800 feet	Strenuous	Silver City Resort
23. Crystal Lakes	10.8 miles	3050 feet	Strenuous	Silver City Resort
23. Crystal–Monarch Lakes Loop	11.1 miles	3400 feet	Strenuous	Silver City Resort
24. Franklin Lakes	10.8 miles	2531 feet	Strenuous	Silver City Resort
25. Eagle Lake	6.8 miles	2210 feet	Moderate	Silver City Resort
26. White Chief Canyon	7 miles	1800 feet	Moderate	Silver City Resort

WESTSIDE TRAILHEADS BY DIFFICULTY

Hike # and Name	Distance*	Elevation Gain	Difficulty**	Nearest Town
3. Indian Pools	1.4 miles	70 feet	Easy	Huntington Lake
4. Rancheria Falls	1.6 miles	200 feet	Easy	Huntington Lake
7. Doris Lake	1.8 miles	370 feet	Easy	Huntington Lake
9. North Grove Loop	1.8 miles	400 feet	Easy	Grant Grove Visitor Center
10. Boole Tree	2 miles	490 feet	Easy	Grant Grove Visitor Center
20. Crescent Meadow	2.3 miles	180 feet	Easy	Lodgepole Visitor Center
16. Little Baldy	3.4 miles	700 feet	Easy	Lodgepole Visitor Center
2. Mystery Lake	3.8 miles	370 feet	Easy	Shaver Lake
17. Tokopah Falls	3.8 miles	630 feet	Easy	Lodgepole Visitor Center
21. Atwell Grove	3.8 miles	980 feet	Easy	Silver City Resort

Hike # and Name	Distance*	Elevation Gain	Difficulty**	Nearest Town
7. Tule Lake	4 miles	370 feet	Easy	Huntington Lake
13. Weaver Lake (Fox Meadow trailhead)	4.2 miles	810 feet	Easy	Grant Grove Visitor Center
19. Big Trees	4.3 miles	300 feet	Easy	Lodgepole Visitor Center
15. Muir Grove	5 miles	450 feet	Easy	Lodgepole Visitor Center
6. Twin Lakes (alternate trailhead)	5 miles	800 feet	Easy	Huntington Lake
1. Bald Mountain	3.5 miles	1293 feet	Moderate	Shaver Lake
11. Cedar Grove Overlook	5 miles	1600 feet	Moderate	Cedar Grove Visitor Center
25. Eagle Lake	6.8 miles	2210 feet	Moderate	Silver City Resort
2. Dinkey Lakes	7 miles	790 feet	Moderate	Shaver Lake
26. White Chief Canyon	7 miles	1800 feet	Moderate	Silver City Resort
6. Twin Lakes	7.2 miles	1100 feet	Moderate	Huntington Lake
13. Weaver Lake (Big Meadows trailhead)	7.2 miles	1110 feet	Moderate	Grant Grove
6. George Lake (alternate trailhead)	7.2 miles	1300 feet	Moderate	Huntington Lake
11. Lewis Creek loop	8 miles	1800 feet	Moderate	Cedar Grove Visitor Center
8. Crater Lake	8 miles	2030 feet	Moderate	Huntington Lake
18. Heather Lake	8.2 miles	2120 feet	Moderate	Lodgepole Visitor Center
12. Mist Falls	8.6 miles	650 feet	Moderate	Cedar Grove Visitor Center
6. George Lake	9.4 miles	1600 feet	Moderate	Huntington Lake

Hike # and Name	Distance*	Elevation Gain	Difficulty**	Nearest Town
14. Jennie Lake (Fox Meadow trailhead)	10.4 miles	1400 feet	Moderate	Grant Grove Visitor Center
22. Monarch Lakes	9.4 miles	2580 feet	Strenuous	Silver City Resort
5. Kaiser Peak	10.6 miles	3170 feet	Strenuous	Huntington Lake
24. Franklin Lakes	10.8 miles	2531 feet	Strenuous	Silver City Resort
23. Crystal Lakes	10.8 miles	3050 feet	Strenuous	Silver City Resort
21. Paradise Peak	11 miles	2842 feet	Strenuous	Silver City Resort
23. Crystal–Monarch Lakes Loop	11.1 miles	3400 feet	Strenuous	Silver City Resort
22. Sawtooth Pass	12.2 miles	3800 feet	Strenuous	Silver City Resort
18. Pear Lake	12.4 miles	2630 feet	Strenuous	Lodgepole Visitor Center
14. Jennie Lake (Big Meadows trailhead)	13.4 miles	1700 feet	Strenuous	Grant Grove Visitor Center

EASTSIDE TRAILHEADS IN ORDER OF THEIR APPEARANCE IN THE BOOK

Hike # and Name	Distance*	Elevation Gain	Difficulty**	Nearest Town
27. Cottonwood Lakes	11.5 miles	1260 feet	Moderate	Lone Pine
27. New Army Pass	14 miles	2400 feet	Strenuous	Lone Pine
28. Chicken Spring Lake	9.6 miles	1292 feet	Moderate	Lone Pine
28. Cottonwood Pass Loop	11.4 miles	1400 feet	Moderate	Lone Pine
29. Camp Lake	10.2 miles	3200 feet	Strenuous	Lone Pine
29. Meysan Lake	11.2 miles	3500 feet	Strenuous	Lone Pine
30. Whitney Portal NRT	1 mile	-360 feet	Easy	Lone Pine

Hike # and Name	Distance*	Elevation Gain	Difficulty**	Nearest Town
30. Whitney Portal NRT	4 miles (one way)	-2720 feet	Moderate	Lone Pine
31. Lone Pine Lake	5.8 miles	1595 feet	Moderate	Lone Pine
32. Trail Camp	12.6 miles	3675 feet	Strenuous	Lone Pine
32. Mount Whitney	22 miles	6306 feet	Strenuous	Lone Pine
33. Mountaineers Route	9.4 miles	6126 feet	Strenuous	Lone Pine
34. Robinson Lake	3.4 miles	1300 feet	Moderate	Independence
35. Flower Lake	5.6 miles	1220 feet	Moderate	Independence
35. Kearsarge Pass	11 miles	2623 feet	Strenuous	Independence
35. Kearsarge Lakes	13.2 miles	3446 feet	Strenuous	Independence
36. Dragon Peak Lakes	6.2 miles	2200 feet	Moderate	Independence
36. Golden Trout Lake	6 miles	2200 feet	Moderate	Independence
37. Second Lake	9.8 miles	2260 feet	Moderate	Big Pine
37. Big Pine Lakes Loop	13.1 miles	3000 feet	Strenuous	Big Pine
38. Brainard Lake	11.4 miles	2660 feet	Strenuous	Big Pine
38. Finger Lake	12.6 miles	3200 feet	Strenuous	Big Pine
39. Tyee Lakes	7.6 miles	1940 feet	Moderate	Bishop
40. Green Lake	5.8 miles	1280 feet	Moderate	Bishop
41. Long Lake	4.6 miles	900 feet	Easy	Bishop
41. Bishop Pass	12 miles	2180 feet	Strenuous	Bishop
42. Treasure Lakes	6 miles	1280 feet	Moderate	Bishop
43. Blue Lake	6.4 miles	1310 feet	Moderate	Bishop
43. Midnight Lake	13 miles	2100 feet	Strenuous	Bishop

Hike # and Name	Distance*	Elevation Gain	Difficulty**	Nearest Town
43. Hungry Packer Lake	14 miles	2200 feet	Strenuous	Bishop
44. Lamarck Lakes	6.4 miles	1670 feet	Moderate	Bishop
45. Loch Leven Lakes	6.2 miles	1493 feet	Moderate	Bishop
45. Piute Pass	11 miles	2173 feet	Strenuous	Bishop
46. Horton Lake	8.6 miles	2000 feet	Moderate	Bishop
46. Upper Horton Lake	11.6 miles	2900 feet	Strenuous	Bishop
47. Pine Lake	9.4 miles	2550 feet	Strenuous	Bishop
47. Honeymoon Lake	12.8 miles	3000 feet	Strenuous	Bishop
48. Dorothy Lake	6 miles	860 feet	Easy	Toms Place
48. Tamarack Lake	10.4 miles	1900 feet	Moderate	Toms Place
49. Chickenfoot Lake	5.8 miles	500 feet	Easy	Toms Place
49. Morgan Pass	7.2 miles	800 feet	Moderate	Toms Place
50. Ruby Lake	4.2 miles	821 feet	Easy	Toms Place
50. Mono Pass	8 miles	1740 feet	Moderate	Toms Place
51. Hilton Lakes	8.8 miles	1530 feet	Moderate	Toms Place
52. Convict Lake	2.8 miles	30 feet	Easy	Mammoth Lakes
53. Sherwin Lakes	5.8 miles	840 feet	Easy	Mammoth Lakes
53. Valentine Lake	12 miles	1910 feet	Moderate	Mammoth Lakes
54. McLeod Lake	1.2 miles	330 feet	Easy	Mammoth Lakes
55. TJ Lake and Lake Barrett	1.7 miles	330 feet	Easy	Mammoth Lakes
56. Crystal Lake	2.6 miles	620 feet	Easy	Mammoth Lakes
56. Mammoth Crest	5.6 miles	1540 feet	Moderate	Mammoth Lakes
57. Emerald Lake	1.8 miles	360 feet	Easy	Mammoth Lakes

Hike # and Name	Distance*	Elevation Gain	Difficulty**	Nearest Town
57. Sky Meadows	4 miles	970 feet	Easy	Mammoth Lakes
58. Skelton Lake	3.6 miles	820 feet	Easy	Mammoth Lakes
58. Duck Pass	8.2 miles	1720 feet	Moderate	Mammoth Lakes
59. San Joaquin Ridge	4.8 miles	990 feet	Easy	Mammoth Lakes
60. Devils Postpile	7.4 miles	-700 feet	Moderate	Mammoth Lakes
61. Shadow Lake	7.2 miles	1020 feet	Moderate	Mammoth Lakes
61. Ediza Lake	14.8 miles	1660 feet	Strenuous	Mammoth Lakes
62. Rainbow Falls	2.6 miles	300 feet	Easy	Mammoth Lakes
63. Glass Creek Meadow	4 miles	680 feet	Easy	June Lake
64. Fern Lake	3.4 miles	1700 feet	Moderate	June Lake
65. Parker Lake	3.8 miles	580 feet	Easy	Lee Vining
66. Lower Sardine Lake	7 miles	2400 feet	Strenuous	Lee Vining
66. Upper Sardine Lake	8.4 miles	2900 feet	Strenuous	Lee Vining

EASTSIDE TRAILHEADS BY DIFFICULTY

Hike # and Name	Distance*	Elevation Gain	Difficulty**	Nearest Town
30. Whitney Portal NRT	1 mile (one way)	-360 feet	Easy	Lone Pine
54. McLeod Lake	1.2 miles	330 feet	Easy	Mammoth Lakes
55. TJ Lake and Lake Barrett	1.7 miles	330 feet	Easy	Mammoth Lakes
57. Emerald Lake	1.8 miles	360 feet	Easy	Mammoth Lakes
62. Rainbow Falls	2.6 miles	300 feet	Easy	Mammoth Lakes
56. Crystal Lake	2.6 miles	620 feet	Easy	Mammoth Lakes

Hike # and Name	Distance*	Elevation Gain	Difficulty**	Nearest Town
52. Convict Lake	2.8 miles	30 feet	Easy	Mammoth Lakes
58. Skelton Lake	3.6 miles	820 feet	Easy	Mammoth Lakes
65. Parker Lake	3.8 miles	580 feet	Easy	Lee Vining
63. Glass Creek Meadow	4 miles	680 feet	Easy	June Lake
57. Sky Meadows	4 miles	970 feet	Easy	Mammoth Lakes
50. Ruby Lake	4.2 miles	821 feet	Easy	Toms Place
41. Long Lake	4.6 miles	900 feet	Easy	Bishop
59. San Joaquin Ridge	4.8 miles	990 feet	Easy	Mammoth Lakes
49. Chickenfoot Lake	5.8 miles	500 feet	Easy	Toms Place
53. Sherwin Lakes	5.8 miles	840 feet	Easy	Mammoth Lakes
48. Dorothy Lake	6 miles	860 feet	Easy	Toms Place
34. Robinson Lake	3.4 miles	1300 feet	Moderate	Independence
64. Fern Lake	3.4 miles	1700 feet	Moderate	June Lake
30. Whitney Portal NRT	4 miles (one way)	-2720 feet	Moderate	Lone Pine
35. Flower Lake	5.6 miles	1220 feet	Moderate	Independence
56. Mammoth Crest	5.6 miles	1540 feet	Moderate	Mammoth Lakes
40. Green Lake	5.8 miles	1280 feet	Moderate	Bishop
31. Lone Pine Lake	5.8 miles	1595 feet	Moderate	Lone Pine
42. Treasure Lakes	6 miles	1280 feet	Moderate	Bishop
36. Golden Trout Lake	6 miles	2200 feet	Moderate	Independence
45. Loch Leven Lakes	6.2 miles	1493 feet	Moderate	Bishop
36. Dragon Peak Lakes	6.2 miles	2200 feet	Moderate	Independence

Hike # and Name	Distance*	Elevation Gain	Difficulty**	Nearest Town
43. Blue Lake	6.4 miles	1310 feet	Moderate	Bishop
44. Lamarck Lakes	6.4 miles	1670 feet	Moderate	Bishop
49. Morgan Pass	7.2 miles	800 feet	Moderate	Toms Place
61. Shadow Lake	7.2 miles	1020 feet	Moderate	Mammoth Lakes
60. Devils Postpile	7.4 miles	-700 feet	Moderate	Mammoth Lakes
39. Tyee Lakes	7.6 miles	1940 feet	Moderate	Bishop
50. Mono Pass	8 miles	1740 feet	Moderate	Toms Place
58. Duck Pass	8.2 miles	1720 feet	Moderate	Mammoth Lakes
46. Horton Lake	8.6 miles	2000 feet	Moderate	Bishop
51. Hilton Lakes	8.8 miles	1530 feet	Moderate	Toms Place
28. Chicken Spring Lake	9.6 miles	1292 feet	Moderate	Lone Pine
37. Second Lake	9.8 miles	2260 feet	Moderate	Big Pine
48. Tamarack Lake	10.4 miles	1900 feet	Moderate	Toms Place
28. Cottonwood Pass Loop	11.4 miles	1400 feet	Moderate	Lone Pine
27. Cottonwood Lakes	11.5 miles	1260 feet	Moderate	Lone Pine
53. Valentine Lake	12 miles	1910 feet	Moderate	Mammoth Lakes
66. Lower Sardine Lake	7 miles	2400 feet	Strenuous	Lee Vining
66. Upper Sardine Lake	8.4 miles	2900 feet	Strenuous	Lee Vining
47. Pine Lake	9.4 miles	2550 feet	Strenuous	Bishop
33. Mountaineers Route	9.4 miles	6126 feet	Strenuous	Lone Pine
29. Camp Lake	10.2 miles	3200 feet	Strenuous	Lone Pine
45. Piute Pass	11 miles	2173 feet	Strenuous	Bishop

Hike # and Name	Distance*	Elevation Gain	Difficulty**	Nearest Town
35. Kearsarge Pass	11 miles	2623 feet	Strenuous	Independence
29. Meysan Lake	11.2 miles	3500 feet	Strenuous	Lone Pine
38. Brainard Lake	11.4 miles	2660 feet	Strenuous	Big Pine
46. Upper Horton Lake	11.6 miles	2900 feet	Strenuous	Bishop
41. Bishop Pass	12 miles	2180 feet	Strenuous	Bishop
38. Finger Lake	12.6 miles	3200 feet	Strenuous	Big Pine
32. Trail Camp	12.6 miles	3675 feet	Strenuous	Lone Pine
47. Honeymoon Lake	12.8 miles	3000 feet	Strenuous	Bishop
43. Midnight Lake	13 miles	2100 feet	Strenuous	Bishop
37. Big Pine Lakes Loop	13.1 miles	3000 feet	Strenuous	Big Pine
35. Kearsarge Lakes	13.2 miles	3446 feet	Strenuous	Independence
43. Hungry Packer Lake	14 miles	2200 feet	Strenuous	Bishop
27. New Army Pass	14 miles	2400 feet	Strenuous	Lone Pine
61. Ediza Lake	14.8 miles	1660 feet	Strenuous	Mammoth Lakes
32. Mount Whitney	22 miles	6306 feet	Strenuous	Lone Pine

APPENDIX 4
AUTHORS' FAVORITES AND FAMILY-FRIENDLY HIKES

*The author's favorites were selected based on the hikes' varied terrain (streams, waterfalls, meadows, wildflowers, wildlife, forests), scenic vistas above the tree-line, scenery along the route, and the picturesque qualities of the final destination.

**The family-friendly hikes were selected with young hikers in mind. The difficulty of the hike, the amount of elevation to be gained, the length, and whether there were interesting activities for young people (such as swimming, wading, or fishing along the trail) were all considered.

AUTHORS' WESTSIDE FAVORITES*

Hike # and Name	Distance	Elevation Gain	Difficulty
1. Bald Mountain Lookout	3.5 miles	1293 feet	Moderate
2. Dinkey Lakes	7 miles	790 feet	Moderate
5. Kaiser Peak	10.6 miles	3170 feet	Strenuous
18. Pear Lake	12.4 miles	2630 feet	Strenuous
22. Monarch Lakes	9.4 miles	2580 feet	Strenuous
22. Sawtooth Pass	12.2 miles	3800 feet	Strenuous
23. Crystal–Monarch Lakes Loop	11.1 miles	3400 feet	Strenuous
24. Franklin Lakes	10.8 miles	2531 feet	Strenuous
26. White Chief Canyon	7 miles	1800 feet	Moderate

WESTSIDE FAMILY FAVORITES**

Hike # and Name	Distance	Elevation Gain	Difficulty
4. Rancheria Falls	1.6 miles	200 feet	Easy

Hike # and Name	Distance	Elevation Gain	Difficulty
6. Twin Lakes (alternate trailhead)	5 miles	800 feet	Easy
9. North Grove Loop	1.8 miles	400 feet	Easy
10. Boole Tree	2 miles	490 feet	Easy
12. Mist Falls	8.6 miles	650 feet	Moderate
13. Weaver Lake (Fox Meadow trailhead)	4.2 miles	810 feet	Easy
15. Muir Grove	5 miles	450 feet	Easy
16. Little Baldy	3.4 miles	700 feet	Easy
17. Tokopah Falls	3.8 miles	630 feet	Easy
19. Big Trees	4.3 miles	300 feet	Easy
20. Crescent Meadow	2.3 miles	180 feet	Easy

AUTHORS' EASTSIDE FAVORITES*

Hike # and Name	Distance	Elevation Gain	Difficulty
28. Chicken Spring Lake	9.6 miles	1292 feet	Moderate
29. Meysan Lake	11.2 miles	3500 feet	Strenuous
35. Kearsarge Lakes	13.2 miles	3446 feet	Strenuous
36. Dragon Peak Lakes	6.2 miles	2200 feet	Moderate
37. Second Lake	9.8 miles	2260 feet	Moderate
38. Finger Lake	12.6 miles	3200 feet	Strenuous
41. Bishop Pass	12 miles	2180 feet	Strenuous
43. Hungry Packer Lake	14 miles	2200 feet	Strenuous
56. Mammoth Crest	5.6 miles	1540 feet	Moderate
58. Duck Pass	8.2 miles	1720 feet	Moderate

Hike # and Name	Distance	Elevation Gain	Difficulty
61. Ediza Lake	14.8 miles	1660 feet	Strenuous
66. Upper Sardine Lake	8.4 miles	2900 feet	Strenuous

EASTSIDE FAMILY FAVORITES**

Hike # and Name	Distance	Elevation Gain	Difficulty
30. Whitney Portal NRT	1 mile	-360 feet	Easy
31. Lone Pine Lake	5.8 miles	1595 feet	Moderate
34. Robinson Lake	3.4 miles	1300 feet	Moderate
35. Flower Lake	5.6 miles	1220 feet	Moderate
41. Long Lake	4.6 miles	900 feet	Easy
42. Treasure Lakes	6 miles	1280 feet	Moderate
43. Blue Lake	6.4 miles	1310 feet	Moderate
45. Loch Leven Lakes	6.2 miles	1493 feet	Moderate
48. Dorothy Lake	6 miles	860 feet	Easy
49. Chickenfoot Lake	5.8 miles	500 feet	Easy
52. Convict Lake	2.8 miles	30 feet	Easy
54. McLeod Lake	1.2 miles	330 feet	Easy
55. TJ Lake	1.7 miles	330 feet	Easy
56. Crystal Lake	2.6 miles	620 feet	Easy
58. Skelton Lake	3.6 miles	820 feet	Easy
59. San Joaquin Ridge	4.8 miles	990 feet	Easy
62. Rainbow Falls	2.6 miles	300 feet	Easy
65. Parker Lake	3.8 miles	580 feet	Easy

APPENDIX 5
EQUIPMENT CHECKLIST FOR DAY HIKES

ESSENTIAL ITEMS

- ❏ map and compass
- ❏ day pack
- ❏ extra clothing—fleece jacket, Gore-Tex or nylon wind pants, waterproof nylon parka with hood
- ❏ hat with sun visor
- ❏ sunglasses
- ❏ wide-mouth water bottle
- ❏ Gatorade or other sports drink (powder form)
- ❏ matches or lighter
- ❏ headlamp or flashlight
- ❏ extra batteries
- ❏ inexpensive watch
- ❏ extra food in case of an emergency
- ❏ personal toiletries—sunblock SPF 40, lip balm, aloe vera gel, insect repellent, toilet paper, handi-wipes, antibacterial waterless soap, bandanna, retractable scissors, pocket knife
- ❏ First-aid kit—ibuprofen or naproxen, moleskin, codeine, decongestant, antacids, elastic bandage, 4" gauze pads, band-aids, butterfly band-aids, adhesive tape, antibiotic ointment, first-aid field manual

OPTIONAL ITEMS

- ❏ light pair of gloves
- ❏ ski pole/walking stick
- ❏ camera and film
- ❏ altimeter
- ❏ GPS (Global Positioning System) reader
- ❏ cellular phone
- ❏ water filter or water purification tablets

LUNCH AND SNACKS

❑ bagels and cheese
❑ canned salmon or chicken or tuna
❑ turkey or beef jerky
❑ potato chips in a cardboard cylinder (for protection)
❑ M&Ms
❑ Gatorade or other sports drink (powder form)
❑ assorted nuts (cashews, almonds, etc.)
❑ fruit (grapes, raisins, apples, oranges)
❑ candy bars
❑ snack bars (that have a balance between protein and carbohydrates)

SIERRA GATORADE SLUSH

1. Find a snowbank and clean off the dirty snow from the top
   surface.
2. Fill a one-liter water bottle with clean snow. Do not pack the
   snow into the water bottle.
3. Add a cup to a cup and a half of water.
4. Add enough powdered Gatorade mix (or another powdered
   drink mix of your choice) to suit your taste.
5. Shake vigorously.
6. Enjoy the your Sierra Slush. It is particularly refreshing on a
   hot day after a strenuous climb.

APPENDIX 6
BIBLIOGRAPHY AND FURTHER READING

CAMPING AND HIKING

Graydon, Don, and Kurt Hanson, eds. *Mountaineering: The Freedom of the Hills*, 6th ed. Seattle: The Mountaineers Books, 1997.

Richins Jr., Paul. *Mount Whitney: The Complete Trailhead-to-Summit Hiking Guide*. Seattle: The Mountaineers Books, 2001.

———. *50 Classic Backcountry Ski and Snowboard Summits in California: Mount Shasta to Mount Whitney*. Seattle: The Mountaineers Books, 1999.

Rockwell, Dr. Robert L. *Giardia lamblia and Giardiasis with Particular Attention to the Sierra Nevada*, or *To Filter or Not to Filter, A Different Opinion*, Yosemite Association News Letter #4, March 18, 2002, and Backcountry Resource Center, *http://pweb.jps.net/~prichins/backcountry_resource_center.htm*.

Secor, R.J. *The High Sierra: Peaks, Passes, and Trails*, 2nd ed. Seattle: The Mountaineers Books, 1999.

Soares, John, and Marc Soares. *100 Classic Hikes in Northern California*, 2nd ed. Seattle: The Mountaineers Books, 2000.

Spring, Vicky. *100 Hikes in California's Central Sierra and Coast Range*. Seattle: The Mountaineers Books, 1995.

Steele, Peter, M.D. *Backcountry Medical Guide*. Seattle: The Mountaineers Books, 1999.

Stienstra, Tom. *California Camping, the Complete Guide to California's Recreation Areas*, 12th ed. San Francisco: Foghorn Press, 2001.

Whitehill, Karen and Terry. *Best Short Hikes in California's Northern Sierra: A Guide to Day Hikes Near Campgrounds*, 2nd ed. Seattle: The Mountaineers Books, 2003.

HISTORY

Browning, Peter. *Place Names of the Sierra Nevada: From Abbot to Zumalt*. Berkeley: Wilderness Press, 1986.

Farquhar, Francis P. *History of the Sierra Nevada*. Berkeley: University of California Press, 1965.

Reid, Robert Leonard. *Treasury of the Sierra Nevada*. Berkeley: Wilderness Press, 1983.

VEGETATION

Blackwell, Laird. *Wildflowers of the Sierra Nevada and Central Valley*. Renton, WA: Lone Pine Publishing, 1999.

Horn, Elizabeth. *The Sierra Nevada Wildflowers*. Missoula: Mountain Press Publishing Co., 1998.

Johnston, Verna. *A Natural History (California Natural History Guides, No. 58)*. Berkeley: University of California Press, 1996.

Little, Elbert L. *The Audubon Society Field Guide to North American Trees (Western Region)*. New York: Alfred A. Knopf, 1980.

Spellenberg, Richard. *The Audubon Society Field Guide to North American Wildflowers*. New York: Alfred A. Knopf, 2001.

Weeden, Norman. *A Sierra Nevada Flora*, 4th ed. Berkeley: Wilderness Press, 1996.

Whitney, Stephen. *A Sierra Club Naturalist's Guide to the Sierra Nevada*. San Francisco: Sierra Club Books, 1982.

INDEX

ABOUT THE AUTHORS

KAREN and TERRY WHITEHILL are the authors of five guidebooks for The Mountaineers. Their adventures include traversing Europe on foot and by bicycle and spending summers in the Sierra Nevada of California. The couple hiked hundreds of miles of trails while researching their Sierra hiking guides. The Whitehills reside in Portland, Oregon, with their three children and a basement full of camping gear.

PAUL RICHINS JR. started hiking, climbing, and backcountry skiing in the Trinity Alps at age twelve. He has more than thirty-five years of experience hiking, backpacking, mountain climbing, ski mountaineering, and whitewater kayaking. He lives in El Dorado Hills, California.

As a longtime member of the American Alpine Club and the Sierra Club, he has participated in major expeditions to Alaska (Mount Hunter and Mount Saint Elias), Canada (Mount Logan), Argentina (Cerro Aconcagua), Ecuador (Chimbarizo), and Tibet (Cho Oyu). Paul and two climbing partners completed the first ascent of the Southwest Ridge of Stortind, in the Lyngen Alps, Norway.

Paul has hiked, climbed, and skied extensively throughout the Sierra Nevada. He is author of two guidebooks, *50 Classic Backcountry Ski and Snowboard Summits in California: Mount Shasta to Mount Whitney* and *Mount Whitney: The Complete Trailhead-to-Summit Hiking Guide*. He maintains the Backcountry Resource Center, a website filled with information for backcountry skiers, climbers, and hikers wishing to explore the mountains of California and beyond.

THE MOUNTAINEERS, founded in 1906, is a nonprofit outdoor activity and conservation club, whose mission is "to explore, study, preserve, and enjoy the natural beauty of the outdoors. . . . " Based in Seattle, Washington, the club is now the third largest such organization in the United States, with 15,000 members and five branches throughout Washington State.

The Mountaineers sponsors both classes and year-round outdoor activities in the Pacific Northwest, which include hiking, mountain climbing, ski-touring, snowshoeing, bicycling, camping, kayaking and canoeing, nature study, sailing, and adventure travel. The club's conservation division supports environmental causes through educational activities, sponsoring legislation, and presenting informational programs. All club activities are led by skilled, experienced volunteers, who are dedicated to promoting safe and responsible enjoyment and preservation of the outdoors.

If you would like to participate in these organized outdoor activities or the club's programs, consider a membership in The Mountaineers. For information and an application, write or call The Mountaineers, Club Headquarters, 300 Third Avenue West, Seattle, WA 98119; 206-284-6310.

The Mountaineers Books, an active, nonprofit publishing program of the club, produces guidebooks, instructional texts, historical works, natural history guides, and works on environmental conservation. All books produced by The Mountaineers Books fulfill the club's mission.

Send or call for our catalog of more than 500 outdoor titles:

The Mountaineers Books
1001 SW Klickitat Way, Suite 201
Seattle, WA 98134
800-553-4453
mbooks@mountaineersbooks.org
www.mountaineersbooks.org

The Mountaineers Books is proud to be a corporate sponsor of Leave No Trace, whose mission is to promote and inspire responsible outdoor recreation through education, research, and partnerships. The Leave No Trace program is focused specifically on human-powered (nonmotorized) recreation.

Leave No Trace strives to educate visitors about the nature of their recreational impacts, as well as offer techniques to prevent and minimize such impacts. Leave No Trace is best understood as an educational and ethical program, not as a set of rules and regulations.

For more information, visit *www.LNT.org*, or call 800-332-4100.